D1538456

Machine, Metaphor, and the Writer:
A Jungian View

MACHINE, METAPHOR, AND THE WRITER
A Jungian View

BETTINA L. KNAPP

The Pennsylvania State University Press
University Park and London

Library of Congress Cataloging-in-Publication Data

Knapp, Bettina Liebowitz, 1926–
  Machine, metaphor, and the writer : a Jungian view / Bettina L. Knapp.

    p.   cm.
  Bibliography: p.
  Includes index.
  ISBN 0-271-00664-1
  1. Machinery in literature.   2. Literature—Psychological aspects.
3. Metaphor.   I. Title.
PN56.M2K57   1989
809′.915—c19   88-7696
                                                       CIP

To Dearest Russell
For Whom the Machine Holds Such Fascination

Contents

Introduction

Before the modern age, machines had been used for three thousand years by Egyptians, Cretans, Sumerians, Greeks, Persians, Romans, Arabs, Chinese, and many other ancient peoples. A dramatic change in the manner in which machines were employed, however, took place during the Industrial Revolution: scientific knowledge, feats of engineering, and utilitarian advances were made available to society in general. Lewis Mumford states:

> Mechanization and regimentation are not new phenomena in history: what is new is the fact that these functions have been projected and embodied in organized forms which dominate every aspect of our existence. Other civilizations reached a high degree of technical proficiency without, apparently, being profoundly influenced by the methods and aims of technics.[1]

Because ancient civilizations had not lifted the physical sciences to the heights known today, the life-styles of their populations were not overly modified. People did not have to adapt to meet the exigencies of the machine. After the Industrial Revolution, however, the course of civilization altered. The plethora of machines that came into existence transformed everyday habits and underlying psychological, spiritual, and cultural orientation.

The march of the machine was cumulative, and by the twentieth century the power generated by machines began taking possession of individuals and societies. High-speed flight and communication over land and air, ease and comfort in daily living, and increased sensory perception so transformed patterns of behavior that problems of adjustment followed in their wake. In many cases, these problems were dramatic and traumatic. Words like *facelessness*, *alienation*, and *identityless* cropped up in speech with increasing frequency. People felt cut off from past traditions and beliefs, and thus insecure and uncertain. Humanity's constantly increasing capacity to wage devastating wars, destroy environments, and eliminate populations has culminated in the potential to destroy the planet itself, arousing terror in many a thoughtful person. Questions concerning the meaning, value, and purpose of life have burgeoned. Is life itself absurd? What is the point of it all?

On the other hand, the invasion and autocracy of the machine and the mega-machine could not have taken place had societies and individuals not allowed technology to dominate them. As Mumford suggests, "society had, by an inner accommodation, surrendered to the machine."[2]

Because machines are the outgrowth of human imagination, inventiveness, and skill, exploring the meaning and the place of these automatic or semiautomatic entities in society is also to learn more about human nature. What, for example, is that inner need, that yearning, that drive in people that compels them to seek out the machine? What factors in the human psyche are fulfilled by the machine? Why and how have these devices succeeded in permeating society and subjecting entire populations to the point of altering their environment?

The machine has its human equivalent in the psyche: the "canalization of libido." Such a force, which transforms or converts energy, writes C. G. Jung, encourages humanity's analogy-making capacity and is responsible for some of the most significant discoveries and works of art. Jung explains:

> I mean by this a transfer of psychic intensities or values from one content to another, a process corresponding to the physical transformation of energy; for example, in the steam-engine the conversion of heat into the pressure of steam and then into the energy of motion. Similarly, the energy of certain psychological phenomena is converted by suitable means into other dynamisms.[3]

The machine aspect of the psyche is deeply rooted in all beings; it is implicit "in the nature of the living organism as such." Living matter, Jung suggests, is "itself a transformer of energy" which makes use of known and unknown physical and chemical factors in order to subsist. "The living body is a machine for converting the energies it uses into other dynamic manifestations that are their equivalents. We cannot say that physical energy is transformed into life, only that its transformation is the expression of life."[4]

The mechanics of the psyche, then, are responsible for conditioning the libido—accelerating or slackening mentation, affects, creativity, and whatever other factors are involved.

> Just as man has succeeded in inventing a turbine, and, by conducting a flow of water to it, in transforming the latter's kinetic energy into electricity capable of manifold applications, so he has succeeded with the help of a psychic mechanism, in converting natural instincts which would otherwise follow their gradient without performing work, into other dynamic forms that are productive of work.[5]

Artists—writers, painters, composers, architects, sculptors, filmmakers—are power stations, so to speak, psychic mechanisms that transform instinctual energy into "an *analogue of the object of instinct*." They react to environment, to society, to culture, to other beings—but mostly to that undifferentiated flame that burns at the core of their being and becomes channeled into a working instrument—or a work of art or some usable mechanical entity.[6]

Creative people are obviously affected by the machine's tentacular hold on them and on civilization in general. However, they register its powers and governing effects by conveying their feelings and ideations in artistic products. The artist may be looked upon as a kind of commentator on what is and a forerunner of what is to be: a prototype, a prophet, a "retort in which [the] poisons and antidotes of the collective are distilled." Artists are able to set down their responses to conditions, latent or present, to transmute the impalpable into the palpable, the evanescent into the eternal, because they react more powerfully to the deepest layers within themselves—to that transpersonal realm which C. G. Jung called the collective unconscious, or objective psyche. The contents and sensations that spring forth from this region of infinite riches—from the unconscious to the conscious in the form of archetypal motifs—are the substance, the *prima materia*, that artists mold and shape into forms, colors, and tones, and the public experiences in poems, novels, paintings, sculptures, musical compositions, and buildings. According to Erich Neumann, nations and peoples are "conditioned by the power of inner psychic realities which often enough appear in the first place as fantasies in the mind of an individual."[7]

Great creative endeavors must be looked upon, therefore, not merely as personal expressions, but as revelations; not simply as individual offerings extracted from their author's depths, but as an indication of what lies hidden "behind the scenes" for the collective and of what is likely to come to pass at some future date in the world of "reality." For this reason the messages of artists—expressed in books, paintings, sculptures, buildings, musical compositions, films—must be taken seriously. Audiences must become aware of the creative works being produced in the world today; for it is the artist who discloses, to those capable of reading his or her language, the effects of the machine and mechanical civilization on the physical world around us and on ourselves.

New physics and new math, quantum theory and the theory of relativity, have revealed universes of electrical fields in which neither absolute space nor time exists, and motion is relative to equally mobile systems. The very notion of the "center," implying a primordial "paradisal state" or Aristotle's "unmoved mover," no longer exists in an expanding universe filled with continuously active molecular events. In the domains of the atom and outer space, the speed of events is not only equal but surpasses the speed of light. "Interdeterminacy" is the rule of thumb for twentieth-century human beings: the solid world, as we know it, dissolves into what has been labeled "a dance of atoms" seemingly unrelated to our senses and perceptions. Nuclei, electrons, protons, neutrons, and other subatomic particles were discovered by modern physicists at a late stage in humanity's continuous probing into nature, a search which has caused human beings and the earth itself to diminish in importance. But did not Voltaire comment on this very notion in his philosophical tale *Micromégas* when he referred to the earth as "a heap of mud," and humans as "atoms"?

Is there a discernible pattern in the way writers or painters reach out to scientific discovery, to universal and transpersonal forces? How do they crystallize their reactions and meanings in metaphors, syntax, images, tones, and rhythms? Like inventors, artists create new forms in the physical medium in which they work, thereby expressing continuously altering and increasingly complex realities. Who better senses the ambiguities, intricacies, contradictions, and miraculous nature of the mechanized world than the artist? Was it not Nathaniel Hawthorne who wrote in *The House of Seven Gables:* "Is it a fact—or have I dreamt it—that, by means of electricity, the world of matter has become a great nerve, vibrating thousands of miles in a breathless point of time?" In *Tomorrow and Tomorrow and Tomorrow*, Aldous Huxley noted: "Applied science is a conjuror, whose bottomless hat yields impartially the softest of Angora rabbits and the most petrifying of Medusas." Nor can anything in nature—and this includes the machine and its effects—be apprehended in toto: the whole is greater than the sum of its parts. That science has attempted to simplify

the ambiguity of nature, Paul Klee explains, has had the reverse effect on
the artist.

> In the highest sense, an ultimate mystery lies behind the ambiguity
> which the light of the intellect fails miserably to penetrate. Yet one
> can to a certain extent speak reasonably of the salutary effect which
> art exerts through fantasy and symbols. Fantasy, kindled by instinct-
> born excitements, creates illusory conditions which can rouse or
> stimulate us more than familiar, natural, or supernatural ones. Sym-
> bols reassure the mind that we need not depend exclusively upon
> mundane experience.[8]

The more mechanized civilization has become, the more profoundly
have twentieth-century artists—be they Symbolists, Cubists, Secessionists,
Futurists, Expressionists, Dadaists, Surrealists, Constructivists, Social Real-
ists, Fluxists—experimented in revealing their inner experiences, their personal but strangely dismembered, mystifying, grotesque, and frequently
horrendous visions. A case in point is Helmut Middendorf's terrifying
painting *Airplane Dream*, expressing the angst corroding his psyche and
that of many contemporaries. Emotions, sensations, and perceptions of all
types—passionate and mystical love, wonderment, hostility, defiance, re-
volt, and rage—are implicit in modern creative works.

New mechanical forms and techniques have given birth to fresh symbols and images; they have also expanded the associations of older ones,
encouraging artists to pursue different directions. Beauty and unheard-of
harmonious reactions have been formulated by such artists as Manet and
Monet, and cacophonous ones by Grosz and Dix. Some artists have reacted
like Marcel Duchamp, who, when walking in front of an airplane propeller
at an exhibition of industrial design in 1911, was stunned by its beauty. He
remarked to Brancusi, who was with him: "Painting is finished. Who can
do any better than this propeller? Can you?" Other artists' responses are
typified by Charles Demuth's 1927 painting *My Egypt*, which features
grain elevators and power generators. The Futurists, so fascinated by
speed, were convinced that movement in a picture could be accentuated
with color, line, and form. They dreamt of a fourth dimension: that of
time in relation to movement as being symptomatic of the new age. For
them, the "roaring automobile" was more beautiful than the *Winged Victory*. The pupil of an engineer and architect and fascinated by movable
partition walls, smooth, straight lines, and an interplay of tense and dynamic forms, Le Corbusier remarked that "a house is a machine for living
in." Oscar Wilde labeled the Chicago Waterworks "the most beautifully
rhythmic thing I have ever seen."[9] Stieglitz manipulated his machine/

camera as a painter his brush and palette. Some of his photographs, such as *Steerage*, came into their own in the machine age, as did the film industry. Who could forget Charlie Chaplin's *Modern Times*—and his humanization of the machine? Industrial designs by Picabia, Fernand Léger, and Mies van der Rohe, not to mention such contemporary artists as Andy Warhol and so many more, became inspirational forces to be admired, ridiculed, or vilified. Hart Crane fashioned his celebrated poem "The Bridge."[10] In *The Education of Henry Adams*, the author compared the Virgin and the dynamo. Considering it far more significant than a mere piece of equipment, Adams saw the dynamo mystically, "as a moral force, much as the early Christian felt the Cross. . . . Before the end, one began to pray to it."[11]

There are as many different aesthetic reactions to our technological civilization as creative individuals to set forth these reactions. In *Machine, Metaphor, and the Writer*, I have explored the notion of the machine as a concrete mechanism: train, bicycle, plane, tank, truck, ship, printing press. These same apparatuses, however, take on an added dimension when viewed in terms of their social, psychological, sexual, and metaphysical functions. The plane, for example, leads into celestial spheres, the train into time/space, the ship into the water element. Each machine endows protagonists and readers with new sets of values, fresh dynamics, poetics, emotional and spiritual centers. The generators or apparatuses in *Machine, Metaphor, and the Writer* are explored along with abstract and symbolic entities as in language, which may be manipulated in such a way as to transform a speaker into a robot, an automaton, or a technician, making him or her easy prey for those who seek to control others. Ideational machines in *Machine, Metaphor, and the Writer* are also experienced in terms of ritual, as in the theatre, guiding protagonist and audience into dramatic and sacred spheres—into the heart of the work of art.

I have limited my study—as of necessity—to only one work that covers eleven twentieth-century authors, embracing both the West and the East. Although other writings and other novelists and dramatists figuring in *Machine, Metaphor, and the Writer* could have been chosen for discussion, my approach was subjective. I also sought a *vision d'ensemble*, a unifying emblem which would trigger questions as well as answers. Conclusions, however, although forthcoming in these pages, are at best only temporary. And this is as it should be. Heraclitus said centuries back that all is flux, nothing is permanent or static. So, too, are ideas and concepts.

The Supermale by the Frenchman Alfred Jarry opens our volume—perhaps rightly so since it underscores specific factors inherent in the mechanics of sex, a provocative theme to say the least. "A Painful Case" by the Irishman James Joyce focuses on the man-machine and the lethal ramifications that come to pass in such an unbending individual. The Polish writer Stanislaw Witkiewicz dramatizes the metaphysics of mechanization in his play *The Crazy Locomotive*. The Italian writer Luigi Pirandello fleshes out theatre viewed as a machine in *Tonight We Improvise*. *Wind, Sand, and Stars* by Antoine de Saint-Exupéry takes readers into celestial spheres, opening them up to a new poetics of space. The Mexican storyteller Juan José Arreola uses the train as a vehicle to depict such concepts as time and timelessness. "Midnight Convoy," Israeli writer S. Yizhar's short story, focuses on the world of war with its tanks and half-tracks and, surprisingly enough, on the dynamics of the feminine principle. In *The Journey*, Japanese novelist Jiro Osaragi fleshes out the machine as implicit in the transformatory process. R. K. Narayan's *The Man-Eater of Malgudi* explores the secret initiatory language revolving around the printing press. *Kaspar*, by Austrian Peter Handke, penetrates the world of linguistic engineering and the dangers surrounding the creation of robotlike beings. In *Operation Sidewinder*, American Sam Shepard probes the mechanics involved in the dramatic event and the interplay of the profane and the sacred.

My intent is to explore the nature of the relationship between the protagonist and the machine. Is it inspirational, satiric, hostile, loving, spiritual, sexual? How do the eleven authors whose works are analyzed in *Machine, Metaphor, and the Writer* channel their reactions in the word? In the metaphor and other figures of speech? Syntax? Plot? Characterization or lack of it? Significant, as well, are the insights readers may glean from the narratives of these novelists and dramatists. Can the information distilled help them better understand their own selves and their relationships to others as they make their way in the mega-complex into which the mega-machine has transformed their world? During the course of a human life, what values are to be preserved and/or rejected in this chaos of ambiguities and imponderables unfolding before each and every one of us? What mysteries are secreted in the printed page—itself the product of this, our machine age?

A Jungian approach to literature has been employed to analyze the purposefully diverse works included in *Machine, Metaphor, and the Writer*. First, the very diversity of these writers illustrates the universality of Jungian archetypal analysis and criticism. Second, archetypal analysis takes the literary work out of its individual and conventional context and relates it to humankind in general. This unique approach lifts readers out of their specific and perhaps isolated worlds; it allows them to expand their vision and thus to relate more easily to issues that may confront them as they come to understand that their own reality is part of an ongoing and cyclical reality. To become aware that people in other parts of the globe suffer from alienation and identity crises, mother or father fixations, sibling rivalry—to mention but a few—and go through harrowing ordeals before they have a chance to know some semblance of fulfillment, if they ever do, may help certain readers face and understand their own gnawing feelings of aloneness and uncertainty.

The material evaluated in *Machine, Metaphor, and the Writer* is designed to enlarge readers' views, develop their potential, and encourage affinities or confrontations with those factors that might please or displease them in the technical civilization in which they live. Such encounters may be painful or joyous, terrifying or serene; hopefully, they will prove enlightening, involving readers in the writings discussed so that they may understand how and why certain creative works speak to and reach them today and others do not. Energized in this manner, readers might go a step further and explore the literary works in question, then through association relate their discoveries to aspects of their own personalities. Self-awareness may thus increase, and understanding of the individual's function and role in society may broaden. Reading now becomes not merely an intellectual adventure but an excitingly helpful living experience.

Although C. G. Jung's vocabulary is defined and redefined in each of the essays in *Machine, Metaphor, and the Writer*, a brief description of such salient concepts as archetype, collective unconscious, anima/animus, shadow, persona, four functions, ego, self, and the notion of individuation will be given here.

Archetypal (primordial) images, which emerge from the deepest layers of the unconscious, are found in myths, legends, and literary works of the world over from time immemorial. Edward Edinger has compared the archetype to the instinct:

> An instinct is a pattern of behavior which is inborn and characteristic for a certain species. Instincts are discovered by observing the behavior patterns of individual organisms and, from this data, reaching the generalization that certain patterns of behavior are the common instinctual equipment of a given species. The instincts are the unknown motivating dynamisms that determine an animal's behavior on the biological level. An archetype is to the psyche what an instinct is to the body. The existence of archetypes is inferred by the same process as that by which we infer the existence of instincts. Just as instincts common to a species are postulated by observing the uniformities in biological behavior, so archetypes are inferred by observing the uniformities in psychic phenomena. Just as instincts are unknown motivating dynamisms of biological be-

havior, archetypes are unknown motivating dynamisms of the psyche. Archetypes are the psychic instincts of the human species. Although biological instincts and psychic archetypes have a very close connection, exactly what this connection is we do not know any more than we understand just how the mind and body are connected.[12]

Archetypes are contained in the *collective unconscious*—also referred to as the objective psyche. The collective, as distinguished from the personal unconscious, exists at the deepest level of the subliminal realm. It is "suprapersonal and non-individual" by nature and as such is usually "inaccessible to conscious awareness." Archetypes are made manifest in *archetypal (primordial) images* experienced in such universal motifs as the *Great Mother, the Spiritual Father, transformation, the Self.* These and other archetypal images will be examined for their import with regard to the metaphor of the machine in the literary works under discussion and their meaning, both personal and collective, for the writers and, by extension, for the readers.[13]

Further discussion will revolve around the anima/animus dynamism. The *anima* has been defined as "an autonomous psychic content in the male personality which can be described as an inner woman;" the "psychic representation of the contrasexual elements in man," which "is depicted in symbolic imagery by figures of women ranging from harlot to saint." The *animus* may be looked upon as "the corresponding representative of the masculine contrasexual elements in the psyche of women."[14] Positive and negative anima/animus conditions, especially in relation to the metaphor of the machine, are probed within the context of the essays constituting *Machine, Metaphor, and the Writer.*

Psychological types are also studied within the context of the literary work: how the energy of the introvert and the extrovert flows inward and outward, acting and counteracting in relation to the dramatis personae (sometimes including the machine) and the empirical world.

Persona problems are also broached in terms of the novels and plays included in *Machine, Metaphor, and the Writer.* The *persona,* which comes from the Latin word meaning "actor's mask," may be looked upon as a "public face" that a person assumes when relating to others. Difficulties arise when an individual identifies too greatly with his or her persona, thereby making it difficult to adapt to the outside world. The persona may also mask a weakened ego, leading to its eclipse.

Attention is likewise focused on Jung's concept of the four functions: *thinking* (using rational faculties), *feeling* (regulating values, especially in relationships), *sensation* (promoting adaptation to reality), *intuition* (perceiving via the unconscious). Each of the four, perhaps alone or at times in pairs, may be discussed in order to explicate the impact of the machine as metaphor in the plots, characterizations, or literary devices used creatively by the writer.

An exploration of the *shadow*—which includes those characteristics that the *ego* considers negative or unacceptable as personified in dreams, myths, plots, characterizations, or other literary devices within the given work of literature—is also undertaken. The ego is that part of the psyche which "stands between the inner world and the outer world, and its task is to adapt to both." The Self, "defined by Jung as both the center and circumference of the psyche," incorporates "within its paradoxical unity all of the opposites embodied in the masculine and feminine archetypes."[15]

Many symbols, images, and motifs are examined in *Machine, Metaphor, and the Writer:* water, cave, earth, sky, clouds, mountains, mandalas, to name only a few. These are discussed in relation to their particular functions in each piece of writing considered—especially in relation to the meaning and impact of the specific machine that is featured (train, plane, bus, car, ship, computer, etc.). Symbolic elements are also considered as timeless, universal components of human expression, used to describe death/rebirth, sacrifice, redemption, salvation, and other mysteries that may be particularized in an author's work but are central to human experience.

The religious and philosophical dimension that comes into focus is inseparable from an understanding of the psychological development or dissolution of the plots, protagonists, and syntax used by the author in the construction or deconstruction of the work. The concept of *individuation*, or the process of "psychic differentiation" that distinguishes an individual as unique and separate from the collective, is adumbrated when implicit in the narratives under scrutiny. The inner life of a character or noncharacter may then be experienced by the reader as a living entity, provoking reflection, admiration, or deep distress at the turn of or dissolution of the events or the philosophical or spiritual message implicit in the text.

The first piece of writing to be considered in *Machine, Metaphor, and the Writer* is by the versatile Alfred Jarry, who wrote about everything that interested him: art, music, sports, literature, theatre, sciences, and the trades. All of his works are different, yet they share a common stamp: a corrosive way of looking at life that is somewhat mitigated by a powerful sense of humor. Monstrous beings emerge alive and grotesque from the pages of his works. *The Supermale* (1902) is no different. Here readers are introduced to a sex machine, a food machine, and bicycles that outdo a speeding train. Although the machines involved are real, each of them points up the detached nature of Jarry's Supermale: unfeeling, unrelated, and identityless. In certain regards he may be viewed as the prototypal man of the future.

James Joyce's "A Painful Case" (1906) narrates the story of a man living a peripheral existence. He gives the impression of being a machine-like person existing in an ordered and methodical world. Beneath this repressed and unfulfilled exterior, however, lies a whole secret realm that emerges only after Joyce's brusque and death-dealing conclusion, which features the image of the train. How does Joyce use this machine as object and metaphor, thereby forcing up the epiphanic experience? How does this event subsequently reveal the protagonist's deeply moving *feeling* realm? Point to the thematics of the chapter.

Stanislaw Witkiewicz's drama, *The Crazy Locomotive* (1923), depicts a surrealist's view of the metaphysics of mechanization. On stage we are dealing not merely with a metaphoric machine, but with a "real live" locomotive that gives the illusion of speeding across the proscenium, then crashing. Witkiewicz's locomotive is viewed as a destroyer of individuals, societies, and cultures; a devourer of rational attitudes, and a despoiler of feeling relationships. Why, then, does it become an object of fascination for the dramatist (and for his audiences and readers), provoking madness in some and morbidity in others?

In Luigi Pirandello's *Tonight We Improvise* (1929), theatre becomes a machine, hungry for poetry, which was in insufficient supply in the early decades of the twentieth century. The poetry needed to nourish the hungry machine is, in this Italian playwright's view, a concoction of imagination and mystery that invites spectators and protagonists alike to substitute for their staid and preconceived notions the *unforeseen* (from the Latin, *improvisus*)—the improvised, the unknown, the world of imponderables. What are the forces at stake in this Pirandellian world of the machine? How is the rejected matriarchal sphere called into question? And in what manner does the dramatist view this "unspeakable" and "reprehensible" domain in terms of theatre and machine?

Antoine de Saint-Exupéry's autobiographical *Wind, Sand, and Stars* (1939) details the author's experiences as a pilot. Focusing most specifically on the psychological, social, and philosophical aftermath of several harrowing and sublime moments in the air and on the ground, *Wind, Sand, and Stars* discloses a soul and psyche in torment. In what way does this work suggest the author's inability to adapt to the needs of the earthly domain and his compulsion to seek solace in his machine/plane? What made him say "I cannot stand this age," with all of its machines, and yet use the machine for his own creative purposes? How were Saint-Exupéry's displacements—viewing the earth from space—instrumental in the creation of his new poetics? Does his vision of life, and the images and symbols he uses, differ from those of the writers on the ground?

Juan José Arreola's short story "The Switchman" (1951) uses the train as an allegorical device to underscore the dichotomies existing between such notions as deception and truth, capriciousness and constancy, eternality and linearity. In its machine-like capacity, the train also heightens the feelings of alienation and powerlessness of finite beings living in the infinite vastness of an impersonal universe. Enigmatic and cryptic, this Mexican writer's narrative ushers in a whole mysterious world—that of the Aztecs and Toltecs—which is secreted in the image of the train. What are we to make of these inner riches? What archetypal significance do they yield for today's readers?

The event narrated in S. Yizhar's novella, *Midnight Convoy*, takes place during one of Israel's many wars. The action revolves around the safe conduct of a convoy of trucks, half-tracks, and jeeps carrying crucial supplies to the army. Metaphorically, it explores a quest for the *right path*, not a path without ruts or wadis, but one that teaches each individual the significance of the gift of life.

Jiro Osaragi's novel *The Journey* (1960) suggests a network of displacements and equivocations viewed from a Japanese point of view. The outer signs of the continuous activity depicted are manifested in the protagonists' constant use of trains, cars, buses, and boats during their multiple trajectories. How do archetypal vehicles and their velocities reflect an inner frenetic, anguished, or serene psychological condition in both individuals and culture as a whole? What is their impact on the Westerner?

R. K. Narayan's novel *The Man-Eater of Malgudi* (1961) focuses on a primitive hand printing press. The letters, syllables, words, sentences, paragraphs, and pages the protagonist sets down in type may also be viewed as factors in activating and actualizing a secret initiatory language. As the Indian Buddhist contemplates or meditates upon the signs or glyphs emerging into view on the blank page, *libido* (or psychic energy) flows inward, catalyzing his subliminal spheres. In what way does such inner combustion act upon the protagonist? How does this affect his lifestyle, the world about him, and, by extension, our own?

Words alone are of import in Peter Handke's play *Kaspar* (1968). Absent in his drama are plot, character, tension, coherence, connecting processes, and meanings of words as we understand them. Subverting the conventional system of relationships and comparisons, words in *Kaspar* become mechanical devices endowed with concretion. Hard and feelingless, they bludgeon well-worn responses to old ways of thinking and understanding. New dimensions are opened up to the protagonist, but they also undermine his security and create a climate of malaise. How are feelings of oneness and cohesion transformed into fractionality? How do these trigger havoc in the mind and psyche of the protagonist? Why do words, as archetypal images, usher in a schizophrenic condition? Is this condition symptomatic of today's society?

Sam Shepard's *Operation Sidewinder* (1970) is a mystery play in the real sense of the word. Two religious ceremonies are enacted onstage: the Hopi Indian Snake-Antelope dance and the electrifying performance of a most up-to-date scientific invention: the sidewinder computer. Both are initiation rituals which lure audiences from the world of the profane to that of the sacred. The intensely patriotic Shepard speaks out openly in his play, urging viewers and readers to become aware of the imminent dangers facing his country if new approaches to life are not forthcoming. Americans have reached a crossroads, he suggests, and their mechanistic and industrialized culture has become obsessive—a threat to life itself with the power to split the earth. What are the archetypal motifs used by Shepard to convey his tantalizing and terrifying views? How does he use religious and mechanical devices to penetrate apocalyptic dimensions in *Operation Sidewinder?*

Where will the machine and the depersonalized and automated nature of technology lead civilization? For those who fear for the future, let us listen to Hölderlin:

> Where danger is,
> Arises salvation also.[16]

1 Alfred Jarry's *The Supermale*—The Sex Machine, the Food Machine, and the Bicycle Race: Is It a Question of Adaptation?

Alfred Jarry's farcical and fantastic novel *The Supermale* (1902) focuses on a sex machine, a food machine, and bicycles that outdo a speeding train. Satiric in intent, the novel uses these as metaphoric devices to further energize Jarry's already supervirile and priapic protagonist. "To survive," the author notes, "man must become stronger than the machine, as happened when he gained dominion over wild beasts. . . . It is simply a question of adapting to the environment."[1]

Jarry's protagonist, André Marcueil, the Supermale, detached, unfeeling, and identityless, may in certain regards be viewed as the prototypical man of the future. Power-hungry, driven to peform outstanding acts, attempting to surpass all others in whatever domain he sets his mind to conquering, Jarry's dehumanized Supermale is victimized by the very machines he seeks to outdo in velocity and dexterity.

To become overly dependent upon machines, as in Marcueil's case, is dangerous. It may lead to a condition of hubris, and, as C. G. Jung has stated, it may divest an individual of his or her independence:

> This proud picture of human grandeur is unfortunately an illusion and is counterbalanced by a reality that is very different. In reality man is the slave and victim of the machines that have conquered space and time for him; he is intimidated and endangered by the might of the military technology which is supposed to safeguard his physical existence; his spiritual and moral freedom, though guaranteed within limits in one half of his world, is threatened with chaotic disorientation, and in the other half is abolished alto-

gether. Finally, to add comedy to tragedy, this lord of the elements, this universal arbiter, hugs to his bosom notions which stamp his dignity as worthless and turn his autonomy into an absurdity.[2]

Although fun and frolic run rampant in *The Supermale*, so, too, do deeply erotic currents. One could, indeed, look upon much of the truculence and verve implicit in *The Supermale* as a twentieth-century reenactment of the Greek *comus:* a joyful procession dramatized by the Megarians and Dorians in honor of Dionysus. These fun-filled celebrations, in which an effigy of the phallus was carried about in merriment and veneration, were expressions of the ecstasy experienced by the participants during their seasonal fertility rites. Like the Greek *comus*, the central image in *The Supermale* is the phallus and everything associated with it. Unlike the phallus in the Dionysian festival, however, the phallus of Jarry's protagonist elicits neither rapture nor delight—nor even hope—as experienced so potently by the ancient celebrants. On the contrary, the modern novel terminates with the destruction of a human being, bringing in an element of sadism that was not part of the *comus.*

Jarry's humor does not evoke belly laughs. It is sardonic, ridiculing, and destructive, closely akin to those spasmodic reactions Baudelaire labeled "laughter" and which he defined as a "perpetual explosion of his [the author's] anger and suffering."[3] The phallus enables Jarry to distill his strange mechanical concoctions with blendings of sexuality—perversions such as sadomasochism, voyeurism, narcissism, homosexuality, priapism, nymphomania, the use of masks, and sundry other rituals designed to enliven the events.

Exaggeration, used as a literary device by Jarry, increases the ugliness of his creatures, who are devoid of any redeeming feature. It also magnifies the humor, irony, and absurdity of certain situations and characters depicted in *The Supermale*, thus mirroring to a great extent the notions concerning comedy set down by Cicero. "The province of the ridiculous lies within limits of ugliness and certain deformity; for the expressions are alone, or especially ridiculous which disclose and represent some ugliness in a not unseemly fashion."[4]

Although prurient images and events are narrated in *The Supermale*, this novel is not pornographic. There are no minute descriptions of sexual acts, nor does Jarry delve into the nonexistent emotional reactions or yearnings of his protagonists. His pen is caustic, leveling blows and counterblows against an ugly society, exhibiting no deep feelings for individuals or their private emotional aberrations. Distancing is Jarry's technique: a plethora of insensitive characters, unable to relate to anyone, including themselves, perform their antics with marionette-like alacrity and verve.

The absurdity of their buffoon-like acts elicits cerebral and morbid reactions, along with macabre grins reminiscent of the rictus worn by the gargoyles of Notre Dame.

Jarry stops at nothing when depicting his views. Whether his humor is raw or sardonic or overflows with instinct, it all serves his goal of devaluing what he finds distasteful in the personal and collective world: the dangers of psychological and spiritual imprisonment for both the individual and society as a whole, as a result of overdependence on the machine.

Jarry (1873–1907) was born at Laval to a traveling-salesman father and a romantic, emotionally unstable mother. Ardent, sarcastic, temperamental, and quixotic, with his penetrating and incisive mind and extreme curiosity, Jarry was considered by his schoolmasters to be an excellent student. After passing both his baccalaureate examinations, he went to Paris in 1891, ostensibly to prepare for entrance to the Ecole Normale.

Once in Paris, however, he immersed himself in the city's artistic and literary worlds, and changed his mind about his future career. He felt an affinity with the symbolists—Baudelaire, Verlaine, Rimbaud, Mallarmé—who searched for and discovered a whole new realm beyond the world of appearances: an unlimited world where things material and immaterial were alive and breathing; where matter and spirit, the mobile and the immobile, the rational and the irrational, were fused into one.

Rachilde and her husband, Alfred Vallette, who directed the magazine *Mercure de France*, took an immediate interest in the "strange" lad who "appeared in their offices, more frequently than not, attired in a bizarre bicyclist's outfit." He attracted their attention with his outlandish antics and the verve with which he narrated his colorful tales about "walking streets" and people who entered their apartments from top rather than from ground floors. Rachilde described Jarry as looking like a "wild animal." His face was pale, almost mask-like, his nose short, his mouth incisive, his eyes black and "singularly phosphorescent . . . at once starry and luminous, like those of night birds." The avant-garde poet, writer, and art critic Guillaume Apollinaire, stunned by Jarry's brio and the manner in which he recited his verses—the metallic ring of their rhymes and the mood created by their varied rhythmic patterns and images—considered him the "personification of a river."[5]

Although Jarry radiated charm and kindliness, characteristics which endeared him to his large circle of friends, he was an anarchist, an impenitent, and a humorist à la Rabelais. From him came neither romantic sweetnesses nor beautiful plastic images, but mordant, satiric, cruel ironies, along with invective, puns, neologisms, jokes, and riddles. Jarry's *Haldernablou* (1894), a narcissistic work pointing up his sexual inversion, relates, in part, the love Duke Haldern harbors for his page Ablou. More significant, perhaps, than almost all of Jarry's writings—including *César Anté-Christ* (1895), *Absolute Love* (1899), *Messaline* (1901), *The Female Pope* (1908), and many other works—was his play *King Ubu* (1896), for it rocked and shocked Paris audiences, and theatre the world over has not been the same since.

Jarry had succeeded in liberating himself from society, in living an uninhibited existence whatever the consequences might be. His dream world had become his reality. In order to create and maintain this state, he fed on alcohol and ether, and spent money before he earned it. His poverty, his unwillingness to eat, his overconsumption of what he considered to be "holy water" (alcohol) and a "sacred herb" ("saintly herb," meaning absinthe) led to physical disintegration and disease. From 1903 on, he wrote with extreme difficulty. His friends tried, unsuccessfully, to draw him away from his erratic existence, his unhealthy haunts, and his nocturnal ventures. Jarry grew steadily sicker. Late in October 1907, after having made an appointment with his friend Dr. Saltas, he failed to show up. Such a lacuna was not like Jarry. Dr. Saltas grew worried. He shared his concern with Alfred Vallette. Both men went to Jarry's small room on 7 Rue Cassette. They found him half-unconscious, dirty, his legs already paralyzed. They took him to the hospital. His last wish, which was granted him, was as "strange" as his life had been: he asked for a toothpick. The wish seems a little less unusual if readers realize that Jarry did not believe in death as a finale. In a letter to Madame Rachilde, written on May 28, 1906, several years after the publication of *The Supermale*, he declared that though the brain decomposes after a person's demise, it still functions, it still dreams, "and its dreams are our Paradise." In any case, it is recorded that Jarry died at the age of thirty-four on November 1, 1907, of tubercular meningitis.

Viewed by many scholars as one of Jarry's most important works, *The Supermale* is far ahead of its time, a forerunner in many ways of the ideas proclaimed by the Futurists and the Cubists. In the *Futurist Manifesto* (1909), Filippo Marinetti suggested that the art to which the machine age gave birth was based on "violence, energy, and boldness." Futurist painters such as Umberto Boccioni, fascinated by the fresh approach that the machine brought to life, remarked: "Everything moves, everything runs, everything turns swiftly."[6] Fernand Léger, inspired by the Cubists, depicted modern urban life in his canvases with all of its harsh, flashing electric lights, its sounds of traffic, its machinelike movements of individuals and crowds. For him, the machine stood mighty and inspiring—like God.

The action in *The Supermale*, purported to take place in 1920, is high-speed, high-tech, high-keyed. Mechanically oriented, it introduces all types of devices and instruments into the story: electric lights and push buttons on doors and in rooms, dynamometers, water-denaturation processes, flying machines (planes), cars in the form of military shells, fecundating and sex machines, and more.

Even as a novel, *the Supermale* is machinelike: devoid of psychological analyses, feelings, and climaxes. Like the fixed or moving parts which make up the framework of the machine, what is of import in *The Supermale* are the facts of the story that is related. The protagonists, robotlike in essence, perform acts and participate in collective situations as if they had been programmed to do so by some invisible transmitter and energy charge emanating from a standarized menu or set course. Like disparate objects brought together for some kind of experiment, these parts of beings, or split-offs, breathe, live, function, and die never knowing themselves plain. In so doing, however, they provoke and elicit reactions from surrounding objects and beings—even from the reader. Never does a flesh-and-blood person make his or her appearance; never do we see into a *real* person's face. Masked and disguised, the *persona* holds sway in *The Supermale:* the outside, the hard, glistening, smooth or corroded metallic entity.

Jarry's protagonist, a Nietzschean *Übermensch* type when it comes to his male prowess, is reminiscent in some ways of other sexually active men, namely Don Juan and Casanova. Like Jarry's protagonist, they, too, were confused as to their sexual identities; their aggression and sadistic approach toward womankind followed a pattern of behavior revealing their unconscious distaste for them. To be an absolute male, in Marcueil's eyes, is to be able to accomplish "the act" more completely, more thoroughly, and more often—eighty-two times in the space of twenty-four hours—than anyone else on earth. Such an outlook has transformed him, in the eyes of the Scientists, into a human machine. Only when this sex machine finally meets his match—the "Machine to Inspire Love" invented by an engineer, chemist, and doctor—are readers made privy to the most fantastic of Futurist, Cubist, Dadaist, Surrealist, and Absurdist situations.

The Bicycle Race and the Perpetual-motion Food Machine

Jarry's disturbing humor is based to a great extent on caricature. This technique, which succeeds in inflating certain patterns of behavior, results in disproportion in the novel's framework, altering its dimension and focus so that protagonists and events are taken out of the world of reality and placed in one of artifice. According to Henri Bergson, caricature, which reveals an aspect of an author's psyche, is a device marked with "insensibility" and "ulterior motive." It enables Jarry to express in veiled terms his paradoxical feelings of inferiority/superiority. The caricaturist, Bergson contends, like the puppeteer can force his creatures to express the most outlandish or excoriating emotions under the guise of folly. "The art of the caricaturist lies in his ability to seize that frequently imperceptible movement, and to make it visible for all to see by inflating it."[7] Jarry performs just such a feat in *The Supermale*.

No one would guess from external appearance that the thirty-one year-old André Marcueil—small, puny, pale, skeleton-like, his relatively long hair curled with a curling iron, his weak eyes assisted by a pince-nez—is a Supermale: an exceptional individual with unlimited energy able to perform the sexual act many times without experiencing the least bit of fatigue. Like eating or sleeping, "love," he maintains, "is an act without any importance, since it can be accomplished indefinitely." Jarry's hero has reduced the sexual act to a mechanical one devoid of feeling and inspiring no need for relatedness by its participants.

Marcueil suffers from an idée fixe: to survive he must outdo anyone and everyone. His first claim to fame occurs during a bicycle race. Like many a competitive sport, bicycle racing fires Marcueil's energy, arouses his spirits, and fills him with élan. At high speeds his body feels electrified, as if imbued by some outerworldly current that gives him a sense of power, exhilaration, and fulfillment.

That bicycle racing should fascinate Marcueil is not surprising. Although not mentioned in English literature until 1769, and not heard of in France until 1799, the sport took on fad-like proportions by the 1880s and 1890s. Indeed, the Tour de France, enlisting the best cyclists of the time to compete over a broad course of more than 2,500 miles, was organized in 1903.

As a means of transport, a bicycle differs from a train, plane, car, and the like in requiring personal effort on the driver's part, thereby affirming his or her will, directive, acumen, and energy. Second, the driver is responsible for maintaining the bicycle's equilibrium and speed, that is, its performance in the outer world. Third, the rider sits astride on the bicycle, as did the horseman in medieval times. The constant motion and friction induced by the motility of the machine also suggest an erotic or masturbatory experience.

Who better than Jarry, for whom bicycle riding was a passion, knew the attributes of this machine and could describe them in ample and accurate detail? He understood how a bicycle could imbue his protagonist with feelings of autonomy as he forged ahead in the open space before him, thereby symbolically declaring his independence from anyone else.

Such hyperactivity, however, has psychological side effects. An introverted and egocentric type, Marcueil is unable to relate to people in a normal way. Living as he does in his own secluded domain, his fantasy world alone is alive as he roams about in unheard-of realms. The source of his constantly generating libido (psychic energy) focuses solely on the gratification of his needs and desires. Never does he examine a situation or a personality. Such a psychological condition is dangerous since it allows an undifferentiated object/subject to gain greater dominion over the ego (center of consciousness), thereby diminishing its importance proportionally. Because of the ego's defective relation to the subject/object, it neither grows nor evolves. Rather than attaining some kind of freedom or independence, it veers continuously between subject and object, increasingly enslaved by the subliminal pulsions which hold sway.

Five bicyclists—one of whom is Marcueil—participate in the frenzied race described with brio in *The Supermale*. The bicycles, vintage 1920 and geared to cover a 10,000-mile course, are described as having tires fifteen millimeters in diameter, no handlebars, and seats that force the rider to practically lie horizontally as he pedals at breakneck speed. Not only do the riders wear masks to protect them from the dust and the wind, but the aluminum cord that binds them to each other is attached to their headgear and bodies in such a way as to prevent them from looking sideways or backwards. Nor can they move about in their seats. Such a vise-like condition suggests a sort of symbolic imprisonment in the manner they live, think, and feel.

That each cyclist wears a mask for protection is understandable. Purposeful anonymity is also suggested by the mask, which implies that the five cyclists are really one: each a facet or mirror-image of Marcueil, the Supermale. Jarry's propensity for using the mask, in this and other works, indicates a need to hide the inner being, to maintain privacy by secreting the individual behind a facade that allows him or her to peer out into the world. In Jarry's essay, "The Uselessness of Theater in the Theater," he suggests that the mask points up the collective quality of the characters involved, imposing upon them a visual expression of a personality trait. In another essay, "Twelve Arguments on the Theater," he further declares that the writer who breathes life into his masked being creates a new existence; a fresh dynamism which comes into being with the exteriorization of an inner conflict. The mask, then, frees the forces within the personality that cannot be integrated, enabling them to crystallize on the stage or in the novel, and there to live out their lives in conflict or in harmony.

The spectators watching Marcueil race take seats in the train against which the cyclists are racing. The lead automobile rolling in front of the cyclists is shaped like a high-explosive shell. When it takes off, like a bullet in space, the racers, following its momentum, keep increasing their speed until they reach 120 km per hour. The excitement generated by the velocity of the cyclists, the automobile, and the train, and the images which catapult forth in paroxysms before the reader spawn tension—which is of course Jarry's goal.

Since the race is to last four days, food is provided the participants by a *Perpetual-Motion-Food* machine. This incredibly nutritive offering, made from a combination of alcohol and strychnine, is, according to the doctor who invented the concoction, highly beneficial. Small, colorless, bitter, broken cubes are placed on five trays (one for each of the riders), then attached to a small table placed in front of each of the riders' mouths. While they pedal, they consume. Not a minute is lost.

At the end of the first day, Marcueil first notices a drumlike mechanism suspended beneath his white speedometer on each side of his bicycle, its function being to attenuate any shock coming from the front wheel. Unfortunately or fortunately, the drum gets caught in the wheels of the lead car, which then pull it and the bicycle along. Although such a situation could be disastrous, Corporal Gilbey, in charge of the racers and unseen by the spectators riding in the train, takes advantage of the automobile's momentum to pull the bicycles "fraudulently" along. Although Marcueil is unable to look about and sees the train only out of the corner of his eye, he notices that it is going at a fast clip, which gives him the distinct impression of being completely immobile. Certainly an optical illusion, he thinks.

Problems arise on the second day of the race. Piercing and strident sounds of grinding metal, coupled with enormous vibrations, almost break Marcueil's eardrums. As he looks in front of him, he realizes that the lead automobile has been replaced by a "flying machine" shaped like a trumpet. This strange apparition seems to be turning on itself in the air, then zooming toward the cyclists, the suction generated by these stunts nearly drawing Marcueil and the other cyclists into a funnel-like whirlwind. Upon recovering from what he considers a surprising situation, Marcueil looks at his ivory speedometer, and discovers he is going 250 kilometers per hour.

Something horrible and unprecedented occurs on the third day of the race. The rider directly in front of Marceuil is Jewey Jacobs, whose knees are but a yard from his own, and who has been going at such a "fantastic" clip ever since the beginning of the race that Marcueil has had to counterpedal several times to slow his pace down, thereby keeping to the schedule. Now Marcueil observes a stiffening of Jacobs's hamstrings. The toes on his right foot, tied to a leather toe-clip, seem rigid, without any ankle play; his marble-colored legs, going up and down isochronously, never waver in their movement. Another apparently minor detail is the unpleasant odor which Jacobs seems to be emanating. Moments later, Marcueil realizes that he is inhaling the smell of a decomposing body.

Stunned, Marceuil screams out the news, but the noise from the train and the "flying machine" overhead is so deafening that it blocks out all other sounds. No one in the train notices anything strange, particularly since Jacobs's bicycle is going more rapidly than the others. In fact, cyclists and observers all scream out their praise of him, unaware that rigor mortis has already set in. Nor does the "Perpetual Motion Food Machine" stop serving Jacobs simply because he is dead. Were it to cease doing so, its inventor would lose a great deal of money since he has contracted to feed five people rather than four.

On the fourth day, Marceuil's speedometer reads 300 kilometers per hour. The riders, including Jacobs, are still traveling at breakneck speed, seemingly unhampered by the smoke issuing from the locomotive, which blows their way and even blinds them momentarily.

In time, Marcueil figures out the number of kilometers they have traversed and notes that he can actually hear the trans-Siberian express in the distance. Speed is increasing still more when one of the riders begins putting all his weight on his back wheel, thereby forcing the others to pedal more rapidly. Then something incredible occurs: a ghostlike cyclist, Pédard, appears as if from nowhere right in front of the train, exceeding its speed as well as that of all the cyclists. Who is this Pédard who sports a pince-nez, a high hat, and short elastic boots? Marceuil wonders, asking himself whether he is hallucinating. When, at a certain moment, a light appears behind the horizon and encircles Pédard's countenance like a halo, then illuminates his entire being, Marceuil thinks he is in the presence of some divine figure sent by heaven to aid the cyclists.

The Terminus finally comes into sight, and the bicyclists win the race. How is it possible for the human machine to surpass the mechanical one? And who is this Pédard who has succeeded in energizing the cyclists to such an extent that they surpass anything and everything? Mystery? Magic? A miracle?

Marceuil's singular interest in cycling indicates an instinctive urge to surpass, to outdo, to transcend others, particularly those he considers weak or even average. Psychologically, he is attempting to destroy what he considers to be his own *shadow* qualities: his small physical stature, his frail appearance, his lack of macho, everything his ego (center of consciousness) cannot accept about himself and therefore seeks to destroy. His obsessive approach to life progressively obliterates his identity, thus encouraging further loss of consciousness of himself as an individual. Rejecting and casting aside characteristics he dislikes is tantamount to self-destruction. Indeed, such comportment is suicidal. The nonpersonal power drive, and the frenzy and excitement of the constant competition between himself and the machine (or himself and the goals he sets), are instrumental in further debilitating his already shaky ego.

Because the ego, the director of the conscious personality, lacks stability, the purely physical (autoerotic) condition aroused by the bicycle and the motion of riding keeps Marcueil imprisoned in the madness of his frenetic activity, thereby preventing him from broadening his view.

Prevalent body consciousness divests Marcueil of any kind of conflict or healthy reactions to situations, acts, or people who might in some way counter his *idée fixe* and so pave the way for psychological growth and broadening of vision.[8]

It might also be suggested that the prolonged concentration and intensity of the energy or libido used to fulfill the racer's objective precludes the necessity of forming any permanent relationships with another person and of delving into his own psyche. No camaraderie or fraternal spirit exists among the cyclists. Indeed, as the race progresses, the reader grows aware of the fact that the five cyclists are but split-offs of Marcueil and not individuals in their own right.

Marcueil's will to succeed as a cyclist conceals unconscious feelings of inferiority as well as superiority. An arrogant belief in his ability to outdo everyone else and the continuous discipline needed to fulfill his goal enable him to gain dominion over what he unconsciously considers his inferior body. This infers a belief in his own perfection—and continuous perfectibility.[9] Intent upon winning the race so that he may prove to the world that he is in fact outstanding and so reveal the Supermale-Deity residing within him, he arrogates to himself what is not properly his. Marcueil, attempting to portray himself as an exceptional person, is in reality the plaything of his instinctual world. As a robotlike individual, unfeeling and unthinking, Marcueil is the puppet of nonpersonal forces within his psyche and as such seeks only to gratify his own needs—nothing more.

The Sex Machine

The same energy expounded by Marcueil as a bicyclist is later focused on sexual matters. Just as the sporting event was different from the norm, so, too, is the sexual act. Marcueil wears a powdery mask while performing his virtually nonstop acrobatics. Such a *persona* is designed to hide what his ego considers his inferior characteristics and reveal only those facets that correspond to and meet with its goals. When Marcueil achieves his end by successfully demonstrating his superior sexual prowess, he earns adulation from his entourage.

Nor does Marcueil enjoy any emotional rapport with his sexual partner. Achievement is what counts, not the depth of the experience. Furthermore, like the bicycle, the female participating in the event is merely a means to an end: a machine whose sole function is to enable him to pursue his goal.

As Jarry resorted to caricature in his description of the bicycle race, so he indulges in imagist portrayal of Marcueil's ribald acts. For the most part he intends to disfigure and unmask what he considers to be a corrosively restrictive notion of morality. Caricature as a technique, Sigmund Freud declared, is one of the artist's techniques for rejecting those who stand for "authority and respect and who are exalted in some sense."[10]

To give credence to Marcueil's sexual feats, Jarry quotes and misquotes statements made by historical and religious figures of old: Diodorus, Proclus, Pliny, Muhammad—the last of whom, he says, had the vigor of sixty men. Rabelais, also mentioned by Jarry, is reported to have stated that Theophrastus (372–287 B.C.), Aristotle's successor as the head of the Peripatetics, wrote about an Indian who performed the sexual act seventy times in one day after taking certain herbs. A pseudoscientific discussion of reproduction, priapism, satyriasis, aphrodisiacs, diet, alcohol, and stimulants is also included.

Under Marcueil's tutelage, Ellen Elson, the daughter of William Elson, a celebrated American chemist (the identification with Edison is intended), develops her proclivity: nymphomania. Like Marcueil, she is devoid of identity. She is all women in one, a collective power. Marcueil's unconscious reaction to what he looks upon as a formidable force is one of fear: she, like all other women, is ready to strike out at the innocent male, to castrate and dismember him. Understandably, then, one of the factors involved in his sexual acts is his desire to subdue and subjugate his partner.

As an *anima* figure (the unconscious aspect of the man's personality), Ellen is pictured as a vamp. Never does she assume the sublime or divinely endowed proportions of Dante's Beatrice or Petrarch's Laura. Although Ellen is frequently depicted as beautiful on the outside, Marcueil sees her subliminally as deformed and grotesquely destructive, particularly when he identifies her with a Siren.

Half-woman or half-bird, this mythical female image (the Lorelei, Mélusine, etc.) is seductive yet negative. She is capable of luring and capturing the young, unsuspecting male, whom she then devours in her embrace; however, frustration and despair ensue since she can satisfy neither him nor herself. Moreover, Sirens, whose goal is to conquer men to acquire power over them, have been featured in literary works as devoid of human feeling. Yet unmediated instinct, which Sirens symbolize, has also been attractive to men since time immemorial. When he knew he would soon hear the mesmerizing songs of the Sirens, Ulysses filled the ears of his crew with wax and had himself tied to the mast of his ship so that he would not yield to their allure. So mesmerizing and frightening were Sirens considered that Aristotle, Pliny, and Ovid wrote about them. In Christian times figures of these maidens with double tails have been depicted on the chapel of Saint-Michel at d'Aiguille at Le Puy, while Sirens in the shape of birds are found at Saint-Benoit-sur-Loire.

On another occasion Marcueil identifies Ellen with her car, which he depicts as a "metallic beast," a "fabulous and lewd God," a "large scarab which flapped its outer wings, scratched, quivered . . ." (64). The chauffeur's mask that she wears, he remarks, transforms her head into a seabird's. Its eyes fascinate him with something supernatural. When peering into them, he feels he is going back to ancient times: Ellen is a reincarnation of the Queen or courtesan archetype—the woman forever ready to satisfy any and all male needs.

Intent upon conveying his great appreciation for the favors she is to bestow, Marcueil takes out his knife to cut some flowers to give her. Moments later he inexplicably thinks better of it.

That Jarry mentions cutting and sticking instruments such as knives and pins throughout the novel is not surprising. Identified with the phallus, activity, and aggression, these sharp objects are also associated with acts of dismemberment. Hindus (Marcueil disguises himself as one during his sexual encounters with Ellen) relate them to some of their "terrible" divinities, who use these implements for cruel and bloody purposes. That Marcueil decides not to cut the flowers, which symbolize spiritual and emotional rapport, suggests that he redirects his libido: that he rechannels this powerful energetic force.

Such dismembering instruments, in Marcueil's case, suggest the presence of murderous instincts. His obsession with death (exemplified in the demise of Jacobs, the cyclist) may be coupled with the love-hate relationship he has with Ellen and his unconscious desire to eliminate what he considers her Lorelei, or Siren-like, characteristics. Those, as previously mentioned, are manifested when he pictures her as a giant bird of prey: a domineering, destructive, and castrating woman.

Marcueil's unconscious fear of failure to reach his goal of seventy or more orgasms in one day becomes obvious in the trip he takes to the zoo on the day planned for this "great" event. It is the animal in him, and nothing more, that he seeks to develop to its ultimate. Amid the many caged beasts on display, he spots something very wonderful and strange: a dynamometer, a machine which both fascinates and threatens him. Because it measures the limits of human strength and performs any activity indefinitely, he views it as dangerous competition. Marcueil wants to be able to surpass everything human or mechanical in the sporting sphere. He decides, therefore, that this automatic power, which the public considers momentarily useful, must be destroyed.

Significant as well is the sex Marcueil projects onto the dynamometer: he identifies its shiny "vertical cleft" or "slot" with the feminine gender. Although the machine is massive, he is convinced that it can be easily destroyed. How? By injecting a 10-centime piece into the proper slot. After doing just that, he grabs the chairlike contraption and shakes its two arms, after which a terrible clanking sound can be heard. Suddenly heaps of broken tubing, screws, bolts, nuts, dials, twisted springs—like animals' innards—fall to the ground before him.

Since the dynamometer, paradigmatic of Marcueil's relationship to the feminine principle and hence representing a threat to his well-being, has been destroyed, the next step is to do away with Ellen, even though she helps him prove his virility. Is Ellen Marcueil's only human victim? According to some reports, several young women on and surrounding his estate have recently been violated innumerable times and died from the experience. No one accuses Marcueil overtly of having perpetrated these acts; nevertheless, the reader senses that he is the culprit.

The great day of sexual acrobatics arrives, and Marcueil accomplishes twenty-four hours of virtually uninterrupted coitus as if participating in a religious ritual. First performing his ablutions, then eating special foods, he dons his Indian mask (consisting of golden powder, rouge, etc.), likening him to the incredible orgiastic performer mentioned by Theophrastus. The room in which Marcueil and Ellen pursue their sexual antics is fitted out like an altar: with candles, incense, soft cushions. As for the act, it is viewed as an apotheosis and an epiphany, two deities becoming one: duality transformed into unity. The successful completion to the climactic drama is marked by the playing of a *Te Deum* on the victrola.

That Marcueil disguises himself as an Indian when performing the sexual act is not surprising. Yogi-tantrics, known for the extraordinary power they have over their bodies, perform the *maithuna* rite—sexual union that is viewed as a transformation ritual. During this ceremony the mortal becomes a divine couple. A period of preparation, including meditation, prayers, fasting, and other such rituals and sacrifices, always precedes the act, which *never* terminates with ejaculation of semen. To permit emission of semen is to fall into the law of time and death, that is, to be the victim of empirical existence. Under such conditions, lovers would be merely libertines and not the detached, Godlike beings they seek to become. Before "supreme great happiness" can take place and "unity of emotion" experienced, all thought and notion of identity (ego-consciousness) must be obliterated. Only then can the condition of *emptiness* be achieved.[11]

Although Jarry was well-versed in Hindu religious practices, there is little resemblance between Marcueil's sexual stunt and the *maithuna* ritual, except perhaps for the number of times coitus is achieved. What does emerge from Marcueil's lovemaking is an emphasis on sadomasochism, implicit in many of Jarry's works. Voyeurism also comes to the fore in this instance, since, to give the sexual experiment a scientific cast, Dr. Balthybus observes the events "discreetly" through a small window in the wall. It is he who confirms the fact that the love act was performed eighty-two times in the space of twenty-four hours; that it could have been extended indefinitely had an artificial rather than a human fecundating machine been used.

Although elated by the fact that he has succeeded in outperforming Theophrastus' Indian, Marcueil still feels a desire to kill Ellen—or Hellen, as he now calls her, after the Greek beauty. He is convinced that only after her demise can his compulsive sexual *desires* be alleviated. He does not kill her, however, since he mistakenly believes her dead when she has only fainted as a result of her ordeal. Then and only then, does he laugh, wax sentimental, and say, "I adore her" (140).

In the days to come, after Ellen has awakened from what has been diagnosed as a hypnotic trance, she tells her father she loves Marcueil and wants to marry him. When Marcueil refuses to comply, *Science* takes over. Ellen's father calls upon Arthur Gough, an American mechanic who has built a most unusual electromagnetic machine, one that can "inspire love." Since Marcueil, the Supermale, considers himself a machine with an iron organism, Gough posits that to combine human and nonhuman machines would transform Marcueil into a loving husband.

The knowledge needed to build the Machine to Inspire Love is predicated on some of Faraday's electromagnetic inventions as well as the electric chair. Here, too, the satiric intent is quite obvious. Since the electric chair causes instantaneous death at 2,200 volts, Gough assumes (though we do not know why) that nothing hurtful can happen if Marcueil is exposed to 10,000 volts. Marcueil is placed in the chair and tied down, after which a strange-looking platinum crenelated crown, with teeth pointed downward, is placed on his head. A diamond-like object carved in the shape of a table appears both in front and in back of the crown. Earflaps made of copper and a sponge-like fabric extend over his temples, thus assuring contact between human and machine. Pieces of semicircular metal, which shine like cabochons, are attached to specific areas of his scalp and hair.

No sooner is the current turned on, electrifying the Supermale's nervous system with 10,000 volts, than something goes awry. Rather than the Machine to Inspire Love influencing the human being, the opposite seems to take place. Dire results ensue; the machine behaves erratically, spiking and sparking madly and uninterruptedly. Its inventor diagnoses the problem: this incredible instrument has fallen in love with the Supermale. Because the scientists had not foreseen such a possibility, they had made no provisions to prevent it.

As the movement of the mechanical parts accelerates, the voltage increases and the metal of the crown turns white-red. Marcueil, in a paroxysmal frenzy, bursts the chains imprisoning him and jumps up from his seat. It is too late. The melting metal flows onto his face like so many tears, explodes, and burns: his demise is preceded by pitiful screams.

As for Ellen, she finally finds a husband—normal in every way.

Although *The Supermale* is a farce and its humor based on man as machine, beneath the bicycle race and the sexual antics is a fiercely macabre and negative note. That a machine kills Marcueil indicates the fragility of the human species and its inability to compete with its own technology. Jarry indeed had a negative view of the machine age and its increasing power over individuals and societies.

The bicycle, the Perpetual Motion Food Machine, the dynamometer, and the Machine to Inspire Love suggest a takeover by the very instruments designed to alleviate pain and suffering and facilitate daily living. Even more dangerous, perhaps, is the fact that machines increasingly cut people off from nature in general and from their own nature, in particular. The dehumanization process, which Jarry foresees as his protagonist competes with machines, encourages a condition of facelessness. Psychologically, neither Marcueil nor Ellen have identities; both are unrelated to others as well as to themselves. Robotlike, they go through life as *others;* insensitive and unable to become emotionally involved. Will twentieth-century men and women succumb to the same fate?

2 James Joyce's "A Painful Case"— The Man-Machine and the Epiphanic Experience

"A Painful Case" (1906), one of James Joyce's short stories in *Dubliners* (1914), introduces readers to the multidimensional world of his protagonist Mr. Duffy. A man who lives only a peripheral life, Mr. Duffy has a *persona* (or mask) that rules his behavior.[1] He gives the impression of being machine-like, his existence ordered, methodical, punctual, and satisfying. Beneath the facade, however, is a subliminal sphere where secret, repressed, unfulfilled, and archaic elements cohabit. The dichotomy in Mr. Duffy's psyche and the tensions aroused by these polarities—the conscious sphere ruling his persona and the unconscious yearning for the realm of feeling—lead him to enter into a relationship with a Mrs. Sinico.

Crucial to Joyce's tale is its brusque conclusion, where a train as object and metaphor induces an epiphanic experience. The trauma of this epiphany, which Joyce describes as "a sudden, spiritual manifestation," heightens Mr. Duffy's understanding of himself and thus opens him up to what he had only sensed until the incident: a whole *feeling* realm.

Machine/Persona Versus Subliminal Mystery

From the very outset of "A Painful Case," we have the distinct impression that despite Mr. Duffy's machinelike and self-satisfied demeanor, this middle-aged man suffers, unconsciously, from some basic antagonism. Such inner hostility is evidenced by the duality of areas he traverses and by the images Joyce uses throughout the tale.

First of all, Mr. Duffy lives in Chapelizod, a suburb of Dublin set apart from the other sections of the city. These Mr. Duffy lumps together and

describes as "mean, modern, and pretentious." Chapelizod is identified
with the medieval Celtic tale of *Tristan and Isolde:* a tale of lovers who
gave up a kingdom and wealth for love. (Izod is a modern decadent form
of Iseult.) Passions once ran high in Chapelizod; flesh, not reason, dictated
the way.

Tristan (or Tristram), one of the most famous heroes of medieval romance, was a fine musician, linguist, chess player, horseman, and fencer;
he was unrivaled in the knightly arts. When he arrived at Cornwall after
multiple adventures, he found his way to the court of his uncle, King Mark,
who accepted him as nephew and heir. After he and Isolde mistakenly
drank the love potion prepared for the king and his wife-to-be, they were
drawn together for eternity.

Scholars maintain that the incidents of this medieval romance, replete
with nostalgia, melancholy, enchantment, and love spells, were historic in
origin and dated from the period of the Viking rule in Ireland. Dramati-
cally antithetical to the Tristan and Isolde story is Joyce's modern setting.
Christian Chapelizod, along with what may at first glance be considered
Mr. Duffy's automated behavior, reveal a condition of aridity, asceticism,
and repression.[2]

That the windows of Mr. Duffy's room open onto a "disused distillery"
might reflect his unlived possibilities. Windows may also serve to encourage this loner to look toward the outside world and not always revert to his
own inner domain. Like bridges, windows permit interchange, flexibility,
and relatedness. Such communication not only allows air to circulate, but
liquefies what has grown static and rigid.

A "disused" distillery also indicates the abrogation of what had formerly provided a source of pleasure for people, expanding their consciousness and filling them with Dionysian fervor. Whiskey liberates a whole
instinctual realm; it frees the individual, at least momentarily, from
social and self-imposed strictures. Whiskey, which in Gaelic means "water of life," is associated with youth, fervor, and eternity. As such, it may
be looked upon as a sacred brew in both a physical and spiritual sphere.
Did not the love potion which Tristan and Isolde drank bring on their
great passion? Mr. Duffy's distillery, however—and anything it represents—is no longer operational.

Even more significant is "the shallow river" (the Liffey) that is also visible
from Mr. Duffy's window. The longest river in Ireland, it turns on itself
continuously, creating circular patterns over a seventy-mile stretch of land.
Not only are the waters of the Liffey a paradigm for all that is nourishing,
fertile, and positive for the Irish, and Joyce in particular, but they also
represent beauty, identified as it is with the feminine principle. (Joyce calls
the river the Anna Livia.)[3] Although Mr. Duffy has a view from his window

of this generative force and aesthetic vision, this source of rebirth and fertility, does he ever really *see* it? That it is there at all may be an indication of its presence in his psyche as an inactive, merely latent force.

Mr. Duffy's "old sombre house" also mirrors his personality. Its Spartan conditions seem to reflect his highly organized routine that functions with enginelike precision. Joyce ironically emphasizes the fact that Mr. Duffy "had himself bought every article of furniture in the room. . . ." The uncarpeted floor and frugally furnished living area—"a black iron bedstead, an iron washstand, four cane chairs," and a few other objects—introduce readers to a man who is seemingly satisfied with bare necessities. Never does he feast, never does he revel; he just pursues his life's course by rote. The hand mirror above the washstand might entice a more curious fellow to peer into himself, to speculate (from *speculum*, the Latin word for mirror) about his life-style. It seemingly has no such effect on Mr. Duffy, who has never really *looked* at himself. As for the white-shaded lamp which stands "as the sole ornament of the mantelpiece," it, too, suggests Draconian severity and a circumscribed existence.

Asceticism, both material and emotional, rules Mr. Duffy's every move and thought. No frivolities detract him from what he considers his rigorous obligations toward himself and society. Nor does he have friends or even relationships. His exilic life, his deeply introverted nature, allow him to pursue his uneventful but secure and routine way.

Joyce does introduce certain clues that permit us to peer beneath Mr. Duffy's persona into that mysterious and hermetic other self buried within his psyche. His bookcase, for example, contains, among other volumes, a complete Wordsworth and a copy of the *Maynooth Catechism*; in his desk lies a manuscript translation of Gerhardt Hauptmann's *Michael Kramer*. What do these literary and religious works imply about Mr. Duffy's intellectual, spiritual, and affective inclinations?

The presence of a "complete" Wordsworth is ironic. This worshipper of nature, seeker of reform, and humanitarian so sympathetic to liberal causes was also an innovative poet—but only from 1795 to 1805. What he wrote thereafter was for the most part "blather." Had Mr. Duffy owned merely an anthology of Wordsworth's poetry, it would indicate taste and knowledge, as well as discernment. That he owns his complete works suggests the opposite. Yet the fact that Wordsworth's romantic writings even garnish his bookshelf underscores the *feeling* side of Mr. Duffy's personality: the very element he has stifled and rejected within himself. Only his persona, or "public face," is revealed to others.

The *Maynooth Catechism* stands at one end of the top shelf of his bookcase, while the complete Wordsworth has been placed on the lowest shelf, underscoring another dichotomy in Mr. Duffy's personality. Significant as well is the fact that the title of the former volume is not visible at first glance since it has been "sewn into the cloth cover of a notebook." Has it been covered because it is worn and needs to be protected? Or is Mr. Duffy simply trying to hide it from view?

Maynooth is the seat of St. Patrick's College—the principal institution in Ireland for training the Roman Catholic clergy that was founded in 1795. Although Mr. Duffy has "neither companions nor friends, church nor creed," the *Maynooth Catechism* nevertheless represents the Catholic credo, with its emphasis on spirit to the detriment of body. Whether Mr. Duffy accepts it or not, the *Catechism* stands as part of his religious heritage, and is therefore very much present in the pattern of his life.

Most important, but tucked in Mr. Duffy's desk, is the manuscript translation of Hauptmann's play *Michael Kramer* (1900).[4] Although this German dramatist usually depicted the suffering of working people and the poverty-stricken middle classes, *Michael Kramer* goes beyond Hauptmann's political orientation. It dramatizes the plight of a young sculptor who is too weak to choose between his love for a waitress and the dictates of a father who wants him to devote his life to art. Highly sensitive and feeling, the sculptor fails to fight his oppressor—a father who is incapable of love and communication with his gifted son. The excoriating tension felt by the young man and the breadth of the sacrifice demanded of him by his father drive him to suicide.[5] That Mr. Duffy has been translating *Michael Kramer*, a play in which the conflict between love and sacrifice ends in death, brings Tristan's love for Isolde to mind. A whole world of passion, latent within Mr. Duffy, has been relegated to a desk drawer.

If we judge Mr. Duffy's taste and psychological needs by the reading material mentioned above, we could point to conflicting undercurrents within his psyche: a painful disquietude between sexual and spiritual spheres, between the recluse and the man so deeply in need of female companionship and love. Mr. Duffy's mechanical, organized, and systematized social self seems unable to fill the growing man within him.

Mr. Duffy, then, may be viewed as a man whose spawning, generating, proliferating inner world is held together by convention, force of habit—and fear. That he "abhorred anything which betokened physical or mental disorder" is, therefore, predictable. To keep the combustible—perhaps even explosive—subliminal contents under control is crucial for him. Such a stance, however, requires preserving a *stable* existence: uniformity, regularity, and a systematic—even rigid—life-style. Hence every minute of Mr. Duffy's life is accounted for—even his evenings spent "roaming" about Chapelizod. Such a clockwork existence, however, denies him the possibility of exploring his inner nature, of thinking, feeling, or even anguishing over something. Plodding along, pursuing his daily routine, is his course.

Mr. Duffy's habits, like the functioning of a machine, are as predictable as his thoughts and reactions. He takes the tram to the city daily, to his job as cashier in a private bank. That he uses public transportation suggests that he is no different from the other passengers. On the surface, then, there is nothing distinctive, unique, or even interesting about him. His habits seem to be the natural outcome of both his culture and his religious upbringing—and so he dons the mask—his social face—that his fellow citizens expect him to wear.

Although Mr. Duffy wants to give the impression of being, so to speak, on top of everything, "a mediaeval doctor," Joyce writes, "would have called him saturnine." Let us recall in this connection the advice given by Paracelsus, a sixteenth-century medical man, to link rather than separate the physical and spiritual sides of being. Thus can disease, which he considered an imbalance in the system, be rectified. Important as well is another Paracelsus dictum that is also antithetical to Mr. Duffy's way: "We are born to be awake, not to sleep! Therefore, man, learn and learn, question and question, do not be ashamed of it; for only thus can you earn a name that will resound in all countries and never be forgotten."[6]

Mr. Duffy is surely asleep. Never does he waver in his comportment. Nor ever think out a problem or allow any obstacle to impede his efforts to achieve a mechanized existence. And so he goes along day after day, keeping to his schedule and preoccupied with only what he considers to be *his* concerns. The outer world exists only insofar as he conforms to its dicta, never in terms of acknowledging *another person's* existence.

The astrological implications in Joyce's use of "saturnine" to describe Mr. Duffy are of import. This adjective refers to a person whose disposition is sullen, surly, gloomy, and sardonic. Lead, associated with the planet Saturn, is not only the heaviest of metals, but also causes severe neurological problems. If too much of this poisonous element infiltrates the body, it can kill. To be psychologically overly saturnine, then, can destroy a personality. Saturn is also the Roman God of the harvest, "the sower" of seeds and thus the god of plenty. When he is referred to in this aspect, he becomes a positive agent. This divinity's symbol, the sickle, may also be viewed as a salutary force: an instrument used to cut down and sever, to prune and destroy dead and decayed branches that sap the vital essence of a plant or tree and hence encourage the generation of new growth. Should Mr. Duffy pursue the sameness of his course indefinitely, the image implies, he will be poisoned by his own noxious sediment. By altering his direction and cutting off the dead branches, he may be renewed and his life enriched.

In later times Saturn was identified with Kronos, the Greek God who swallowed his children for fear of being overthrown by them, which sheds a still different light upon Mr. Duffy's character. Like Kronos, he is unable to come to terms with the fear that corrodes his psyche: he is afraid of losing his social face. What would people say? Rather than dealing with the possible overthrow of his daily routine, he represses any force that might alter his restrictive and restricted existence. (Let us recall that Zeus, with the help of the ocean nymph Thetis, made Kronos disgorge his children, after which he overpowered him. Will Mr. Duffy be forced to succumb to a similar ejection? The expulsion of those nascent fertile, feeling forces living within him *in potentia* would allow a whole vital and creative dimension to burgeon. For the time being, Mr. Duffy seems to prefer a condition of stasis and paralysis to the trauma upheavals generate.)

Joyce adds other details concerning Mr. Duffy's personal appearance. His face, for example, has taken on the "brown tint of Dublin streets," indicating an affinity with the archaic aspects of his city: an atmosphere layered, so to speak, with centuries of soot, dirt, and grime. Yet Dublin, this "black pool" built on bog, is also a nourishing and infinitely fertile area, the source of much creativity for its inhabitants—even this middle-aged man, if he would only take advantage of them. But Mr. Duffy insists on maintaining his persona, as exemplified by his "dry black" lifeless hair, his "tawny" mustache, his "unamiable" mouth, and the layout of cheekbones that reveal a "harsh character." His eyes, however, disclose another domain: the other secret and unlived side of his psyche.

That Mr. Duffy "lived at a little distance from his body" suggests the disconnection of his physical and spiritual worlds. Understandably so, since according to the Platonic view—and that part of the Christian ethic influenced by it—the physical or animal side of the human being is denigrated and therefore must always be subdued, while the thinking or spiritual factors—the Godly aspect of humankind—must be encouraged to expand and grow. That a top-heavy creature emerges from such disparity is not surprising.

The word "distance" implies spatial separation in the empirical domain, as well as in humankind's inner spheres. Because Mr. Duffy is not *in touch* with his body, he is, in effect, repudiating and starving it. Repressing this earth force requires a rigid, strong-willed asceticism and an outward silence that renders him unable to communicate with and relate to people. He dreads the thought of making a poor impression on others because he is never certain as to the validity of his behavior—"regarding his own acts with doubtful side-glances." Mr. Duffy cannot face the world at large and unconsciously looks away, disclosing fundamental evasiveness and elusiveness—weak and shifty qualities. Indeed, he is incapable of coming out of his shell; it serves as protection from the possibly cruel collective.

Duffy so identifies with his outer attitude that he has no consciousness of his subliminal inner process. His repressed functions therefore remain unconscious and embryonic. Were he to *see* himself plainly, he might suffer distress at the discovery of the unlikable, stiff, selfish, unfeeling fellow that he is.

Mr. Duffy, unlike the autonomous man he considers himself to be, resembles the tram he takes to Dublin every morning. Throughout the working day he follows his timetable course, never varying his punctilious practices. Such a mechanical existence does have its positive side. His employers, the directors of a private bank in Baggot Street, know that they have an honest and reliable cashier. His habits are Spartan: a meager and mundane lunch consisting of a bottle of beer and arrowroot biscuits; dinner at the George's Street eating house, "safe" from the "gilded youth." His programmed routine keeps him secure, as do his daily tram rides. There is nothing new in his scheduled existence, nothing exciting—but nothing dangerous either. So rigid is Mr. Duffy's schedule, so serious-minded is his approach to life, so specialized is his work in the growing industrialized society of the time that he has little or no occasion to give vent to his affective side; his life is regulated to the last second, "without room for harvest."

However, the archaic *feeling* side of his psyche does find a convenient outlet in music. In the evenings after work, Mr. Duffy frequently plays his landlady's piano. This seemingly inflexible and inaccessible man is deeply moved by Mozart. His love for the works of the Austrian composer lures him to the opera and to concerts. He projects feeling onto music, incorporating into melody what has become estranged or alienated from him and thereby sublimating those very elements he looks upon as burdensome. Thus he rids himself of passion and frenzy—those potentially uncontrollable tendencies within his psyche—amalgamating in this manner both subject and object.[7]

Under such circumstances Mr. Duffy will never suffer humiliation: his persona is always firmly attached, his manner remains unvaried. Although he gives the impression of being an integrated person, the very contrary is true.[8] Opposites are present, but since Mr. Duffy is unaware of their existence within himself (the world of instinct remaining unconscious), they are for all intents and purposes nonexistent. His machinelike persona is at odds with his hidden and secret musical or feeling world; it continues to function, however, thereby sheltering him against harm. He is, so to speak, *out of reach.*

Nevertheless, sound, tone, timbre, melody, harmony, and rhythm trigger dangerous reactions within Mr. Duffy; the world of emotion and instinct is volatilized. In psychological terms, his feeling world can be identified with the *shadow:* that subliminal part of the personality which the ego (center of consciousness) considers inferior or weak and rejects. Like the Stoics or the ascetics—Christian or otherwise—Mr. Duffy has learned to control passion and desire, renounce the pleasure principle, and behave in a detached manner in the external world. Stoic philosophers and patristic church fathers taught that emotions were evil and had to be overcome by cognitive or spiritual means. For them ethical progress was a matter of reason.

What are the psychological implications of such a route? First and foremost, the instinctual world—which is part of the whole human being—is not taken into account. To suppress the entire "weak" affective side (including love, affection, relatedness) is tantamount to starving it. Such extreme deprivation may eventually lead to a loss of control and destroy the personality's precarious balance.

When the Stoics and religious ascetics tried to annihilate what they considered humankind's inferior characteristics, that is, the instincts, they did not take into consideration the fact that when instincts are properly understood and accepted, they act in harmony with other aspects of the personality as positive forces. When unattended, however, they seethe beneath the surface and become virulent and mutilating. Not to take into account a person's earthly half (*physis*), and merely to cultivate the intellectual, spiritual, or godly side, is to cut the individual off from life, to create a top-heavy being whose illusions and delusions will cause him or her to wax in self-deception or narcissistic egocentricity.

Mr. Duffy is such a being. Unconsciously he is always attempting to do away with that vital, earthy, carnal side of his psyche that he considers inferior and worthy of pulverization. Unlike the Stoics and religious ascetics, however, he has no spiritual life to fill the void left by sexual or instinctual divestiture. Nor does he have companions or friends. The rituals he imposes on himself for "dignity's sake" focus on family matters. These consist of visits to relatives at Christmas or to the cemetery after funerals.

Music, which plays such a significant role in Mr. Duffy's life, may be considered, psychologically, as an *anima* figure: an unconscious and abstract feminine power living an autonomous existence within his psyche. Music's tonalities excite him, fill him with an inner and subdued glow. Not of flesh and blood, music does not threaten him as a fearsome, monstrous, and corruptive force that can shred his persona, or "public face." On the contrary, it permits him, so to speak, to get out of himself—to enjoy in safety.

As an anima force, music assumes a kind of autonomy over his ego. It inspires him to go out into the world to listen to concerts and operas. At these moments, when reason recedes into the background and the anima functions overtly, he becomes most vulnerable and impressionable.

That Mr. Duffy should prefer Mozart not only suggests fine musical taste on his part, but also a superior understanding of the creative principle. While the average tram-taking Dubliner reacts enthusiastically to popular little Irish ditties, Mr. Duffy's attraction to Mozart reveals a more sensitive and evolved power at work.

Operational within him, then, is the music/anima force that entices him to the Rotunda. When, on one evening, the lady sitting next to him conveys feelings of pity for the singers performing to an almost empty opera house, Mr. Duffy responds immediately to her warm and compassionate nature, interpreting her statement "as an invitation to talk." He is impressed by her handsome and dignified countenance, which is as follows:

> The eyes were very dark blue and steady. Their gaze began with a defiant note but was confused by what seemed a deliberate swoon of the pupil into the iris, revealing for an instant a temperament of great sensibility. The pupil reasserted itself quickly, this half-disclosed nature fell back again under the reign of prudence, and her astrakhan jacket, moulding her bosom of a certain fullness, struck the note of defiance more definitely.

Mr. Duffy's meeting with Mrs. Sinico may be viewed as a *synchronistic* event (a meaningful coincidence).[9] Her presence is a living recognition of a deep-seated need within him. Unconsciously, he not only longs for the new, the different, and perhaps even the *defiant*, thereby destroying the routine and paralyzing *steadiness* of his life, but also for the flesh-and-blood woman. Something within Mr. Duffy seems to have crystallized during their encounter.

Another synchronistic happening occurs a few weeks later when Mr. Duffy meets Mrs. Sinico at a concert at Earlsfort. During the course of their conversation, he learns that her husband's great-great grandfather had come from Leghorn, that the husband is captain of a mercantile boat which sails between Dublin and Holland, that he is frequently away from home, and that the couple have one daughter.

In a third synchronistic episode, Mr. Duffy finds "the courage" to ask her to see him again. She accepts. Their rendezvous are always set for evenings in quiet neighborhoods. Later, after Mr. Duffy—unwilling to pursue what he considers "underhand ways"—has "forced" her to invite him to her house, he meets Mr. Sinico, who encourages his visits, believing his intent is to court his daughter and never thinking for a moment that his wife, whom he "had dismissed . . . so sincerely from his gallery of pleasures," is the focus of Mr. Duffy's interest.

Although Mr. Duffy visits Mrs. Sinico frequently at her "little cottage outside of Dublin," it is not surprising that he fails to build any kind of *personal* relationship with her. Their discussions are intellectual (abstract), revolving around music and politics for the most part. Because neither Mr. Duffy nor Mrs. Sinico has had any previous adventures, they see no harm in pursuing their relationship. As Joyce describes it: "Little by little he entangled his thoughts with hers. He lent her books, provided her with ideas, shared his intellectual life with her. She listened to all."

During their rendezvous, Mrs. Sinico, a deeply understanding and compassionate woman whose lonely existence has given her insights into the human heart, treats Mr. Duffy as he needs to be approached, with "maternal solicitude." In so doing, she activates a whole feeling dimension within him. When she urges him to open up, to give vent to his nature, she plays the role of "his confessor." So impressed is she with Mr. Duffy's "theories" that she urges him to commit his thoughts to paper. Replying rather scornfully, he says he does not consider it fitting to "compete with phrasemongers." Professional writers he regards as an "obtuse middle class . . . incapable of thinking consecutively for sixty seconds."

That Joyce alludes to Mr. Duffy's concert- and opera-going as his only "dissipation" is an irony. He is thereby associating his hero's love for music with all that is intemperate, extravagant, pleasurable, hedonistic, or dissolute. Despite such a negative identification, however, Mr. Duffy continues to indulge his bent, aware of the fact that since his indulgences are restrained within conventionally approved meeting places and his feelings are displayed overtly, no harm can come to his public image.

As the days pass, Mrs. Sinico, the anima figure, becomes a living repository for Mr. Duffy's feelings: a world always kept separate from his outer attitude. The fact that he never considers Mrs. Sinico as an individual in her own right, with her own likes and dislikes, indicates an identification with his unconscious feminine image. Since this psychological condition does not allow for any discrimination, reason is functionless. Thus Mr. Duffy overvalues her insight, sensitivity, and understanding.

When losing himself in music, an abstract principle, Mr. Duffy is in no danger of losing his self-control. He is master of the situation. When dealing with a flesh-and-blood human being, however, the relationship becomes multilayered and behavioral patterns go askew. Should Mrs. Sinico—at any time—step out of the role Mr. Duffy has envisaged for her, he would reject her.

Onto the little world that Mrs. Sinico's home has become for the pair, each projects a very different meaning. For Mr. Duffy, it symbolizes a maternal breast as well as a hierarchy of abstract states: everything connected with Mrs. Sinico is an outgrowth of his own needs. Even as the two broach "less remote" subjects during their conversations, no *real* meeting evolves between them. She is the positive source of energy for which he has yearned, the origin of a new life. But he remains oblivious to her needs, her yearning for love and tenderness brought about by her husband's absences and contempt for her. Joyce, as narrator, reveals the subhuman function that has been assigned her when Mr. Duffy views himself as a tender plant and Mrs. Sinico as merely "a warm soil about an exotic."

Nor is it surprising that as they talk deep into the night, she allows "the dark to fall upon them, refraining from lighting the lamp." As a seed gestates in black and moist earth, so does a dream in the unconscious. If light, to which the rational function is traditionally compared, beats down too intensely on this seed, it will become dry and vanish. The longer the room remains in darkness, the greater becomes Mr. Duffy's sense of security, the more daring his forays into fantasy and self-inflation. As a shadow figure, Mrs. Sinico represents, paradoxically, everything that Mr. Duffy's conscious attitude rejects in the empirical domain. This includes whatever is incompatible with his rigid persona—love, feeling, understanding, passion, gentleness.

"The dark discreet room, their isolation, the music that still vibrated in their ears united them." These elements set the stage for an initiatory ritual, a rite of passage that takes the acolytes from a tightly sealed and closed world to one of openness, that is, from the rational to the irrational sphere, from exile to integration. Indeed, the "discreet" or secret room— reminiscent of those underground chambers used in the Eleusinian mysteries of old—might have been instrumental in leading Mr. Duffy and Mrs. Sinico from death to life.

So deeply "entangled" do his thoughts become, that he, increasingly cut off from the world at large and from himself at a certain point, feels "exalted," "emotionalized," and uplifted by what *he* considers to be a "union" of two beings, a meeting of the minds. That he experiences an *exaltatio intellectus* allows him to become assimilated into the highest realms of true intelligence: the world of the Idea and Ideal—the Angelical. "He thought that in her eyes he would ascend to an angelical nature." There, the quintessence of ethereality and life can be known.[10]

So deeply entrenched is Mr. Duffy in his own ideations, so alienated is he from the empirical sphere, that he becomes increasingly sensitive to audible tones and vibrations. As he talks, his ear transformed into an organ of comprehension, a canal, an echo of his thoughts and feelings, he catches "himself listening to the sound of his own voice," its timbre and intensity disclosing a whole arcane realm for him that perhaps he likens to the breath used in speech and sound—*ruah* or *pneuma*, which represents the Spirit of God (Gen. 2:7). The exaltation he feels as music, respiration, word, and feeling fuse transcends human dimension, endowing his voice with archetypal power. Emanating as it does from an objective psyche, it has grown strangely "impersonal," speaking of "the soul's incurable loneliness" in the third person, of its inability to give of itself to others.

A transpersonal force now, Mr. Duffy peers into Mrs. Sinico's eyes and feels himself ascending to "an angelical stature," thereby growing increasingly remote from the world of phenomena. Angels, considered ethereal, aerial, and sexless beings, have multiple functions: they may be messengers, protectors, guardians. As a sublimated being, Mr. Duffy is now an untouchable and unapproachable presence.

While angelical stature indicates, paradigmatically, Mr. Duffy's inability to descend to the real world, it also suggests sexual deprivation. Caught as he is between the world of the spirit and that of sexuality, he can live comfortably in neither realm. Hence his identification with angels may be considered an unconscious rejection of life, a salute to his peripheral existence. In any case, any departure from the roles he and Mrs. Sinico are now playing will destroy the delicate balance between the two. Most particularly, if Mrs. Sinico modifies her behavior, it will be interpreted by Mr. Duffy as a violation of his fantasy image, earning her his immediate rejection.

And indeed, one evening Mrs. Sinico shows "every sign of unusual excitement" during the course of her *spiritual* encounter with Mr. Duffy. He, however, immersed in his angelic identity, never once considers her reactions to his talk, encrusted as he is by his solipsistic world. She, not inured to his mechanical ways, acts on impulse; catching "his hand passionately," she "presse[s] it to her cheek." Such an outburst is unacceptable to Mr. Duffy and worthy of instant dismissal.

The hand, representing activity and aggression, also indicates the *manifestation* of an unconscious force. (The root of "hand" in French, *main*, and in Latin, *manus*, is the same as that of "*man*ifestation".) To use the hand, then, gives concretion or empirical reality to what has only been sensed on an abstract level. Mrs. Sinico's action therefore inscribes meaning in space, transfers feeling out of the "discreet," "secret," and dark room to the realm of light and alters Mr. Duffy's image of her.

Predictably, this *real* act puts an end to their relationship. So out of tune is Mr. Duffy with his feeling world that he fails to adapt to the situation. So outrageously has Mrs. Sinico violated the moral code that he is overpowered. She has depotentiated what he looks upon as sacred. Nature has triumphed where heretofore he saw only spirit. His one-sided and distorted attitude has been toppled. Disillusionment and a sense of betrayal and deception follow. Mrs. Sinico must be banished from his world so that some semblance of balance may be restored.

On a cold autumn day a week following the incident, Mr. Duffy arranges to meet Mrs. Sinico at a cake shop near the Parkgate. Even the season is inauspicious: the end of a fruitful summer, the beginning of seasonal defoliation and divestiture. He suggests, and Mrs. Sinico agrees, that they should not see each other again: " 'Every bond,' he said, 'is a bond to sorrow.' " As they walk to the tram, Mrs. Sinico, unable to contain her emotions, begins trembling violently. Fearing that she might "collapse," and unwilling to deal with her trauma, Mr. Duffy bids her farewell. He wants no commitment; no outside obligations that bind him to the real world.

The bond which has been theirs has been broken, putting an end to Mr. Duffy's fantasy world. The mystical and magical domain, where he lived in the moist, brown-black earth of the psyche, has given way to the routine empirical world. "They walked in silence towards the tram. . . ."

Mr. Duffy returns to his mechanical existence: relentless like the tram, in the sameness of *its* and *his* circular routes. Ensconced once again in his safe, sexless, and detached existence, his automatonlike and pedestrian persona rules supreme.

The Train: The Epiphany

The train, a more powerful machine than the tram, will be instrumental in bringing on what James Joyce calls the epiphany. Joyce defined the epiphany as "a sudden spiritual manifestation, whether in the vulgarity of speech or gesture or in a memorable phase of the mind itself," and as "the most delicate of evanescent moments;" it brings awareness to the individual experiencing its numinosity. Joyce did not look upon the epiphany as the revelation of Christ to the Magi, but rather as a metaphor for that moment when "the soul of the commonest object" takes on radiance; when the "whatness of a thing" is suddenly revealed; when an unforeseen joy or sorrow opens up onto an infinite domain.[11]

Four years pass after Mr. Duffy severs relations with Mrs. Sinico. More deeply entrenched than ever in his systematized and patterned existence, he now even refrains from going to concerts for fear of meeting her and exposing himself to the danger of her affects. Nevertheless, some changes in his habits are evident. He has bought some pieces of music and two books: *Thus Spake Zarathustra* and *The Gay Science.*

That Mr. Duffy has bought two of Nietzsche's works is understandable in that he considers himself a kind of *Übermensch* superior to the rabble walking the streets of Dublin. Unlike Nietzsche's hero, however, Mr. Duffy is in no way Dionysian in outlook or makeup. His life is therefore antithetical to the one prescribed in *The Gay Science:* "The secret of the greatest fruitfulness and the greatest enjoyment of existence is *to live danger-*

ously."[12] To attempt to depotentiate instinct was for the German philosopher poet to denature natural values.[13]

Zarathustra represents the reverse of self-abnegation, restraint, and asceticism. As a promoter of the Dionysian archetype, he encourages humankind to experience nature instinctually, to emphasize earth factors—the visceral and the sexual—which many Christians, said Nietzsche, considered "evil." Suffering, weakness, pain, and punishment of the body are for Zarathustra negative and harmful, leading to decadence, to a "slave morality." Strength and courage, joy, and an affirmation of life's pleasurable aspects should instead be encouraged.

Such duality as Mr. Duffy experiences—his unconsciously rejected sexual needs versus his proclivity for the spiritual sphere and the conscious set of moral precepts this connotes—creates internecine warfare within his psyche. He is a dissociated human being. Only by reconciling the sexual and the spiritual within oneself, rather than repressing one or the other, can an individual come to terms with such disparities and lead a harmonious existence.

Mr. Duffy seems fated to be a man at odds with himself until one evening, while eating his usual supper of corned beef and cabbage, he happens upon an article in the paper—"The Death of a Lady at Sydney Parade—A Painful Case"—and is stunned. The lady in question is Mrs. Sinico: "while attempting to cross the railroad line, she was knocked down by the engine of the ten o'clock slow train from Kingstown, thereby sustaining injuries of the head and right side which led to her death." The article also states that she had become an alcoholic. Her death, however, according to the assistant house surgeon of the City of Dublin Hospital, was not due to the injuries sustained, but to the "shock and sudden failure of the heart's action."

Rather than reacting with compassion and sorrow, Mr. Duffy is "revolted." He is convinced that he has been twice deceived: once when she took his hand and put it to her cheek and again when she debased herself by taking to the bottle. Let us recall in this connection the image of the "disused distillery" which Mr. Duffy can see from his window. That Mrs. Sinico's drinking overwhelms him with disgust is proof of his utter lack of understanding of her suffering after his departure from her life. It is as if he has been the catalyst: that very power that wrenched Tristan from Isolde and led to the *Liebestod*, or Love-Death. Rather than thinking of Mrs. Sinico, Mr. Duffy focuses on *his* defilement: he tarnished his purity by speaking to a commonplace and vulgar woman "of what he held sacred." The very thought of such contact with this "miserable and malodorous" woman makes him feel utterly "degraded." Indeed, she was "unfit to live," he thinks, her life having no "strength of purpose."

So disturbed is Mr. Duffy by his sense of degradation that he goes to the public house at Chapelizod Bridge and orders a hot punch. He seems unaffected as he watches the smoke filter into the room, the spittle drop onto the floor. Not so: when remembering his own acts and motivations, they make him "feel ill at ease." But only momentarily. Seconds later, he absolves himself. "How was he to blame?" He could not have possibly continued the pretense by seeing her. He was blameless, he muses, having cut off their relationship cleanly. A sense of infantile innocence fills his being. Remorse vanishes as he heaps the blame on Mrs. Sinico. She was the sinner. He behaved ethically by adhering to the collective moral code. It was his dignity that was sullied for keeping company with an alcoholic.

So acute is his distress that images begin flooding his memory, particularly that of the solitary woman who "must have been sitting night after night alone in that room." This is the first time Mr. Duffy thinks of her life and not exclusively about himself. Some inner power has begun to strike his built-in defense mechanisms, dismembering what has been so pat and stultified. As he starts to question the meaning and impact of his acts, he slowly experiences a collision between the reasonable approach to the affair—a rejection of what he considers Mrs. Sinico's immorality—and his own unconscious feeling world, which she has come to represent. It is the latter, which I have called the shadow side of his personality, that yearns for love, relatedness, and sexuality. He tried desperately to annihilate these for fear he might fall prey to their lawless insubordination. Mr. Duffy is, to use Nietzsche's phrase, a "pale felon" who cannot confront his acts.[14]

Mr. Duffy leaves the public house after nine o'clock and enters the park where he used to walk with Mrs. Sinico. It was in this fertile forested terrain, identified with Isolde's well, that this legendary love figure had pledged herself for all time to Tristan. That Mr. Duffy seeks out the park, although its trees have grown "gaunt" and barren with approaching winter, indicates his inner need to commune with the past, with Mrs. Sinico and the nourishing, fertile earth forces for which she stood.

The world of abstraction has to be dissolved so that nature—Mr. Duffy's basic nature—can come to the fore. Fluidity must break down the rigid carapace he has built up. Only when a liquid relationship exists between conscious values and unconscious contents can an individual begin to experience wholeness. As Mr. Duffy walks through "bleak alleys," following the same paths he and Mrs. Sinico had taken four years previously, he seems to experience her presence, to "feel her voice touch his ear, her hand touch his." He stops. At last he questions himself: "Why had he withheld life from her? Why had he sentenced her to death?" Mr. Duffy feels "his moral nature falling to pieces." Liquidity that now exists between the various segments of his psyche slowly dismembers his rigid moral concepts, so filled with arid abstractions and so removed from nature's bounties. As he relives his memories, his gaze shifts to the River Liffey and its waters, forever spawning life. Let us recall that although the river is visible from Mr. Duffy's windows at Chapelizod, as mentioned at the outset of the story, he has always been impervious to the waters' riches. He has never really *seen* them. He does now.

Other life-giving factors also come into view. The lights of Dublin "burned redly and hospitably in the cold night." Never before has Mr. Duffy felt any kind of rapport with others, and certainly not with the city that he has identified only with his work, his routine, his scheduled existence. It has all changed: the lights kindling with energy and fire seem to warm him. Then he looks around at the "venal and furtive" lovers lying about in the grass. Why does their presence fill him with despair?

Where Mr. Duffy has until this moment experienced only his own rectitude, his own persona, a bridge is now being built between himself and the world outside, between his unconscious and repressed secret realm and his consciously structured world. He understands what he has missed: "He gnawed the rectitude of his life; he felt that he had been outcast from life's feast." He begins to understand that he has been the sinner. He has sentenced to death the one person who loved him, even to "ignominy" and "a death of shame." No one wants him now, least of all the lovers in the park around him. Again he looks at the source of nature's riches, the "grey gleaming river, winding along towards Dublin," and beyond the river he hears the goods train, "like a worm with a fiery head winding through the darkness, obstinately and laborously." His ears pound with the engine's "laborious drone" that translates itself into "the syllables" of Mrs. Sinico's name.

Mr. Duffy's epiphanic experience, metaphorized in the train image, has opened him up to the fire of his own being, shedding luminosity where there had only been darkness, reality where there had only been fantasy, cohesion where there had only been divisiveness.

Although Mr. Duffy turns back the way he had come, all is different now. No longer does he hear the sound of the engine or the syllables of Mrs. Sinico's name. Nor does he *feel* her presence. Cut off from extraneous matters, he even begins "to doubt the reality of what memory told him."

The silence that so completely pervades Mr. Duffy's world compels him to face himself, to peer into that inner maw, that void—that mirror which, Joyce tells us at the outset, "hung above the washstand." The numinosity of the epiphany is such that it opens him up, for the first time, to both sides of the life experience *simultaneously.* "He *felt* that he was alone."

The very train that was instrumental in Mrs. Sinico's demise has also brought on the epiphanic experience. As reality and metaphor, the train serves to dismember both Mr. Duffy's anima figure (through the death of the living woman) and his automated persona. These have remained dissociated from each other and thus prevented him from experiencing "life's feast." The ensuing revelation causes Mr. Duffy to know "the most delicate of evanescent moments" he has ever encountered on earth.

3 Stanislaw I. Witkiewicz's *The Crazy Locomotive*—A Surrealist's View of the Metaphysics of Mechanization

Stanislaw I. Witkiewicz's two-act play *The Crazy Locomotive* (1923) deals not merely with a metaphoric machine, but with a real locomotive which gives the illusion of speeding across the stage, then crashing. Symptomatic of machines in general, Witkiewicz's locomotive is viewed as a destroyer of people, societies, and cultures; a devourer of rational attitudes; a despoiler of feeling relationships. Nevertheless, it is an object of fascination: it mesmerizes and haunts, provoking madness in some and morbidity in others.

The Crazy Locomotive may be viewed as a dream: a manifestation of the irrational sphere which keeps gaining in ascendancy while concomitantly provoking a loss of adaptation to reality. The continuously accelerating speed of the locomotive during the course of the play suggests a heightening of psychic function—a desire to transcend the space-time category of consciousness, and therefore dissipate its energy. Under such conditions, the ego (center of consciousness) virtually ceases to function, allowing the collective unconscious to take over. The progressive diminution of potential energy in the rational domain causes a schizophrenic condition.[1]

The Crazy Locomotive is arresting theatrically as well as psychologically. Disconcerting lighting techniques coupled with strident sound effects have an impact on spectators' auditory and visual senses. The brutality and gore of the happenings underscore the visceral atmosphere, demonstrating the prevailing condition of spiritual bankruptcy. Another electrifying effect characterizes this surrealist play: the protagonists are not flesh and blood. Like wooden puppets, they ambulate, gesticulate, and speak out as alienated beings who feel no real rapport with one another. Faceless and identityless, they shift about, masking and unmasking themselves amid sequences of irrational acts and dialogue. Sentences do not necessarily follow ideationally; nor are actions and reactions logically set forth. Anything can mean everything or vice versa.

The Crazy Locomotive, like many a surrealist play, does reveal certain unpalatable truths: it seeks to shatter the values of the once-active but now decadent bourgeois society, but it also attempts to dismember the tenets of Futurism, a movement begun in 1909 by Filippo Tommaso Marinetti.

Along with his followers Balla, Severini, Carra, Boccioni, and others, Marinetti called for a revolutionary attitude toward life, including contempt for women and exaltation of the machine and everything associated with it: speed, danger, energy, ecstasy, courage, daring, aggression, heroism, militarism, and war. Transliterating into painting and poetry the kinetic rhythms and chaotic qualities inherent in contemporary life and rejecting sentimentality, apathy, and the conventional past, the Futurists concentrated their attention on motorcars, trains, planes. "These sources of emotion satisfy our sense of a lyric and dramatic universe, better than do two pears and an apple," Severini wrote. "Poetry must be a violent onslaught upon the unknown forces, to command them to bow before man," stated the initial Manifesto on Futurism (1909). "Time and Space died yesterday. Already we live in the absolute, since we have already created speed . . . broad-chested locomotives prancing on the rails . . . destructive and incendiary." In their 1910 declaration, the Futurists wrote "that all subjects previously used must be swept aside in order to express our whirling life of steel, of pride, of fever and of speed . . . The name of 'madman' with which it is attempted to gag all innovators should be looked upon as a title of honour."[2]

Although Witkiewicz sought, ostensibly, to abolish everything the Futurists represented, he was nevertheless bedazzled by their concept of modernity, their love of speed and excitement, and their focus on insanity, making these the very core and substance of *The Crazy Locomotive*. Although he satirized and derided machines for their dismembering and dehumanizing power, Witkiewicz imitated the Futurists, who broke up line and color in their canvases by fragmenting mind, body, and psyche, in his stage happening. Ironically, in using the techniques of the Futurists to debase their philosophical and artistic credo, Witkiewicz became so caught up that he used these same techniques to convey his own creative élan in surrealist fashion!

Warsaw-born Stanislaw Ignacy Witkiewicz (1885–1939) was the son of a well-known painter, cultural anthropologist, and critic whose ideas were out of tune with the times. Dissension between father and son manifested itself when the young man enrolled at the Crakow Academy of Fine Arts (1904–5) and indulged in numerous and passionate love affairs. Having gone to Paris to study the canvases of the Fauves, Cubists, Futurists, and others (Braque, Picasso, Dufy, Vlaminck, Derain, van Gogh, and Gauguin), the budding artist began painting truncated and dismembered figures and distorted landscapes. He discovered in himself a growing predilection for the unnatural—monsters, caricatures, grotesque and eerie sites—which was mirrored in the subject matter and titles of his canvases: *A Man with Dropsy Lies in Ambush for His Wife's Lover*, *The Prince of Darkness Tempts Saint Theresa with the Help of a Waiter from Budapest*.

Upon his return to Poland, the tension between father and son grew more pronounced. An unhappy love affair increased Witkiewicz's grief and led to a nervous breakdown. Freudian analysis followed, then optimism. Witkiewicz became engaged, but shortly thereafter his fiancée committed suicide and her body was found in a strange manner: at the bottom of a cliff with a bouquet of flowers next to it. The shock of her death caused another breakdown. This time Witkiewicz's father arranged for Stanislaw to accompany the anthropologist Bronislaw Malinowski to the South Seas, Australia, India, and Ceylon in the capacity of secretary, draftsman, and photographer.

When World War I broke out, young Witkiewicz enlisted in the Russian army, suffered shell shock, and in 1916 was decorated for bravery. He spent the rest of the war years in Russia, painting and studying the works of the avant-garde: Malevich, Tatlin, Rodchenko, Kandinsky, Chagall. It was then that he experimented with cocaine, peyote, morphine, nicotine, ether, and other drugs. In 1918 he returned to Poland, ready to concretize his pictorial and dramatic fantasies.

Witkiewicz is a seminal force in modern theatre. Like Alfred Jarry (1873–1907), he rejected the framework of the so-called well-made play so popular in his day and banished sentimentality and rational coherence from his dramas. Both men saw corrosively, but this view was mitigated by their powerful sense of humor. Not perhaps so monstrous and grotesque as Jarry's vengeful and brutal King Ubu and his cohorts, Witkiewicz's characters are equally memorable. Jarry, in his use of provocative words, strange verbal associations, harsh alliterations, and unusual rhythmic patterns, was more shocking than Witkiewicz, whose creatures speak in a more socially acceptable manner and bear more conventional physical traits. Both playwrights, however, succeeded in destroying all semblance of logic between character and situation.

Witkiewicz peoples his stage with creatures from both dream and waking states. They are archetypal forces gesturing their way through dramatic sequences and ushering in a world of mystery and magic. The techniques of dissociation, displacement, dislocation, and distortion used by Cubists and Futurists, and later by Surrealists, were adopted by Witkiewicz with the effect of disrupting rational coherence between the characters and the world about them. Spatial language (gesture, movement, lighting, stage accessories) created a new optic, allowing for greater dimensionality. As the playwright intended, the preeminence of the unconscious succeeded in stirring spectators and luring them into a new state of awareness. Dichotomy was the rule rather than the exception in his theatre.

Witkiewicz describes his aesthetics in the introduction to the *Theory of Pure Form in the Theatre* (1918) and in *Theoretical Introduction to Tumor Brainard* (1920), among other essays. Plays, he says, must express intuitively the livingness of each individual existence, and tensions must be aroused with the purpose of inspiring a "metaphysical sense of the strangeness of existence."

Witkiewicz was plagued by the philosophical and metaphysical notion of "*Unity within Plurality.*" Each person functions as a unit, an individual biological entity, as well as a unit within a social organism, which is a plurality of biological entities. Similarly, each human being is made up of an infinite number of particles ("monads," as he called them), forever tugging at each other within the body ("unit"). These single and plural entities may be measured spatially (exteriorly, in the so-called real world) and also as duration (in the inner, autonomous realm).[3] The tension arising from the one and the plural creates anxiety within a feeling and thinking being. The creative act is capable of relieving this conflict of polarities, and Witkiewicz therefore described painting and the theatrical as composites of "oriented tensions."[4]

Witkiewicz stresses the absurdity of life in his theatre in general, and *The Crazy Locomotive* in particular, by deforming "the external world, by violating the logical feeling principle." Going beyond the linear time scheme, he advocates the abolition of a chronological approach. The vicissitudes experienced by his protagonists, therefore, are realized as impulses and affects, brittle spasms and movements, enacted in conglomerates of disconnected sequences. The goal of his theatre, he stated, "is to put the audience in an exceptional state, which cannot in its pure form very easily be attained in the course of ordinary daily life, a state where the mystery of existence can be apprehended emotionally."[5]

The Superfast Locomotive

The superfast locomotive in Witkiewicz's play is the center of focus. Its engineer, Tenser, who keeps accelerating the speed of this mechanical "beast," identifies with it. Tenser is filled with a false sense of freedom, power, and courage. Nicholas, the fireman, assuages the appetite of this metallic force by carrying out Tenser's orders and feeding it coal throughout the stage happenings. The transformation of the combustible substance into energy that in turn fuels the locomotive may be associated with emotional heat, or affects, suggesting a gradual change from the physical world of concretion to the psychological realm. Since the psyche, according to C. G. Jung, possesses its own mass—an extension of time-space—it may be understood physically: emotions have intensity which may be looked upon as frequency. The heightening of intensity or frequency activates the unconscious, thereby inviting visions and ecstatic experiences— or schizophrenic episodes.[6]

For Witkiewicz, and in accordance with Einstein's theory of relativity, mentioned in the play, neither space nor time is a separate entity, nor is there a universal flow of time, as posited by Newton. On the contrary, they are related and inseparable, forming a four-dimensional continuum. Observers moving about will order events in keeping with the velocities relative to the action observed. For example, when one person views two actions as simultaneous, they may really be taking place in another temporal sequence for another observer. There is, then, no *absolute* space any more than there is absolute time. As Einstein postulated, mass is nothing but a form of energy: $E = mc^2$.[7]

Witkiewicz's sets, if Einstein's space/time continuum is kept in mind, are particularly arresting. The spectator, although observing a seemingly inert mass, nevertheless sees a mobile happening in a variety of space/time schemes. "The stage represents the back of a locomotive and the front of the tender. The locomotive can be gigantic—a model which hasn't yet been invented." The train moves onstage, to the right or to the left, depending on the action. Two brightly lit lanterns are visible from within the engine, as are rods, pipes, levers, and the firebox, from which "blood-red flames shoot forth." Every now and then, to make matters even more realistic in this incredibly surrealist play, "steam shoots out from the front taps and covers everything."[8]

To give the impression that the locomotive is going somewhere and to increase the illusion of mobility onstage, a movie projector has been placed behind the train, flashing scenic views at appropriate times at the back of the stage. Changes in the relative speed and position of the images affect the viewers' notions of space and time, establishing a variety of relationships. In so doing, tensions and encounters, depending upon the associations made on the basis of time and position, act on form, character, and dialogue.

The play opens in a railroad station. All is static. Once the camera begins projecting landscape scenes, the locomotive gives the impression of movement. As the images interact with one another, welding together or dispersing light and darkness, form and non-form, they create or fragment concretion, thus giving the impression of frantic, even shattering activity. The ensuing atmosphere of restlessness and fragmentation parallels an inner psychological condition of dislocation and disquietude.

Because of the blend of theatre and film in *The Crazy Locomotive*, the stage play not only inspires an active performer/audience relationship but provides the technical factor, so dear to the Futurists and so unconsciously fascinating to Witkiewicz. The viewer can experience the space/time continuum—a past existing in a present reality which is lived at the very moment it comes into being and may be recalled ad infinitum. While uncertainty and mystery reign during a theatrical performance, the fortuitous does not prevail in film. The combination agitates and expands consciousness.

A semaphore, the lights of a city in the distance, and the noises of a station (the clanging of coupling railroad cars, ringing bells, the hubbub of a crowd) generate excitement. Since the pitch of a tone depends on the frequency of its vibrations (the number of vibrations per second), higher and lower pitches suggest spatial relationships based on oscillating sensations experienced in higher or lower parts of the body. Spectators of Witkiewicz's play are assaulted aurally according to the number of higher or lower tones emitted from the stage happenings. At certain times the stridency and amplitude is so acute as to be nerve-wracking.[9]

Conflict, opposition, and duality are evident from the very outset of *The Crazy Locomotive*. The nonpersonal image of the train, with its blood-red coals, its fire and steam, slowly takes shape, provoking visceral reactions. Julia, the eighteen-year-old fiancée of Nicholas, the instinctual fireman, comes on stage. Her beauty is described as "animalistic." That she has brought Nicholas a basket of victuals parallels his act of feeding coal to the "monster." His rapid descent and ascent into and out of the locomotive is described as being accomplished with "apelike agility."

Using the word "ape" when referring to Nicholas suggests a kind of clownishness, something disconcerting, perhaps even priapic, tricksterish. Is he dominated by his appetites? Is he cynical, insensitive, cruel? Does he have a child's mentality? Julia certainly is detached and unfeeling; she warns Nicholas not to go too far in his invective. Antipodal to normal couples en route to marriage, this pair converses with hate and rage rather than love and understanding.

Nicholas's coal-stoking job also sheds light on his personality. It indicates a need to participate in life's activities, no matter what the outcome. Black coal stands for potential energy, light, activity, and warmth. To become an active force, to engender life and thereby reveal its real nature, coal needs a spark, flame, fire, or some other energetic source. Only then can black be transmuted into red. Coal alone, like Nicholas, is dead matter. He needs a catalyst.[10]

As soon as Tenser—the engineer and the driving force of this dream-drama—arrives onstage with his wife, Sophia, he asks Nicholas for a reading of the "steam pressure." A revealing request, indeed, since steam is a gaseous substance as distinguished from liquid or solid matter; it also powers the train's engine. Furthermore, the creation of vapor or a steamlike substance gets rid of dross and impurities. Translated into psychological terms, coal, flame, and steam suggest volatility and heightened tension: a condition that could either reach a boiling point or set off an explosion.[11]

After Tenser orders Nicholas to "stoke up the fire,"actual flames shoot out of the locomotive and the "beast races along at a frantic clip." Traditionally associated with purification, illumination, and transcendence, flames indicate a strong state of excitement as expressed in the phrase, "burn with desire." If aimed at the outer world, such emotional frenzy may lead to killing; if channeled within, it can encourage suicide.

The epithet "beast," which Tenser applies to the locomotive, and which is reminiscent of Emile Zola's novel *The Human Beast*, also dealing with a train, indicates the archetypal nature of this machine. The visualization of Witkiewicz's locomotive emanates from the deepest levels of the unconscious, the instinctual realm. If instinct is not integrated into the whole psyche and remains unchanneled and undirected, passion, as in Witkiewicz's play, may result in dire consequences. Tenser's sense of reality, even at the outset of *The Crazy Locomotive*, is so disturbed that he finds it impossible to relate emotionally to people in general. His sexual attraction for Julia, for example, is alluded to as "perfectly diabolical!" Indeed, he sees nothing human in it. On the contrary, he links Julia with the devil, with doubt, with dark and demonic aspects of the psyche, which, though lying below collective life, relate to an individual's personal problems. Tenser views Julia as a temptress, serpent, night demon, and magic power who knows well how to persecute man.[12]

As the train increases its pace during the course of the action, it seems to become caught up in universal motion, engulfing forms and highlighting shadows, thereby creating sequences of counter and conflicting rhythms, shapes, and colorations. In keeping with Futurist paintings, the moving object is not seen in isolation but takes in its surroundings, affecting actual forms in space and humanizing the locomotive rather than mechanizing the men.

Noise, energy, and tension increase to such a point that Nicholas warns Tenser that the valve can no longer contain the pressure. The engineer, manning the throttle, reaches such a state of ecstasy—sexual and spiritual—that he feels empowered to remove his psychological mask, thus exposing his *inner* being to society. So, too, does Nicholas. As both men return to their childhood fantasy lives—to the desert island where the master, Robinson Crusoe (Tenser) and his man Friday (Nicholas) lived—they begin playing the same game and indulging in the same mystifications as they had when the world was young and the fantasy world reigned eternal.

Regression now takes precedence on stage: archaic impulses surface as childish responses and pleasurable patterns of life are reactivated. If such a situation is allowed to run its course indefinitely, however, the psychic structure can deteriorate. Let us recall that when the biblical Jonah regressed, living in the great whale's belly—a symbol of the womb—he experienced the chaos of undifferentiated beginnings (the ocean), the shelter of the pre-born state. Jonah's regression, or, psychologically speaking, his schizophrenic episode, was not complete since he fought against the continuous tossing about and possible dissolution within. In the darkness, we might say, God allowed Jonah to experience light. Such was not Tenser's situation. Only when the train sped along did he feel he was living fully. Unlike Jonah, he neither could nor wanted to return to the human world.[13]

Heightened speed allows Tenser to live out a progressive *abaissement du niveau mental* cut off from empirical reality. When experiencing such disorganization of archaic matter, his consciousness is fertile field for an invasion of unadapted and unassimilated material from the unconscious. Although many of these unsorted ideas might be potentially creative, they can also indicate the onset of a morbid condition. As Tenser's exuberance grows in proportion to the locomotive's increase in speed, so, too, does the impact of proliferating fantasy images. As he lives out his multiple displacements and dispersions, tossed here and there by shifting currents welling up from his collective unconscious, his mind and psyche become progressively devoid of any judgmental factors. Such continuous and unassimilated activity reveals not only a deterioration of consciousness but a split, thereby increasing the possibility of a full-fledged schizophrenic episode. Is Tenser acting out Marinetti's statement when he sees himself "alone with the black phantoms that rummage about in the red-hot bellies of the locomotives launched at furious speeds"?[14]

As the two men talk during the locomotive's speeding trajectory, Nicholas brings up a delicate subject: Is Tenser in love with Julia? Tenser answers by asking Nicholas to throw more coal into the furnace and by pushing down the throttle to the accompaniment of a volley of shooting flames. The sequence's volatility and dizzying effect is increased by the projector's rapid alteration of landscape images.

Relativists consider the four-dimensional world depicted in Witkiewicz's play to be transcendental: time is observable only through the movement of actions taking place during a certain time span. For example, as Tenser watches the landscape in the distance, time passes—duration in flux. On the other hand, as the locomotive speeds ahead, Tenser is divested of his identity—the personality behind the husk or mask. Within the locomotive, then, there exists a pitiful creature, one whose ego is slowly disappearing, whose persona is engulfed by an inner vision—a man lost to himself.[15]

In keeping with the speed of the projected images are Tenser's repeated orders to Nicholas to continue stoking coal. The sensations of heightening flame, steam, and speed not only allow Tenser to "break through all normal day-to-day relationships" but further scatter his psyche, continuing to deplete an already weakened ego-consciousness. Such atomization allows him to identify with primitive forces within him, thereby paving the way for further regression into his collective unconscious—to an earlier level of civilization.[16]

Other interesting factors also come to light. We learn that Nicholas has read about Einstein's theory of relativity as he discusses its pros and cons with Tenser in a deeply amusing dialogue, and the two men also broach the theory of Pure Form, a concept derived from the chief exponent of the Formists, Leon Chwistek (1884–1944), which Witkiewicz adapted to suit his own needs and make-up.

Chwistek's *The Plurality of Realities* (1921) censures the notion of a single and uniform reality, suggesting instead the existence of different kinds.[17] Witkiewicz's notion of Pure Form and the acceptance of a plurality of realities may, if properly understood, free individuals from psychological and material constraints—and theatergoers from conventional plots, characterizations, and sound effects, luring them into unheard-of dimensions. However, Pure Form also encourages alienation and metaphysical anguish. There is no center, no common denominator.

As Tenser seeks to experience Pure Form intensely and subjectively, he pushes down the throttle still further, additionally increasing the locomotive's speed. Nicholas warns him that his "plan means death." No matter. Tenser, the master, orders him to continue stoking coal, inviting fulgurating incandescence to prevail.

The madness of the moment encourages both men to discuss the Mystery of Existence in its infinity, after which they admit to not being Nicholas or Tenser, but two famous criminals: Travaillac and Prince Karl Trefaldi, respectively. The latter, a very high-class individual, is "an inspiration" to the lower-echelon Travaillac. (The name may have been modeled on Ravaillac [1578–1610], the murderer of Henry IV.) Nor is Tenser's wife's name Sophia, but Erna Abracadabra, the famous chanteuse, who helped Trefaldi murder his aunt, the Princess di Boscotrecase.

The change of identities is not surprising in *The Crazy Locomotive*, where protagonists are not only identityless but dissociated. Nor are Trefaldi's and Travaillac's goals of rising "above the turbulent pulp of international depravity" out of the question in a world of unlimited horizons. As the two discuss the complex nature of criminality, Trefaldi suggests they do something "diabolical" like causing an accident. If they could be successful in this endeavor, they would be able to lose themselves in time as well as space—able, thereby, to make sense out of the "whole unsavory comedy" of existence.

To make matters still more disconcerting, absurd, and irrational, we see Julia and Sophia, who have climbed on the tender just before it pulls out, creeping on all fours through the coal pile toward the locomotive. Trefaldi is delighted to see Julia, to whom he confesses his love, and disheartened at the sight of his wife, whom he rejects. The thought of being loved by the most notorious criminal in the world in addition to riding a speeding train—even if it means certain death—sends Julia into a state of rapture. "Something is being created right here and now, the way it was in the beginning before the world began," she states. Erna, however, conventional in her way, considers them all demented as she screams out her desire to live: "Close the throttle: Put on the brakes!"

The regression which Julia now experiences permits her to return to the undifferentiated world of childhood, where she can live out her gleeful fantasy images—her Pure Form. Psychologically, however, since the floodgates to subliminal spheres have opened for her as they have for Tenser and Nicholas, her ego-consciousness drowns amid the duality of the schizophrenic episode she now experiences.

There is no ritual combat in Julia's case any more than in Tenser's or even Nicholas's, no conflict between the forces of life and death, good and evil. Speed and hyperactivity, which dictate the lives of these atomized psyches, have obliterated all differentiation.

Plurality of Realities, Psyches, Persona

Trefaldi announces the possibility of derailment as the locomotive rushes by at an increasingly fast clip, flame and steam emerging from its cylinder cocks. So tense is Trefaldi's excitation that if a "normal person" were to touch him at this point, he would be killed instantaneously, as if "struck by lightning."

Travaillac, echoing Trefaldi's intense joy, sputters: "My head is hurtling into the infinite cosmic abyss, like a bullet along its trajectory." The ecstatic Julia is only too "willing to die a thousand times for a moment like this!"

Like Empedocles, the three are fascinated by flame and everything associated with incendiary and electric charges. Their great enemy is repose, those moments when meditation and thoughtfulness force people to face themselves. Although fire and its emotional effects provide warmth and comfort, they also burn and destroy. Like the energy of the physical world—which is never lost, but continuously transformed—emotional intensity is related to a continuously mobile process. When, for example, the inherently energetic atomic particles that make up mass collide with one another at high velocities, their apparent inertness is changed into kinetic power and redistributed among other particles.[18] The same occurs with Witkiewicz's characters, who seek to experience a four-dimensional continuum where space and time are fused and forms and objects exist dynamically as energetic powers. As each individual interpenetrates space and time, the group blends into a flowing and changing mass. Dying flamboyantly, as was Empedocles' willed fate when he jumped into Mount Etna, is said to be the least solitary of deaths—indeed, it is looked upon as a cosmic death.

As machine madness takes over, Trefaldi could reiterate Marinetti's statement about the positive nature of "motorized masses," suggesting that "we are immoral, destroyers, disorganizers; we want death and madness," and prophesying the dehumanization of people when "the Animal Kingdom comes to its end and the Mechanical Realm begins."[19]

Neither Trefaldi nor Travaillac pays attention to the "seven separate destinies" meeting at this one point on the locomotive—the single reality obliterating the multiple as the locomotive's passengers speed on, unaware that another train is rushing at them full speed. Crash! Steam covers the entire stage, after which the engine bursts into fragments.

As the steam dissipates, spectators learn that the throttle has penetrated at least twelve inches into Trefaldi's belly and that his guts are spilling out. He even confesses to the fact that he is "almost dead." Julia, by some miracle, is safe, though she considers everything "strange and horrible" and really wants to experience "a black abyss, soft and impersonal"— death (107). Travaillac lives on and is sentenced to six months in a lunatic asylum, but because the prosecutor of the appellate court is a friend of one of the surviving passengers, he is freed.

Clearly, the locomotive is the machine leading to self-destruction. Its increasing speed may be viewed as a metaphor of the repressed elements within the protagonists' unconscious. When activated as a machine, the tremendous energy charges which take over allow a breaking through of the time/space continuum. In Witkiewicz's play such folly has led to blindness: the inability to see an oncoming train results in death and destruction.

As a psychological metaphor, the train is the ego that can no longer resist the intensity welling up from the subliminal sphere. Thus the individual undergoes a personality change. The constantly shifting conditions provoked by the intensely volatile libido further disable an already weakened ego. The rich archaic material dredged up from the unconscious proves to be unadaptable to the world of contingencies. If dissociation in a state of emotion does not last, it can adapt to the objective, external situation and conclude with a coming together of disparate contents. In schizophrenia, however, once the container is smashed or explodes, it cannot be returned to its original unity. Dismemberment occurs for Tenser/Trefaldi, and to a lesser degree for the other protagonists. When he can no longer relate to his Self, it is unable to protect him since he is not even conscious of its existence. Once the loss of the Self comes about, an identification with the world of things takes over and no distinction between the object and the I is operational. A turning point in Tenser/Trefaldi's personality comes to pass. What had formerly been a neurosis becomes a psychosis.

Untamed powers lurking within the unconscious have been differently labeled throughout history. When, for example, Siegfried challenged the dragon, Fafnir, in a cave, he replied: "Leave me alone, I want to sleep."[20] In the case of Witkiewicz's protagonists, when the dragon is aroused it comes out fighting, spreading death and destruction in its wake. Psychologically, I suggest that Witkiewicz's play is in part the living out of a schizophrenic episode:

> There is something . . . in the schizophrenic subject's blood which seeks out and responds to the violence and dread of the daemonic unconscious forces. Something in him shouts the devil's laughter as the ship is battered and broken by the attacking sea. The renegade in the psyche is archaic and nihilistic, seeking violence involuntarily, as an insecure ruler seeks war. Men of insight can perceive the presence of this renegade voice in their own make-up.[21]

Dragons in ancient times—and the locomotive in Witkiewicz's play—represented fabulous mythological creatures of the inner world, personifications of nonpersonal forces in the depths of the psyche capable of either aiding or devouring consciousness. When Tenser/Trifaldi identifies with the locomotive, he becomes that dragon, that bull, that *beast* alluded to previously, with virtually suprahuman power and energy, a potential destroyer of cultures, civilizations, and humankind in the process. The beast dies; so, too, was the Minotaur slaughtered. The price is great in both ancient and modern times.

The image of light, flame, and energy which appears throughout *The Crazy Locomotive* symbolizes destruction rather than an increase in knowledge. A blinding and flaying force, light as manifested in Witkiewicz's play precipitates its victims into a devouring and explosive maw: the belly of the machine. Conflict is then abolished, as it was for Empedocles when he jumped into Mount Etna—as it was for Witkiewicz, who committed suicide in 1939, first by taking sleeping pills, then, after awakening, by cutting his wrists with a razor. His farewell sentence reveals the depth of his own harrowing condition: "I won't go on living as less than myself."[22]

4 Luigi Pirandello's *Tonight We Improvise*—Machine, Magus, and Matriarchate

> You see, ladies and gentlemen, the theatre is the yawning mouth of a gigantic machine that is—hungry: a hunger, I should add, that these gentlemen the poets— . . . profoundly err in not trying to satisfy. It is deplorable that the invention of our poets, far behind everyone else, no longer succeeds in discovering adequate nourishment for this vast machine we call the theatre that, like other machines, has in recent years enormously and wondrously grown and developed.[1]

So speaks Dr. Hinkfuss, director of the play within the play in Luigi Pirandello's *Tonight We Improvise* (1929). For Pirandello, then, the theatre is a machine, hungry for poetry, which is in insufficient supply in the early decades of the twentieth century. The poetry needed to nourish the hungry machine is, for Pirandello, a concoction of motility, imagination, fantasy, mystery, and illusion that would invite spectators, protagonists and readers alike to substitute for their staid and preconceived notions the *unforeseen* (from the Latin, *improvisus*)—the improvised, the unknown, the world of imponderables. And thus the title expresses an aspiration: *Tonight We Improvise.*

What is the significance of machines, that creators of twentieth-century works of art are so fascinated by these rhythmic/spatial constructs? How have Pirandello in this play, as will be seen later in connection with the airplane, and the Futurist and Metaphysical painters and sculptors been able to create an illusion of motility, even though the observer knows the object to be immobile?

The machine may be looked upon as a positive force, a *transformer* of energy from kinetic to electric whose uses are virtually unlimited. Machines may also distort vision and perspective, thereby dislocating former concepts of reality and encouraging further probes into nature's infinite secrets. The term "machine" is applicable not only to inanimate objects, but to the body and psyche as well. (A good literary example of this is provided by another great Italian author, Pirandello's contemporary, Italo Svevo, whose protagonist in *Zeno's Conscience*, having been told that every rapid footstep he takes requires fifty-four mechanical movements of his body muscles, is so discomposed by the discovery of this "monstrous machine" within him that he henceforth limps!)

Inanimate machines use fuel to fulfill physical, energetic, and chemical functions. Animate machines convert or channel raw instincts, or libido (psychic energy), directing them away from their own unregenerate course toward purposeful goals. Like the machine, theatre and psyche plow through an uncharted time/space continuum, participating in a *transformation* ritual which is the creation of the living work of art. *Tonight We Improvise* presents unresolved conflicts that arise between actors and director during a dramatic performance. Both audiences and protagonists are compelled to make choices and force out solutions. For Pirandello, however, there are no final answers. Like Heraclitus, he believes that *all* is in a state of flux. To probe and question on the religious, psychological, or theatrical level is to fragment and divide, and to open up new thoughts as one discards old or even archaic modes and beliefs. Pain and suffering are important factors in the transformatory process which brings about a renewal. The process is circular and cyclical: to recharge or innovate implies a destruction of former ways followed by the birth of fresh ideas and new polarities. However, it is also the birth of different antagonisms, which must then be balanced again, but only temporarily since equilibrium is followed by fresh contradictions.

A brief plot summary of *Tonight We Improvise* is in order. Dr. Hinkfuss, the theatrical director of a play within a play by Pirandello (his double, or alter ego), begins by denigrating the dramatist's role in his creative production and then proceeds to read the scenario (which has been reduced and printed on a scroll) of a tragic play revolving around a Sicilian family. The actors, in *commedia del l'arte* style, have been given only the bare essentials of the plot, the rest being left to improvisation. Hinkfuss finds himself in conflict with his actors, who demand more and more freedom in interpreting their characters. A continuous struggle rages between the actors, who are determined to gain their creative independence (the theme of *Six*

Characters in Search of an Author), and Dr. Hinkfuss, who wants to pay them no heed.

A large, buxom, domineering mother, Signora Ignazia—also called "General"—is full of life and spirit and has transmitted her *joie de vivre* to her four daughters—Mommina, Nene, Dorina, and Titina—who sing and dance for her and for the entertainment of the local air-force officers as well. Ignazia's husband, Sampognetta, is a weak, pusillanimous mining engineer who seeks escape from his wife by getting drunk at a cabaret and falling in love with the singer there. The play unfolds in a climate of mounting hostility. Jealousy is the reigning passion. Sicilian patriarchal culture imposes its rigid laws, oblivious to all feminine values, and the play ends with an enactment of the tragedy of Mommina's marriage to a typical Sicilian male, Rico Verri. The actors perform this illusory play within the play so convincingly that both audience and protagonists are stunned by the verity of the fictitious tragedy. Dr. Hinkfuss struts in pride over his theatrical triumph, but when the leading actor calls for the author, Hinkfuss refuses to introduce Pirandello, who nevertheless has triumphed by bringing the action of his play beyond reality, into the realm of the unknown.

Dr. Hinkfuss: Director, Master of Ceremonies, and Magus

Dr. Hinkfuss was modeled, some critics say, on Max Reinhardt and Erwin Piscator, German stage designers and directors who used dramatic texts to serve their political and aesthetic needs. Pirandello, however, imbued with notions of freedom and fluidity, would not allow his creative élan to be suffocated by any "given scenic style."[2] Averse to limiting a dramatic work of art to conventional techniques, sets, auditory devices and lighting, Pirandello, like Strindberg, insisted on the necessity of introducing on-stage dances, acrobatics, and other diversions to flesh out and dramatize the written text.

Although Dr. Hinkfuss may be considered Pirandello's alter ego and/or a copy of Reinhardt and Piscator, he may also be viewed as a collective being or an image of archetypal dimension. Archetypes, which are manifested in archetypal images, emerge from the deepest layers of the unconscious. They are "suprapersonal and non-individual," and are universally implicit in legends, myths, and literary works from time immemorial.

As one such archetype—the Spiritual Father—Hinkfuss is a composite of opposites. Machinelike in that he is a dynamic entity that follows a prescribed course, he is geared to relating chance factors to causality. His very presence as an agent of transformation engenders conflict by inciting speed and motion. As Director, Master of Ceremonies, and Magus, Dr. Hinkfuss is the paradigm of consciousness. His *rational* function being highly developed, he may be classified as a *thinking* type. That he chooses to have his performers *improvise* indicates an unconscious need to compensate for his extreme cognition. Endowed with perspicuity, Hinkfuss would like to enter the domain of uncertainty and mystery, but at the same time senses the dangers of the *improvisus*—the unforeseen. He therefore gives his actors little leeway. The locale of the play to be performed is Sicily. Passions must conform to the patriarchally oriented Sicilian society. The unconscious, the visceral, the mysterious—the feminine sphere, in sum—represent dangerous, fearsome powers. In Pirandello's time, and indeed even today, it is believed that a whole shadowy female world lies in wait for the unsuspecting male. Ideally, Dr. Hinkfuss envisages a taut theatrical production, in keeping with highly structured procedures, identifiable characters, and channeled creative forays. The machine-theatre must at all times pursue its sleek and neat run through the time/space continuum, in a fashion reminiscent of Plato's black and white horses in *Phaedrus*. Here the white horse is docile to reason, while the black one, unruly, representative of appetites and desires, must be forever whipped into line by the charioteer. Likewise Dr. Hinkfuss attempts to keep a tight reign on his cast and all the technological aspects of the production.

As an archetypal figure, Dr. Hinkfuss is endowed with transpersonal qualities. He is both somber and luminous, positive and destructive, rational and impulsive, and frequently at odds with his own conflicting personality traits. How do these characteristics manifest themselves? His actions speak for him: Dr. Hinkfuss, controlled and methodical, makes a sensational entrance into the stage space. The house lights and footlights are turned up; buzzers and other noise-making devices sound off.

Most important, however, in pointing up the dichotomies in Dr. Hinkfuss's psyche is his physical portrait: "Dr. Hinkfuss is one of those unfortunate creatures whose fate it is to be a tiny man hardly five feet." His very small stature is compensated for by his grandiose views of the role of director and the theatrical performance in general. Archetypally, he may be identified with the dwarf figures in the Norse *Eddas*. Dwarfs, created by the Gods prior to their creation of humankind, represent, psychologically, semiconscious impulses. Many dwarfs are named after certain crafts—the Builder, the Burner, the One Who Colors in Brown, the Iron Smith, etc. They live in the earth's cavities or caves, or, symbolically, in the inner theatres of the mind. They are quickwitted, industrious, intelligent, and frequently quarrelsome. They are affective and emotional in nature. The dwarf is subject to flashes of creative flickerings, or *Einfall*, which are sparks or impulses that fall into the conscious sphere from the uncon-scious. Because dwarfs are small, they may be overpowered by their titanic inner impulses; emotional affects seem far bigger in small beings than in normal-sized humans.

On the other hand, since the *Einfall* is a mere flickering of intuition—a hunch—it may at times be considered insignificant and cast off lightly. Overly rational persons frequently discard good ideas that do not fit with their previous plans, setting them aside or repressing them rather than evaluating and airing them.[3] In keeping with the concept of the *Einfall*—those sparks of light or intuitive forays—Dr. Hinkfuss focuses most of his attention, particularly in Acts II and III, on lighting effects. Like Lucifer (from the Latin, *lux*, "light," and "bring"), he is a *bringer of light*. To shed light on some part of the shadowy psyche is to arouse consciousness of joy or pain, but it may also instill terror in the face of a world of imponderables and the menace of chaos. Herein lies the challenge: to find the perfect formula whereby mystery, underlying both theatrical and religious specta-cles, may be revealed with clarity, conciseness, and ever-increasing tension.

Dr. Hinkfuss, as previously mentioned, is a composite of opposites: thinking and impulsive, rational and instinctual. Because of his own inner turmoil, as he enters the stage space he shows his irritation and impa-tience by throwing open the door with violence, then hurrying down the central aisle of the theatre. Agitation having thus been injected into the atmosphere, actors and spectators now begin speaking their minds to the accompaniment of clanging and buzzing sounds. Because these outpour-ings are unplanned, they embarrass Dr. Hinkfuss, who apologizes to his audience for the "momentary confusion." A thinking type, he seeks to dominate the unpredictable, impulsive, passionate actors, but logic, intel-lect, and objectivity cannot always prevail—in the ordinary world or the theatre or the composite makeup of Dr. Hinkfuss. Chaos reigns with the eruption of the chance factor. Unorganized matter stands opposed to the sought-for sequential and comprehensible elements. To stop the continu-ous physical and emotional activity that is taking place onstage and to fix the fleeting moment, Dr. Hinkfuss reads from his scroll, thereby securing the plot and concretizing feelings, at least momentarily.

For Dr. Hinkfuss, "art is the kingdom of perfected creation, where life is as it ought to be, in an infinitely various and continually changing state of becoming" (13). On the key words in his definition of art—"an infinitely various and continually changing state of becoming"—hinges the very notion of creativity. Using a solitary and immutable statue cast outside of time as his point of reference, Dr. Hinkfuss further explains that the statue, as a true work of art, experiences many lives. It may inspire thoughts and arouse feelings and sensations in the viewer. In so doing, the statue breathes, acts, and absorbs everything and everyone gazing at it, thereby changing and renewing its surroundings. A painting in a museum, to take another example, alters in shape and dimension depending on its placement in the room and its proximity to other works of art, as well as the temperaments that people project onto it. The art object may also take on special qualities and a ghostly appearance, inspiring terror in some and awe in others. What is of import in Dr. Hinkfuss's rational/irrational scheme of things is the dynamic factor set in motion by the interplay between the object and its environment.

The theatre is fluid and subject to flux. It is not outside of time, as is the statue; nor is it immobile and immutable. No matter. As long as Dr. Hinkfuss is there to intervene "whenever necessary to lead the play back if it goes astray ever so slightly," all will be well. He is the infallible mechanical factor, the perfectionist, the logical, rational entity that supplements what is faulty and clarifies what is ambiguous. He is that self-regulating machine that "makes efforts at improvisation amusing."

The actors, however, are not amused. The Leading Actor (as Rico Verri) protests against the presentation of the cast before the play begins, and voices his resentment of Dr. Hinkfuss's search for effects in his production— tricks, surprises, "accidents," "little games of light and shade," to "amuse the audience." Actors, he maintains, are *feeling* types, who must spontaneously live out the truth of the characters they incarnate. As if to demonstrate this, the Character Actress (as Signora Ignazia) slaps the Character Actor in the face, which resounds through the theatre. The Character Actor (as her husband, Sampognetta) loudly protests that his makeup has been spoiled. She was merely playing her part in slapping him, she asserts vehemently, indulging in "a perfectly instinctive gesture." Pointing to her stomach, she says: "My lines come from here." She is *in* her role. Had her husband been in his he would have gotten out of the way. Confusion sets in. Was Signora Ignazia *really* behaving that way or is her conduct part of the *role?* Dr. Hinkfuss informs the spectators that he had directed his cast to improvise in this manner—"it pleases me to carry it this far"—yet it seems that he is trying to save face with the audience as the actors go their own way.

The Character Actress then presents her four daughters, the men from the local air-force base introduce themselves, and everything seems to be "going like clockwork" as the players step forth in a natural, easy way. Dr. Hinkfuss, however, had intended to introduce them himself, and he thinks that the cast has countered his orders in a form of "rebellion." Again to save face, he tells his audience that everything being witnessed has been prearranged—even the rebellion. It makes the "performance more authentic." The actors, however, protest that they have really been improvising and begin creating additional turmoil in order to emphasize the artificial side of the theatre: "You really want to make people believe that this emergence of our roles was agreed on between us ahead of time?" The entire theatre is now in bedlam.

Dr. Hinkfuss puts an end to this "shameful" behavior by ordering a *religious procession!* Not only will the ceremony lend the play the necessary color, but *religion* (from the Latin *religare*, meaning "to bind together"), with its accompanying rituals, will serve to amalgamate the group and enforce discipline through a self-regulating force.

The Mechanics of the Religious Procession

Religious processions are collective acts, manifestations of deity or epiphanies. Let us recall that theatre was born of religion: in India, with the Natyashashtra; in Japan, with the display of feelings of the Sun Goddess, Amaterasu; in Greece, with the Eleusinian mysteries; in Christian countries, with the dramatization of Holy Family myths.

When observing or participating in a religious procession, believers project themselves onto the effigies, hierophants or fetishes parading before them, which fill them with feelings of wonderment, security, and a sense of belonging. By reliving the stories that religious objects conjure up in the mind, the devout—be they Roman Catholics in Sicilian processions, or Taos Pueblo Indians in New Mexico—are able to transcend their temporal existence and experience an *illo tempore:* past merges into the present, death takes on life, and renewal thus comes about. As an act of faith, the religious procession infuses a sense of the divine into the participants, thereby serving as a bridge to link ancestors with contemporaries and generation to generation. In this way the individual is rescued from an inborn sense of isolation and distress.

For Dr. Hinkfuss, the spectacle factor—the local color in the religious ceremony—preempts all others. He is delighted with the Choirboys, the Young Girls, the Old Man, the Virgin and Christ Child, the Shepherd, and the Group of Peasants filing down the central aisle. The procession walks onto the proscenium, and then into the church onstage, amid the sounds of an organ and chiming bells. In sharp contrast is the jazz music emanating from the nightclub on the other side of the proscenium. When its walls become transparent, thanks to the expert manipulation of lights, heavily made-up girls, dancers, and clients appear. The juxtaposition of the religious procession and the visceral world of the night club creates further dichotomies in both stage play and the psyche and heart of spectators and participants.

The Mechanics of the Interlude

Dr. Hinkfuss performs yet another feat of technical magic in what is referred to as the Interlude, which is based on *simultaneous* action and takes place in the theatre lobby during intermission. Here actors and actresses, grouping themselves in four different areas, continue playing their parts freely and naturally, as though they were part of the audience milling around during the entr'acte.

"All things move, all things run, all things change rapidly," says the Futurist dictum.[4] Such is Dr. Hinkfuss's rule of thumb in the Interlude, revealing his expertise in stage mechanics and his technical mastery of sound and lighting effects. By creating several centers of gravity and having each sequence unravel its own scenario at the same time, audiences are exposed to different visions of the play's action. This kind of collage quality encourages audiences to conceptualize forms in space and to react in multiple ways to lighting and sound. Multiplicity, fragmentation and dissociation are all willed by Dr. Hinkfuss, preordained by this *magus* to create new optical and aural perspectives and a panoply of surprises and strange juxtapositions.

In contrast to the hypermotility of the Interlude is the stillness and utter immobility of Dr. Hinkfuss's mechanical marvel which concludes the scene. Onstage, "an airfield at night, under a magnificent starry sky. Everything on the ground is small, to give the impression of infinite space bounded only by star-strewn sky; in back, the white buildings that house the OFFICERS, with their small lit windows; here and there scattered about the field two or three airplanes, all very small. One hears the roar of an airplane out of sight, flying in the tranquil night." The small illuminated windows of the white buildings housing the officers lend a storybook quality to the image. The sound of the roaring engines of the two or three small model airplanes on the field reverberates throughout the theatre, giving the impression of flight through vast expanses of tranquil heavens. The additional impression of limbolike suspension of planes in flight gives audiences a fresh vision of mechanistic iconography. The planes themselves, representative of speed, noise, and pulsation, are harbingers of a *new poetics*. Airplanes have taken the place of the Pegasus of past poets and painters. As Marinetti suggested, mechanical powers have been injected with new lyrical qualities: "these sources of emotion satisfy our sense of a lyric and dramatic universe, better than do two pears and an apple."[5]

Like Leonardo da Vinci's detailed drawings of mechanical birds and other flying objects, Dr. Hinkfuss's scenic marvel is designed to stir the imagination of the spectators, who through their inner eye see the planes flying higher and higher. Fresh associations, dynamic impulses, and broader perspectives take shape from the new vantage points offered by the presence onstage of these mechanisms. Another factor is also involved: the sight of planes accustoms individuals to a new age, inviting them to adapt and relate to the world of the machine—to this "jarred reality," in de Chirico's terms. Feelings of estrangement and alienation, which some experience, in a world where the machine inhabits the heavens, may vanish, and with these feelings, the sense of alienation from the society that gave birth to them. By interweaving such mechanical forms into the poem, the painting, or the drama, feelings of joy, power, and renewed creativity may replace those of dread.

Representative of aggressive and assertive feelings rather than submissive qualities, the plane in all of its lustrous beauty may be envisaged as breaking through the atmosphere, or, concomitantly, through the shell surrounding each individual. It does so by means of its own power and energy. Like an *Einfall* it catalyzes its new surroundings, fragments what is whole, brings new vistas, materials, and perspectives into consciousness, thereby broadening the vision—even reaching apocalyptic dimensions—of both laypeople and artist.

Not only have planes and aviators replaced the ancient Pegasus and fabulous birds in literature, but, psychologically, in contemporary dreams they have taken on the qualities of fabulous ascensional animals and monsters of the past. Representative of spiritual aspirations and of liberation from gravity and earthly dross, planes carry their passengers to vertiginous heights, purifying those who soar within their sleek metal frames. As sublimating powers of archetypal dimension, planes, like magical forces, are emanations from the collective unconscious. Materialized spiritual contents, they are energetic factors containing spellbinding and awesome powers similar to those of religious processions.

One can readily understand why Dr. Hinkfuss calls the theatre "the yawning mouth of a gigantic machine." The machine—Pirandello and the Futurist and Metaphysical painters understood this so well—lives boldly and powerfully in the contemporary psyche. It nourishes the imagination, activates the senses, and grows wondrously beautiful as its smooth, glossy, silvery form soars through the heavens.

The Matriarchate

Signora Ignazia may be viewed as both a personal mother who has given birth to four daughters and as the collective Great Mother, like Gaia, Rhea, Isis, Ishtar, Kali, the Virgin Mary, and others. As an archetypal mother, she is a transpersonal figure invested with authority and numinosity who functions according to traditional modes of behavior. Earth-oriented, strong and dominating, she stands as a constant threat to the patriarchate. The more she refuses to submit and the more she struggles against the limitations imposed upon her by the male-dominated society, the more terrifying she becomes to men and the more forcefully she is reviled by them.

In patriarchal cultures, of which Sicily is a prime example, woman is not only repressed but divested of all individuality. She is looked upon as a vessel and a procreating agent to be fertilized. Germination of the woman's individual personality is of little or no consequence. All innovative, creative, and pleasurable experiences—outside of giving birth—are extirpated from her life. The joys of girlhood, of youthful romance and love, are forbidden and immediately crushed.

Signora Ignazia, whose name derives from the Latin *ignis*, meaning "fire," is indeed a firebrand, an electric charge, a catalyst who encourages her daughters to express their own flamboyant feelings through music in order to sublimate a whole, unlived part of their psyche. As a combustive agent, her presence is a disturbing factor in the Sicilian environment. She is the harbinger of extreme views—a natural outcome of the repression of woman in Sicily. Indeed, the woman in such a culture is so cut off from her instinctual world, so channeled into submission, subdued, and enslaved to church and man, that she never really has a chance to develop as an individual in her own right.

Whenever instinct is inhibited, as is the case with Sicilian women, it becomes blocked and regresses, leading to all types of aberrations. Sexual disturbances are not uncommon, manifesting themselves either in a reactivation of infantile situations or in forms of rebellion.[6] Signora Ignazia is the living incarnation of active sexuality. She is a Fellini-type Earth Mother, who wants to reap the pleasures of this world and not be bound and fettered while she waits for beatitude in the next.

Her husband Sampognetta is, as to be expected, weak, passive, and undirected. Unevolved as husband and father, Sampognetta's psyche is characterized by what Westerners in patriarchal societies consider feminine characteristics: dependence, irresponsiblity, and emotionality. He not only never developed an identity of his own, but led a counterproductive life as the Great Mother's servant and votary. Had he followed in the tradition of the archetypal Sicilian male, he would have been conscious of his power over the woman and comported himself as a father figure, the mother acting merely as the "soil" in which the father's "seed" grows.[7]

Signora Ignazia, the catalyst, does not want her daughters to play into the stereotyped image of the young girl, attending a convent school, being incarcerated in a prison-like home, and remaining deprived of the joys of *this* world. Nevertheless, she is a good mother and has prepared them for marriage: they "have virtues of good little wives." Mommina "is wonderful in the kitchen" and in addition has a fine voice.

Music governs the mood and patterns of behavior for these two daughters. Not only does it enable them to channel their energy along certain paths, it also dictates the manner in which they convey their fantasy images and express the intensity of their feelings. Singing, which combines *voice* (the collective creative breath of spirit, *pneuma*) and the individual breath of the performer brings into being a whole world of emotion. Unlike the music-making of the instrumentalist, singing has no mechanical intercessor. No force intervenes between performer and the emanations of the tones. Song, then, is particularly important in societies such as the Sicilian, where the instinctual world is repressed with such brutality. Song allows the soul to soar and transforms volatile emotions into volcanic forces which can be lived out in the imagination and the *feeling* realm, even though they remain forbidden in the ordinary world.

That something is amiss in the Great Mother's excessively flamboyant approach to life is evident at the outset of Act III, when she complains of an excruciating toothache. In that teeth help with the intake of food by cutting, blending, and crushing particles too large to be ingested—thus providing the individual with vital energy—they may be said to represent strength, direction, and the ability to assimilate whatever is beneficial. The toothache Signora Ignazia experiences, therefore, indicates some infected or diseased element in her life and may be looked upon as a premonitory breakdown of her power within the family structure. Her daughters are extremely sympathetic to the agony she is now undergoing. Mommina tries to comfort her, while Rico Verri, her fiancé, goes to the pharmacy for medicine. As for Nene and Dorina, they waltz about the room with their aviator friends, trying to take her mind off her pain. No palliatives seem to be effective and she concludes: "It's the rage, it's the rage that these people in town raise in me; just fire in my blood. They are the cause of all my grief."

Indeed. Signora Ignazia knows she is out of place, out of touch with the Sicilian life-style. That her infected tooth grows more and more painful throughout the scene indicates a further whittling away of her defenses, manifested by a loss of vitality, a diminution of that fiery quality which had made her an active and crepitant force.

Nene suggests that she recite the *Ave Maria*. It had helped her once before. The "miracle" might be repeated. But to be really effective, she must recite the prayer in Latin. At first, Signora Ignazia refuses; then she acquiesces. The stage is perfectly appointed with every accoutrement of piety, as during the religious procession scene in the previous act. Dr.

Hinkfuss has seen to it that the stage lights have been turned down; that the candle which now burns gives off a quavering illumination—a "miracle light;" that the statue of the Madonna is placed on a small table, thus creating the impression of an altar. Signora Ignazia, seated before these objects, clasps her hands and recites "in a slow, deep voice, the words of the prayer."

Prayer, as is true of other rituals or invocations, is a most effective way of channeling spiritual energy, and therefore of opening oneself to God. As a *rite d'entrée* and *rite de sortie*, it moves from the terrestrial to the celestial spheres. It unties the "knots" that bind one to the material world which blocks off so much of the psyche, thus preventing a free-flowing interchange between the two spheres. As a transformatory ritual, prayer stirs that archaic heritage within human beings, blending its findings with present situations. The psyche is not only aroused and energized by this spiritual exercise, but the doors leading to unknown inner spheres are unblocked, releasing a kind of animal vigor into uncharted areas.

The beatific mood is suddenly interrupted with the introduction of "the devilish glare of a bright red light." Titina, dressed in one of the air-force men's uniforms, enters singing. Such a travesty, paradigmatic of her unconscious desire to take over the male powers, reveals a need for independence and a yearning to escape from an authoritarian situation.

The word "devilish" is crucial to the situation. Lucifer, as previously mentioned when referring to Dr. Hinkfuss, was a light bringer. A rebellious angel, Lucifer used his free will to disobey God. In so doing, he provoked an imbalance in the smooth-running patriarchal sphere of Eden, arousing panic, disorientation, and chaos. To alter what is fixed— spiritually, politically, or emotionally—is to destroy the security of what is old and staid. The birth of the new—be it that of a child or an idea— invites fear and trembling. Such agonies are known to all pathfinders— Abraham, Christ, and Lucifer included. As a source of light, Lucifer divided what had been whole (paradise) and allowed darkened realms (the earth) to become illuminated by his presence. Division into two engenders conflict and tension; the struggle may, however, also serve to enlighten individuals by bringing problems into focus. Understandably, the number two was considered evil by the medieval philosophers since it not only broke up the entire senex-directed sphere, but introduced the *thinking process*—always considered a danger in Western cultures. Thinking paves the way for argumentation and therefore change; it is also instrumental in effecting revolutions. He who lights the fire of cognition creates conflict.

That Dr. Hinkfuss, after having been ejected as director of the stage play by the performers, remained hidden in the theatre, maintaining his post as regulator of lighting, is significant. He continued—unbeknown to the performers—to play the role of devil's advocate. In that way he not only paved the way for conflict, but for a coming to consciousness of the problems at hand. Representing the *thinking* factor—the mechanical, logical, objective aspect of life—Dr. Hinkfuss had to put an end to Signora Ignazia's overly instinctual, earthy, and aggressive attitudes, just as it had been necessary for the performers to ask him to leave the theatre when his extreme rigidity became incompatible with their own feelings. The psychological law of opposites, or *enantiodromia*, becomes operational when the energetic process of the psyche reacts to the tension and interplay between opposites, or, in Signora Ignazia's simple terms: "Maybe it was the devil—or the Madonna."

Matriarchal Martyrdom

The Madonna, as well as the Earth Mother, are anima images, defined as an autonomous complex that represents man's unconscious inner attitude toward woman. Anima figures, as they appear in dreams, myths, and literary works of all types, range from saint to sinner. They are usually the repository for feelings or notions that are not discernible in man's outer comportment. They are therefore revelatory of an inner unconscious state.

In the male-oriented Sicilian society, few compromises are possible: young girls must either resemble the immaculate and spiritual Madonna or be identified with a whore. In either case, the role of the woman is devalued. As Madonna, the man looks up to her as an ideal, an abstract principle to be worshipped but not to relate to since she is not of this earth. As a whore, although reviled, she remains an object of obsessional fascination. The depreciation of the physical side of life and Christianity's emphasis on the spiritual frequently invited the crudest show of brutality and violence on the man's part, reflecting his unconscious discomfort with his anima, or his own feminine principle—his "inner woman."[8]

Since the prayer ritual is not effective in healing Signora Ignazia's toothache, a second one—song—is tried in an attempt to exorcise her pain. It may "charm" distress away. Signora Ignazia asks Mommina to sing Azucena's aria, "Stride la vampa!" from *Il Trovatore*, while the other daughters and their aviator friends perform other roles, including the gypsy chorus. Mommina, however, refuses to sing. Her future husband, Rico Verri, wants her to remain withdrawn at all times. He expects her to devote her days to religion, the home, their future children—and mostly to him. Mommina feels that to countermand his orders is unthinkable, yet she yields to both her mother's wishes and her own inner need for music—that *feeling* force that will convey her sorrow and pain in the mysterious and unarticulated language of sound.

Mommina, Rico Verri's anima figure, *must* fulfill the requirements of the Madonna archetype: remain immaculate, untouchable, and pristine in her purity. No earthly contact is to sully this spiritual vision. Ties to her "sinful" family must be severed, and "sensual" music, which exposes her body and feeling sphere to the outer world, must be banned. In that she exists as an abstract principle in Rico Verri's mind, Mommina dwells in a timeless, irremediable realm. She is not, therefore, a full-fledged human being, but rather a *sacred* force, set apart from others, like the hyperdulian Mary. Any divergence from this set image would be an offense to Rico Verri's principles, punishable by death.

Interestingly enough, even the Virgin Mary had been downgraded by the early Fathers of the Church. Epiphaneus wrote: "Let the Father, the Son and the Holy Spirit be worshipped, but let no one worship Mary."[9] Anastasius declared: "Let no one call Mary the Mother of God, for Mary was but a woman and it is impossible that God should be born of a woman."[10] Mariolatry, embodying the need to worship the mother figure, was always problematical in Christian patriarchal teachings. As the centuries passed, a reverse position grew. St. Bernardine of Siena believed that Mary's mystic powers were more miraculous than God's. Louis-Marie de Montfort, a French priest and author of *True Devotion to the Blessed Virgin*, went so far as to write that Mary had absolute power over God.[11]

In view of the above, we cannot consider Rico Verri's attitude toward Mommina as expressive of jealousy, but rather of his inability to distinguish the *ideal* from the *real*. A primitive type with an anthropoid psyche, Rico Verri is undeveloped and therefore incapable of discernment. So undifferentiated is his ego (center of consciousness) that he cannot distinguish between Mommina's actual character traits and those he projects upon her. Any destruction or destabilization of his spiritual or psychological well-being must be exterminated lest he experience an eclipse of his ego, i.e. insanity.

That his *passion* for the ideal, the pure, the sacred image of womankind obliterates all reason indicates the extreme power of the archetype which victimizes Rico Verri. It also reveals a fundamental inability to relate to an earthly, or *real*, woman and to the feminine sex in general—a sign, perhaps, of his own unconscious fear of sexual impotence. The loftiness of his ideal shapes and forever reinforces his narrow view of the feminine principle, thereby damaging any kind of relationship he could have with a flesh-and-blood woman. If Mommina and Rico Verri were involved in a true life experience, they would be in tune with their instincts, and opposites could be reconciled in the flow of life. Although the cultural and psychological problems might not be solved, a *modus vivendi* might be found. But because Mommina's and Rico Verri's egos are so unevolved and wavering, the conflictual sides of their personalities fall apart and identity is lost in the process.[12]

Since Rico Verri does not waver in viewing woman as saint or whore, his actions are predictable. Returning from the pharmacy with medication for Signora Ignazia's toothache, he sees Mommina singing. Taking the entire incident personally and out of context, he becomes so enraged that he pulls the piano player off his stool, hurls him to the floor, and damns them all. "So this is the way you make fun of me behind my back, is it?"

Mommina, equally unintegrated, had sung the part of the gypsy Azucena, identifying closely with her. A sense of foreboding had marked the scene. In her aria "Stride la vampa" ("Harsh roars the flame"), Azucena describes the harrowing sight of her mother being burned to death at the stake. In the gypsy's need to avenge such infamy, she throws what she thinks is the perpetrator's infant brother into a fire. When she discovers later that it was her own child, her life thereafter is one long agony.

Mommina is likewise destined to a life of heartbreak. Having apologized to Rico Verri for singing, she then bursts out: "I *am* the victim! The victim of my sisters, of the house, of you; the victim of everyone." Victimization leads to sacrifice, and ultimately Mommina is to play the role of the martyr.

Martyrdom was and still is looked upon as an *ideal* in the Roman Catholic religion. The image of the suffering Christ suspended on the cross, his festering flesh pierced through with nails, lives as an archetypal image in the psyche of all Westerners no matter which religion they embrace.[13] Pictorial, literary, and philosophical renditions of the *imitatio Christi* are plentiful. Countless artists, for example, have depicted Saint Sebastian's glowing, tender, beautiful flesh pierced by arrows, as he lives out his pain in *ekstasis.* The Christian idea of flagellation later became a regular feature in monastic life. The scourging and bloodying of oneself allowed the devout to reach consummation in torn flesh and degradation.[14]

Unlike the Roman archetype of power, domination and physical beauty, the Christian archetypal image emphasized punishment, torture, humiliation, and shame. Such excesses have been identified with the sadomasochistic syndrome. These examples of psychological aberration not only indicate a fragile ego and an inability to cope with the realities of life, but a condition of *hubris.* The performers of such painful/joyful acts which take them from excoriating pain to the ecstasy of fulfillment are indulging in an *imitatio Christi*, through which mortals identify with the transpersonal principle of deity.[15]

Mommina's marriage to Verri is tantamount to religious martyrdom and psychological sadomasochism. She has sacrificed her life as an individual, as a member of her family, and as a singer in order to fulfill her husband's anima figure. In so doing, she has divested herself of everything that is human—even her own identity. She and Rico Verri are so cut off from the archetypal foundations of their psyches, so dissociated and schizophrenic, that each plays into the delusionary world of the other, falling apart in the process and dissolving into a cluster of disorganized reactions.

In Act III, although barely thirty years of age, Mommina is being made up to look wrinkled and deformed. To emphasize the incarcerating life she has been forced to lead, and the destruction of her freedom, the stage sets call for three bare walls resembling those of a prison. These can be seen only when Mommina, alone onstage, presses her forehead against one wall, then against the others, whereupon a "blinding light from overhead makes the walls visible for a moment, and then they disappear." That she hits the walls with her *head* and *forehead*, the seat of wisdom and intuitive powers, paves the way for *gnosis*, or understanding. Athena, let us recall, was born from her father's head. In *Timaeus*, Plato asserts that "the human head is the image of the world." In the *Zohar*, a Hebrew mystical text, the head stands for astral light.

Walled up in her home, Mommina has allowed whatever healthy elements existed in her psyche to disintegrate. She can no longer relate to the world around her except through fantasies and hallucinations. Archetypal images issue forth from an unduly active subliminal sphere. Her conscious attitude, which is passive and womblike (walled-in), is at odds with her unconscious need for love and tenderness, which encourages her to sing out her feelings in operatic arias. Because she cannot integrate the estranged contents that battle within her, and can only express them indirectly, her world is peopled by unexpected and apparently inexplicable apparitions.[16] So deeply entrenched is Mommina in her unconscious and so oblivious is she to her surroundings that she continues knocking her head against the three walls "like a crazed animal in a cage."

Walls, considered protective when built around towns and cities, have been identified with the feminine element (uterus). Since they also serve to limit, imprison, and separate, they pave the way for a condition of exile. Once communication with the outside world is cut (which implies, psychologically, a severing between conscious and unconscious spheres), whatever lies within may be stifled and eventually smothered to death.

Repression is Mommina's way of evading conflict by pretending that problems do not exist. In her case, it has led to regressive reactivation of earlier relationships with her family, now reinvested with actuality via the apparitions she sees. When St. Theresa of Avila had her visions, they were called "visitations from Deity;" in Mommina's case, they may be classified as aberrations due to schizophrenia.

Rico Verri, whose reality is equally dislocated, enters the room, and, seeing her seated motionless on her chair, questions her brutally. What was she thinking about? Mommina's utter fixity, reminiscent of the inanimate objects in de Chirico's painting *Seated Manikin*, and Carra's *The Oval of the Apparition*, injects the atmosphere with a disquieting solemnity. The phantom-like appearance of the stilled form onstage conceals a *daemon* within it—soon to be revealed in the dramatic unfoldings to come.

Having locked all the doors, barred the windows (out of which Mommina is forbidden to look), and deprived her of all mirrors, Rico Verri adds another dimension to his sadistic foray. She is forbidden to think about her past and to dream, lest she be plunged into unfathomable realms over which he would have no control.

When Mommina tells her husband that she does not think or dream of her past, he does not believe her. He accuses her of sinning and shaming her family. His madness forces up from abysmal realms terrifying apparitions of the Terrible Earth Mother and her equally sinister daughters. Signora Ignazia spits out her anger, verbally flaying her son-in-law.

The room, like one of de Chirico's *Metaphysical Interiors* or *The Disquieting Muse*, is alive with phantoms and spirits. The already harrowing claustrophobic atmosphere is made even more terrifying by the brightening and dimming of the lights, in rhythm with the appearance and disappearance of the mother, sisters, and walls of the room. The Kafkaesque quality of the scene increases the tension. The climax occurs when Signora Ignazia accuses Verri of "slowly *murdering* our Mommina with your cruelty." Still Rico Verri pursues his accusations: denounces Mommina for having let other men kiss her. So possessed is he by his need to divest her of her past—her life—that he stands over her, hugging and kissing her—biting her—violently and spasmodically, imitating her embraces of other men. The greater his frenzy, the more he hurts her.

Mommina, bruised and shaking, screams. Her two little girls, terrified by the noise, come toward her. They cling to her. She shields them from Verri, unleashing her real feelings for the first time, ordering him to get out. He leaves. Her mother and sisters approach her. The ghostlike appearances vanish and Mommina begins to sing *Il Trovatore*, virtually repeating the earlier scene. Although she barely has a voice now, she sings out her pain. The extraordinary lighting effects not only intensify the melodramatic nature of Verdi's opera, but also increase the various levels of reality implicit in the protagonists' psyches. The intensity of Mommina's feelings—repressed for so long—is too great for her to bear and her failing heart stops beating. She collapses on the floor. Dead. Shock! The stunned spectators, in the throes of identifying with the melodramatic scene just enacted, now hear Dr. Hinkfuss's voice: "Magnificent! A truly magnificent scene!" He runs down the aisle onto the stage. "You did it just as I told you to. *This* is not in the story at all."

So intensely did the Character Actress perform her role as Signora Ignazia that she cannot rise from the floor at the end of the final scene. The members of the cast, fearing for her life, go over to her. She has, however, only fainted.

Friedrich Nietzsche had warned of the dangers involved in depotentiating instinct. He was one of the first to speak of the "denaturalization of natural values" and to suggest that "we must liberate ourselves from morality in order to be able to live morally."[17] To codify morality is to ossify it, to transform it into an absolute. If morality is considered an end in itself, it can become an evil. To seek perfection indicates a repression of whatever unconscious forces are alive within an individual that do not conform to the collective social outlook. Only by reconciling polarities, rather than rejecting them, can a person or a culture come to terms with the multiple and fluid factors that make up human and social behavior patterns.

Although the protagonists in *Tonight We Improvise* never evolve and do not succeed in facing the unintegrated forces within their psyches. Dr. Hinkfuss—the logical, mechanical, cerebral power behind the spectacle— is that Luciferian force that casts light, through his stage production, on their problems and conflicts, thereby inviting humankind to examine the vast sea of energy that lies deeply embedded within and outside human consciousness.

The rigid mechanics of the prevailing patriarchal culture where freedom is banned for women leads to the physical degradation and disintegration of the family: symbolically society. The living organism—women in this case—is no longer able to participate in the life process. Psyche and body as machine can no longer convert the energy at their disposal, thus bringing the dance and song of life to an end.

5 Antoine de Saint-Exupéry's *Wind, Sand, and Stars*—The Pilot and a New Poetics of Space

Antoine de Saint-Exupéry's autobiographical *Wind, Sand, and Stars* (1939) details the author's experiences as a pilot as well as the psychological, social, and philosophical aftermath of several harrowing and sublime moments in the air and on the ground. *Wind, Sand, and Stars* reveals a soul and psyche in torment. Only through the airborne experience could Saint-Exupéry begin to heal—albeit temporarily—his increasingly corrosive anxiety. The inner wound which bored deep and bled until the end of his days prevented him from adapting to the needs of the earthly domain.

Saint-Exupéry's relationship with the planes he piloted in *Wind, Sand, and Stars* is of utmost significance. These machines enabled him to escape from the monotonous and unpleasant world of contingencies into what he considered the free world above. To ascend to astral spheres, where imagination roams unimpeded, blending into seemingly infinite fluid expanses, endowed him with a sense of liberation. Such a need indicated a nostalgic yearning to surpass the human condition; it also afforded him a spiritual experience. The weightiness of earth was left behind.

The plane, associated with the modern age as the horse is with ancient and medieval times, may also be viewed as an instrument of self-discovery. Within its sleek, solid, and shiny metallic body, the pilot, Saint-Exupéry, looks out into space, at suns, moons, planets, and burned-out remnants of stars that have collapsed under their own gravity and then exploded. Do these images replicate his own inner climate?

Within the confines of Saint-Exupéry's firm, lustrous plane exists an intensely active emotional and intellectual power: a human microcosm attempting to understand the inhuman macrocosm. As the pilot seeks to further his knowledge about space, perhaps affording him access to another mode of existence, he begins to personify the plane. Endowed with human dimensions, it is transformed into a friend, companion, nurturer, and protector. Also imbued with spiritual attributes, it provides Saint-Exupéry, the narrator of *Wind, Sand, and Stars*, with the power of a *hierophany:* a manifestation of the sacred.

Flying alone inspired Saint-Exupéry with feelings of *transcendence* and freedom, transforming the pilot's earthborne spiritual and psychological discomfiture into a sense of achievement and joy. Fascination with the dangerous aspects involved in flying—very real in 1926, since planes were far from being perfected at the time—also fueled his already active sense of excitement. Flying could obliterate, at least momentarily, an overwhelming sense of despair and helplessness. But it was also a flirtation with suicide.

Psychologically, the Saint-Exupéry of *Wind, Sand, and Stars* may be associated with the *puer aeternus* type: the eternal adolescent, weightless, liberated, and unfettered, perpetually wandering throughout into the aerial spheres of the globe and universe. Unable to commit himself, except superficially, unwilling to be bound to any job, group, or ideological view for any length of time, Saint-Exupéry was forever piloting and getting *high* in rarefied elevations. He never probed the heart of his problems, nor dealt with his periods of deep distress directly. He preferred to detach himself from worldly entanglements and confrontations, shearing off all that was mundane and pedestrian.

To seek sublimated or aerial spheres is to reject solid elements and substances. Such yearnings reveal a longing for the impalpable, the incorporeal, the atomized. A deeply rooted individual, on the other hand, one whose will to live and acceptance of life are uppermost, accepts the earth with all of its solid, concrete, and material entanglements. Saint-Exupéry, I suggest, never wanted to outgrow his youthful years, his *puer* existence, which offered him a rich fantasy life, a creative and perpetually new and fervent experience. In no way did he accept reality—the flow *into life.* Rather, he was forever flying out of it.[1]

Saint-Exupéry's introduction of a new *poetics of space* in *Wind, Sand, and Stars* is experiential and reveals a spiritual necessity. Since earth and sky are no longer viewed from a single vantage point by someone standing on *terra firma* looking upward, feelings of immanence and visionary gleanings emerge. Because the pilot beholds the cosmos from within a moving vehicle traveling in the air, each entity in this densely populated area becomes an active partner in a celestial encounter. Space, then, is not passive, as it had been when Newtonian physics reigned sacrosanct, in that space is not three-dimensional and time is not a separate entity. Instead both are connected to form a four-dimensional continuum—

perceptions have been altered. In his description of the constellations, the heavens, and the earth, therefore, Saint-Exupéry cannot and does not talk about space without mentioning time. Nor does he consider mass anything but a form of energy. Empty space for Saint-Exupéry has no meaning since it is filled with subatomic units of matter. Not only does the author of *Wind, Sand, and Stars* challenge outmoded perceptions and concepts, but while he stares out of the window of his plane at giant clusters of galaxies, increasing light seems to merge into his line of vision. (Light here is synonymous with understanding, and is multivalent, its multiplicity of meanings replicating the many forms Saint-Exupéry sees around him.) The words needed to translate the feelings generated by the excitement of the seemingly unlimited horizons that come into view are endowed with a sense of free play, of fluidity—a new liberty and power. Different perspectives reveal variegated chiaroscuros created by cloud formations, the interactions between the sun's radiance and the moon's reflected tones, and the perpetually altering glimmerings and rhythmical patterns of the stars and planets. Each of these visualizations constitutes a link in the cosmic chain of processes and properties which the observer, Saint-Exupéry, seeks to comprehend.

Ascensional images have, since the very dawn of history, implied an attempt to understand metaphysical truths. The *Rig Veda* states: "Intelligence is the most rapid of birds" (VI, 9, 5). Heights invite Saint-Exupéry to decode messages in startling images, metaphors, oxymorons, and paradoxes, opening up both the writer and reader to unheard-of realms of solid and gaseous, liquid and fixed matter. Disorientation and confusion ensue: dangerous conditions which so frequently precede a broadening and deepening in understanding baffling ideations. In Saint-Exupéry's case, they lead to an encounter with the universe and his experience within its folds.

The poetics of space introduced in *Wind, Sand, and Stars* discloses an archetypal world based on a reappraisal of the time/space continuum. Since time can be measured only by bodies in motion, Saint-Exupéry's perspectives—topography, climate, and his relationships to these entities—are constantly shifting. There is nothing stable in his description or his outlook, except, paradoxically, the plane itself. From within its belly, the author—all eyes—reacts literally and emotionally to the luminous spectral centers which force their way upon him. He listens carefully as they cry out their paradoxically toneless sonorities in harmonic and cacophonous rhythms. Equally responsive to all aspects of the earth's personality—its moods, mounds, and folds, consistencies and divergencies—Saint-Exupéry succeeds in catapulting his readers, in the most sensual manner, into the very heart of embodied and disembodied images, each exuding its unique tactile, olfactory, auditory, and visual sensations. Amid these connected and disconnected expanses of atomized abstract and concrete masses, a new understanding of reality may be gleaned, which leaves readers floundering in a *somewhere* which is *nowhere*.

Saint-Exupéry was aware of the fact that classical sentences and clauses could no longer be used to conceptualize or represent the world or the events experienced from space. Words had to take on materiality, to become part and parcel of the physical surroundings they suggested, even while remaining incorporeal. Meaning, sound, idea, emptiness, and silence inherent in morphemes had to be interrelated with everything in the cosmos both rationally and irrationally. Their presence became an aggressive force ready to disrupt people's preconceived and limited perceptions or they were transformed into passive recipients of *eros*.

When reshaping his imaginary universe, Saint-Exupéry remarked that he saw white gluey substances in the heavens above, which not only "took on unknown value" but lured him into the confines of the real/unreal. Nor was he to be duped. He understood from the very start of his writing career, and most particularly in *Wind, Sand, and Stars*, that to convey the essence, the very fiber of the spectacular sights he saw from the window of his cockpit, required detachment on his part, along with objectivity and disentanglement—those very factors of which he had divested himself when leaving the empirical world. Detachment was necessary "to make the airline pilot discover new meanings in old appearances."

The very texture of space, the fibers and lacerations which Saint-Exupéry conveys in so many of his descriptions, leaves the pragmatic meaning of ordinary language behind. Words, discourse, and feelings, became apprentices to a new freedom, to the unforeseen, where language, like the plane, channels a different path as it penetrates its new habitat—a sphere where duration is deprived of its thickness. No longer the victim of fossilized words, with immobile and solidified contents, Saint-Exupéry molds his phrases and sentences to space and silence, to past, present, and future solitudes.

Like Nietzsche, Saint-Exupéry animalizes his experiences by magnifying the rhythms and sonorities of his morphemes, and amplifying the motility of their continuously mobile representations.

> Down currents sometimes fill pilots with strange sensations of malaise. The engines run on, but the ship seems to be sinking. You jockey to hold your altitude: the ship loses speed and turns flabby. And still you sink. So you give it up, fearful that you have jockeyed too much; and you let yourself drift to right or left, striving to put at your back a favorable peak, that is, a peak off which the winds rebound as off a springboard.

And yet you go on sinking. The whole sky seems to be coming down on you. You begin to feel like the victim of some cosmic accident. You cannot land anywhere, and you try in vain to turn round and fly back into those zones where the air, as dense and solid as a pillar, had held you up. That pillar has melted away. Everything here is rotten and you slither about in a sort of universal decomposition while the cloud-bank rises apathetically, reaches your level, and swallows you up.

By mixing metaphors, fusing analogies, and creating oxymorons, Saint-Exupéry's syntax takes on a liberty of its own. Intending to startle readers out of their usual torpor and the false security of their earth-oriented ways and concepts, the writer propels them into a sphere where sound footing is nonexistent. Cut off from human habitation and anxiety, even their fear mounts at the thought of being alone in space—as does the frenetic joy at the sight of this unlimited realm with its giant masses of impalpable rarefied regions: anti-life.

Saint-Exupéry was not alone in aspiring to know spatial climes. To reach the Moon and Sun, those glowing and constantly beckoning planets and stars, has been the goal of human beings since earliest times. The great Sumerian and Persian star gazers yearned to understand the flow of these divine powers, as did Pythagoras, when studying mathematics in the ancient mystery schools in the pyramids of Egypt. Plato and Aristotle created their theories, and Leonardo da Vinci drew flying machines based on the principle of birds in flight. In 1609, Johannes Kepler wrote a plan for a projected moon flight, which he sent to Galileo: "Who could have believed before Columbus that a huge ocean could have been crossed more peacefully and safely than the narrow expanse of the Adriatic or the Baltic Sea, or the English Channel? . . . Provide ships or sails adapted to the heavenly breezes, and there will be some who will not fear even that void of interplanetary space. So for those who will come shortly to attempt this journey, let us establish the astronomy."[2] In 1783, a balloon manned by Joseph and Jacques Montgolfier lifted off the earth. In 1842, an Englishman, W. S. Henson, patented a design for the machine that foreshadowed a modern monoplane. In 1890, Clement Ader, a French engineer, achieved a flight of 150 feet in his power-driven monoplane which looked like a bat. But it was not until 1903 that the Americans Orville and Wilbur Wright produced the first manned, power-driven, heavier-than-air flying machine with two propellers chain driven by gasoline motor.

Fictional journeys into space date back to pre-Platonic times and have continued throughout the ages. The seventeenth-century Cyrano de Bergerac's *Voyages to the Moon and the Sun* introduced a machine powered by rockets. In Samuel Johnson's *Rasselas*, we learn of the possibility of aerial travel and space flight by an aeronaut reaching an area outside of the earth's gravitational field. A report of an airship's journey from Vienna to Lisbon was printed in a newspaper a hundred and fifty years prior to Edgar Allan Poe's depiction of Hans Pfaall's trip to the moon in a balloon. In *Typee*, Herman Melville declared that by the end of the nineteenth century air travel would permit people on the West Coast of America to spend their weekends in Hawaii.[3] Nor can we discount Jules Verne's *From the Earth to the Moon* (1860), in which the concept of steering rockets to maneuver spaceships from the earth to the Moon and around it evolved. H. G. Wells, in *The First Men in the Moon*, depicted spacemen entering a sphere by means of a gravity-defying substance called "Cavornite."

Antoine de Saint-Exupéry (1900–1944) was born in Lyon into an old French family. Even as a child he demonstrated a fascination with mechanical objects like boilers, pistons, and engines, spending hours on end drawing all different types of apparatus. When a young lad, he built a flying machine by stretching a pair of sheets over the frame of bamboo struts attached to the handlebars of his bicycle.[4]

At twenty-one, Saint-Exupéry began his two years of military service. He asked for and was assigned to the new air branch; he was then sent to join the Second Aviation Regiment in the suburbs of Strasbourg. After obtaining a civilian pilot's license, he became a commercial flyer piloting mail all over Europe, Africa, and South America.

Saint-Exupéry's relationship with his mother, a domineering woman who sought to direct his life as best she could, was close. His affairs were for the most part unhappy, including his early rebuff by Louise de Vilmorin, and his marriage to Consuelo, née Suncin de Sandoval. No woman could fill the void within him; nor could he fill the limitless emptiness he felt throughout his earthly existence.[5]

Saint-Exupéry served as a pilot in the first year of World War II, after which he came to the United States, only to return to North Africa and the war zone in 1943. A year later, while flying on a reconnaissance mission over France, his plane was lost. His writings, such as *Southern Mail* (1929), *Night Flight* (1931), *Wind, Sand, and Stars*, and *Flight to Arras* (1942), are deeply moving explorations of one man's struggle with the elements, his relationships with people, his harrowing and heroic missions, and his attitude toward danger and death. His best-known and perhaps most-loved work, *The Little Prince* (1943), has been regarded as a masterpiece of its kind: a modern fairy story with immense psychological and philosophical ramifications.

Wind, Sand, and Stars narrates a physical, spiritual, and psychological adventure. Divided into eight parts, it takes its readers into the very heart of the airman's world: those with whom he must deal, the plane or instrument itself, and the elements confronted. It relates the story of the first mail route from France to Dakar and down the coast of South America; the pilot's struggle against a cyclone on the Argentine coast; his hallucinatory vision of infinite night; his entrapment after crashing in seemingly endless snows; and his imprisonment in the desert—where he faced thirst and seemingly certain death.

The Plane as Anima

Flying as a transoceanic aviator, breaking speed records, piloting the mail, and escaping physical mutilation and death several times draw Saint-Exupéry, the narrator of *Wind, Sand, and Stars*, ever closer to his machine. He depends upon it to fulfill his empirical and spiritual goals and to see to his well-being. Frequently alluded to as a tool, such as a plow, the plane is also endowed with emotional powers. A companion, a presence, a mate, a positive force in his life, the plane makes it possible for him to gain a new kind of understanding and *feeling* about himself and the world at large.

A mediating factor, the plane/machine takes on the function of a soul mate: his *anima*. Defined as the unconscious side of a man's personality or the "inner woman," the anima has been personified in dreams from time immemorial by images of women ranging from whore to saint to spiritual guide. An autonomous psychic content—she—the plane stands for *eros*, a relational factor which paves the way for the birth and progress of love.

As anima, the plane plays the role of the *ideal* woman existing in the narrator's fantasy. Unlike the *real* woman, it does not disappoint. Although it may break down or crash when its mechanism malfunctions or when it is overpowered by a storm, if it weathers these situations, it responds to the pilot's touch, to his commands, to his yearnings in the most efficient, perfect and beautiful of ways. It is *beauty* for Saint-Exupéry; it is *love*.

That the plane takes on the function of an anima for the pilot in no way suggests that it is a passive force. On the contrary, it is an aggressive power, shooting through the air, ripping and tearing it asunder. The anima/plane is that factor that creates turmoil and ushers in the birth of new ideas and fresh sensations. A sense of bewilderment and confusion dominates as old concepts are broken up or concretions dismembered. Sure footing and a sense of security disappear. Instead, fresh and unexperienced images, forces, and feelings come into being, endowing the pilot with the necessary strength to confront the unknown—even death. Like the plow that breaks up the earth, an instrument to which Saint-Exupéry refers several times in the book, as mentioned above, the plane penetrates the atmosphere, fulfilling its own destiny. As this powerful feminine principle reaches higher celestial altitudes, equated since ancient times with the archetype of the Spiritual Father, opposites seem to coalesce: *eros* comes to the fore and immerses the flyer in a sense of well-being.

Since the plane encloses the pilot, it may be considered a protective device, saving him from the perils of the atmosphere and thus taking on the traditional characteristics of the feminine principle. In that it takes him on a journey that will nourish his imagination and warm his feeling world, it also plays the role of a loving and stimulating agent. When, physically speaking, it is identified with the bird, the anima/plane becomes an agent for communication between heaven and earth. It is the soul escaping from the weight of the body. The plane may be looked upon as a modern counterpart of the ancient images of bird as soul depicted on the walls of the Lascaux caves; as intellect in the *Rig-Veda*; as angel in the Koran; as an initiatory quest in Attar's *The Conference of the Birds*; as the imagination becoming operational for Saint John of the Cross. All these may be associated with the plane as a feminine force.

Such positive views of the plane/anima/bird cannot but call their counterpart into play: the plane as an agent of destruction. We may envisage its devouring metallic jaws—the *vagina dentata*—as cutting, jarring, abrasive and dismembering devices, destroying the pilot and itself during periods of rage or torment, when, for example, it loses its battles with tornadoes, thick cloud formations, and powerful downdrafts.

Even though the plane is instrumental in guiding the pilot to the land of his dreams—to celestial spheres, the dominion of the Spiritual Father—it also removes him from what has been identified from time immemorial with woman: the earth and the world of encumbrances and obstacles but also life itself. One side of the anima, then, makes it possible for Saint-Exupéry to strip himself of woman's constricting and tentacle-like grasp, even while paradoxically he encourages, accepts, and loves her aggressive side, which empowers him to fulfill his fantasies and connects him with the Spiritual Father.

Among the Hebraic and Christian mystics of old, the burden of ascension to celestial spheres is placed upon the human mind and is not, as in the nonmystic doctrines of these religions, given as a gift from heaven. The plane/anima for Saint-Exupéry, who had abandoned the tenets of Roman Catholicism, was experienced as a mighty catalyst, a religious power that helped him ascend into pleromatic spheres, as well as a manifestation of his own creative force as writer and artist.

The Initiation

For the plane/anima to penetrate celestial spheres the pilot must undergo an initiatory process. The word *initiate*, derived from the Latin *initium* ("going within"), means "to enter." The initiate, then, is one who enters into a new way of viewing things by following the path he or she has chosen for fulfillment: it means realizing full potential by passing from a so-called inferior to a superior state.

Aristotle remarked, in referring to the mysteries of Eleusis, that the lessons learned by an initiate cannot be taught: they must be *experienced*. Since secrets cannot be communicated, they must be lived through, viscerally and emotionally. The same applies to the mysteries surrounding flying: these must be understood physically and practically, accepted emotionally, and fulfilled via personal effort. To complete an initiation as a pilot—or a priest, composer, writer, or painter—requires great discipline on the individual's part.

Saint-Exupéry's initiation into the world of airmen, as revealed in *Wind, Sand, and Stars*, required the completion of a difficult physical, spiritual, and psychological indoctrination process. It was believed that strength and fortitude enable the pilot to cope in a more lucid manner with the hazardous vicissitudes facing a flyer. The rituals involved in the initiation process also taught such necessities as independence and resourcefulness under the most intolerable and dangerous of conditions. During Saint-Exupéry's training period—or time of trial, to use the words of the mystic—he was forced to do without sleep, to perform all sorts of exercises designed to overcome inertia, fear, hunger, and pain. To receive his pilot's license he had to complete one hundred flights in three weeks: this meant flying three to four times a day. Landing in soggy ground or on sun-drenched sands, learning to repair his machine's frequent breakdowns, and always remaining lucid and functional were not easy disciplines.[6]

a. The male community: To complete a group's initiation, be it mystical or professional, usually demands that the acolyte learn to function harmoniously within a male community. Saint-Exupéry, the pilot in training, entered a patriarchal community where he underwent a variety of tests designed to toughen him and enable him to face danger.

Living in an all-male group is not always desirable, but in Saint-Exupéry's case it had its compensations. Not only did it increase his knowledge as a mechanic and engineer, but it broadened him socially, developing his ability to get along with men from all walks of life. Above all it put him in touch with *archetypal heroes* like Jean Mermoz, whose character and feats as depicted in *Wind, Sand, and Stars* were those of an incredible pilot. In his Breguet 14 (a "square-nosed biplane driven by a 300-horsepower Renault engine"), which resembled a "flying crate" rather than the sleek machine he later piloted, he fascinated crowds at Casablanca and elsewhere with his stunt flying. His spectacular loops, his incredible climbing bank, his landing on the exact spot marked out in white chalk on the field, were virtually miraculous.[7]

Saint-Exupéry the novice questioned superiors like Mermoz, listened to their stories, and experienced the *mysterium tremendum* vicariously. Their curt but *revered* answers disclosed a fabulous world filled "with snares and pitfalls, with cliffs suddenly looming out of fog and whirling air-currents of a strength to uproot cedars. Black dragons guarded the mouths of the valleys and clusters of lightning crowned the crests—for our elders were always at some pains to feed our reverence."[8]

Henri Guillaumet was another hero pilot. It was to him that Saint-Exupéry dedicated *Wind, Sand, and Stars*. Fearless always, when his plane crashed on the snow-covered Chilean slopes of the Andes he not only survived the impact, but also had the stamina to make his way alone down the frozen mountainside and walk for five days. He then collapsed, but an Indian woman saw his virtually lifeless body and called for help.

Guillaumet, who had been over the route from Alicante to Casa Blanca, *initiated* Saint-Exupéry, the novice, into the mysteries of flying without a radio and of landing on poor emergency fields. The young pilot felt as if he were entering an ancient mystery cult—celebrating the rituals involved in honoring Osiris, Orpheus, Pythagoras, or Christ. Like the acolytes of old, he received secrets, and therefore considered himself different from the ordinary person, virtually dead to the profane world and reborn into higher celestial and spiritual domains.

The perils implicit in each of Saint-Exupéry's missions endowed him, he wrote, with the status of "a warrior in danger" and "the proud intoxication of renunciation."

Danger and renunciation are part of the initiate's disciplines; they are also intrinsic to the flyer's vocabulary in *Wind, Sand, and Stars*. To emulate the great hero types, such as Mermoz and Guillaumet, the pilot must identify with these fearless *masculine* powers within the community of legendary men or Spiritual Fathers. It is not surprising, then, to discover that during Saint-Exupéry's training or initiation period, emphasis was placed on the formation of leaders. As the life force of a male initiatory group, the Mermozes and Guillaumets are viewed as models for younger novices to emulate and look up to as ideals. Such a psychological situation nevertheless has its dangers. Should blind admiration or idealization of Great Individuals (psychologically viewed as Father figures) continue for any length of time without the application of judgmental faculties which serve to fracture or fragment such archetypal images, the initiate's maturation process may be stunted. He might never learn to think for himself and remain content to wax in perennial idolatry.

Unlike authoritarian or dictatorial male groups such as the Nazi Youth Movement or Islamic terrorist factions in recent times, the patriarchal sphere as depicted in *Wind, Sand, and Stars* encouraged individual development. This implies, psychologically, that the adolescent ego (center of consciousness) of each of the initiates was to be strengthened, taught to survive and to dominate fear while also carving out its own destiny. To accomplish such a goal requires separation from the group once the basics have been taught. According to Erich Neumann, such a rite of passage is crucial in preparing and vitalizing the ego so that it may forge ahead as an independent force.[9]

b. "Baptism" in the air: Saint-Exupéry's "baptism" in the air was fraught with real and psychological dangers. The former because of the rudimentary nature of the flying equipment at the time and the difficulties involved in coping with the lack of adequate directional devices and unforeseen storms. On a psychological level, *inflation* or *hubris* is always a condition to be dreaded. The novice/pilot, once in the air, sometimes becomes dizzied and dazzled by feelings of grandeur and power, forgetting his human and limited nature and neglecting to let wisdom guide his actions.

The myth of Icarus is a case in point. Icarus was the son of the great architect Daedalus, the designer of the Cretan labyrinth and the fabricator of wings which would allow him and Icarus to fly out of the labyrinth, where they had been imprisoned. He warned his son not to fly too high because the sun would melt the wax he used to glue the wings onto his back. So imbued with joy and power was Icarus as he sailed over the sea that he disregarded his father's sage advice and drowned in the Aegean. Daedalus, who followed a more cautious course, reached safety.

Saint-Exupéry's narrator, though more like Daedalus, does have a bit of Icarus in him. Like the father, he adheres to the rules and regulations of his craft. The earth forces him to deal with mundane matters and the obstacles confronting him; it engages him in the life experience. Like Icarus, however, he is sometimes overcome (perhaps unconsciously) by an inflated sense of his own worth, marking him with feelings of superiority. He feels he is part of an elite group, and superior to those "lowly" mortals forced to walk on Mother Earth. Indeed, he is, since few flew in the 1920s.

A "baptism" in the air suggests other considerations: spiritual aspirations as well as a passionate desire to lead a life of action. To enter aerial domains for protracted periods of time, as we have seen, is antipodal to an earth-oriented reality. It indicates a yearning for amorphous, pliable realms, and an existence without the entanglements of daily living. Despite the fact that Saint-Exupéry, who had been sent to parochial schools when a child and youth, had given up his faith, he uses religious language throughout *Wind, Sand, and Stars*. With such words as *ordination, consecration, novitiate,* and *renunciation,* he refers to his probation in 1926 as a student airline pilot with the Lateocoere Company (predecessors of Aeropostale, now Air France), imbuing the entire period with sacrality.

The word *renunciation* had very special significance for Saint-Exupéry. It indicated a need to cut himself off from anything and everything that was not vital to gaining expertise in his chosen field. To renounce, however, implies the kind of asceticism necessary to succeed in facing tests and ordeals. In Saint-Exupéry's case, extreme rigor and self-discipline were required to fulfill the imperatives of his craft. His great will power, courage, and determination to reach his goal point to other psychological factors: his need to escape into a world of his own and, at the same time, an inability to relate to others as well as, perhaps, an unconscious longing for death.

The sense of mystery he experienced in the solitude and silence high above the earth energized his entire being, transforming his feelings, sensations, and perceptions into a verbal experience. The visions of endlessly mobile storm centers, of strange lucent clouds, of fiery constellations whose eerie glimmers pulsated with seemingly mechanical regularity, of azure space brilliantly lit by the sun's nuclear holocausts—each had ideational as well as psychological content. The complexity of the imagery solidifying before him took on both a real and unreal countenance, these spatial fossils becoming replicas of his own inner climate. Invigorated by the forever-dazzling array of unreal powers, of pure *sublimated* essences, Saint-Exupéry felt strangely rejuvenated. Higher altitudes opened a gateway to anterior existences, to an interplay of multiple, silent resonances. Time and space were deprived of their thickness; their weightlessness allowed him the joy of indulging in his metapoetic flights. As an *elixir* for Saint-Exupéry, flying was comparable to the imbibing of a magic brew; it had the power of communion wine, endowing him with a sense of infinite beatitude.

A life of action, with a need to dominate events and destiny and an unwillingness to participate in stasis, or *ataraxia,* filled Saint-Exupéry's life with perpetual activity, excitement, and a sense of power—always coupled with anxiety. Test after test. Solo flights. Flights with and without an engineer. Some trajectories which took him over the Sahara. On one occasion, he and his technician felt as though they had "slipped beyond the confines of this world."

Once the *professional airborne baptism* was over: the *work* would follow. That meant that Saint-Exupéry would have to deal directly with the unforeseen and the unpredictable, the harrowing as well as the supernal. Episodes beyond human imagination took on the patina of reality, catalyzing the pilot. It was as if he and his anima/machine had been *ordained* to ascend to higher spiritual spheres—to experience the headiness of being lost in the wilderness of amorphous transparent matter. A prey to "errant signs, delusive flashes, phantoms," Saint-Exupéry would find himself able to leap into uncharted territories, baffling and tortuous convolutions of masses of evanescent particles. Within the mazes that amaze, the fissures and fullnesses of interplanetary space, amid the infinite, uninhabitable, and unreachable stars and planets, he *knew* the solitude of the measureless regions surrounding him and bathed in the sensual joy of the experience.

Like the heroes and knights of old, Saint-Exupéry, the pilot, became the defender of his religion: the safe deliverer of mail from one land to another. Having learned to decipher, in a rudimentary way, the signs of danger—snow, clouds, storms, peaks, rocky corridors, or oncoming night, all of which could bring on a cosmic accident—he pursued his hazardous course—after his *ordination*—with courage and fortitude.

Invested into the order of pilots, Saint-Exupéry, no longer the acolyte, entered the ministry of the air, *consecrating* himself to his future flights, imbued with the high sense of the "magic of the craft," and loving that sleek, smooth feminine power that took him closer and closer to the stars and heavenly planets whose presence he yearned for always.

The Work

Like the carpenter who faces his block of wood, or the alchemist who blends his amalgams in his *athanor* (oven), or the believer before the host, or religious statue, so the pilot with his plane—a hierophany—pursues his course with love, fervor, and tremulous rapture.

During the course of Saint-Exupéry's initiation, the plane, while drawing him away from rational and empirical spheres, had taken on an increased human dimension. That this lustrous, calm, and cool instrument that soars from temporal to atemporal spheres also possesses its own organs, muscles, and personality indicates the pilot's deep-seated need for a woman companion and the plane's fulfillment of this yearning. He delineates his feelings of extraordinary expansiveness when penetrating a hydroplane, which he describes in loving terms as it *plows* through the sea's surface and mounts into the spheres above. Hypnotic and spectacular, its gleaming, polished, and sensual body cuts through the air, moving with the lascivious beauty of the most perfect woman—into outerworldly space.

Under the dizzying whirl of the scythelike propellers, clusters of silvery water bloom and drown the flotation gear. The element smacks the sides of the hull with a sound like a gong, and the pilot can sense this tumult in the quivering of his body. He feels the ship charging itself with power as from second to second it picks up speed. He feels the development, in these fifteen tons of matter, of a maturity that is about to make flight possible. He closes his hands over the controls, and little by little in his bare palms he receives the gift of this power. The metal organs of the controls, progressively as this gift is made him, become the messengers of the power in his hands. And when his power is ripe, then, in a gesture gentler than the culling of a flower, the pilot severs the ship from the water and establishes it in the air.

The pilot and his plane, like the lover and his beloved, can no longer be parted. They are mystery as is woman, as is the slab of marble which the ancient myth tells us contains the sculpture the sculptor will hammer, chisel, and scrape from its mass, sometime in the future, bringing forth creation from brute matter. In indissoluble partnership with his airplane, Saint-Exupéry—pilot, writer, and mystic—will go forth to do his ordained work: to bathe in celestial spheres. The *spiritual* wind, synonymous, for mystics, with Divine Spirit (*rouach*) or Divine Breath—that same force which "breathed into his [Adam's] nostrils the breath of life" and enabled him to become "a living soul"—will also inspire the poet (Gen. 2:7). Saint-Exupéry will go through a sacramental ceremony reminiscent of Arthur Rimbaud's experience as a *seer* when his gaze is opened onto the ineffable. The pilot/mystic will intuit the right airways to take: "Roads avoid the barren lands, the rocks, the sands. They shape themselves to man's needs and run from stream to stream." He feels supremely confident; he possesses the power to blaze new trails while flying his missions—and disclose to his reader realms no one has ever seen before.

My world was the world of flight. Already I could feel the oncoming night with which I should be enclosed as in the precincts of a temple—enclosed in the temple of night for the accomplishment of secret rites and absorption in inviolable contemplation.

Already this profane world was beginning to fade out: soon it would vanish altogether. This landscape was still laved in golden sunlight, but already something was evaporating out of it. I know nothing, nothing in the world, equal to the wonder of nightfall in the air.

Although consciously occupied with the complicated control apparatuses before him when flying his plane, Saint-Exupéry also absorbs the
wonders of the limitless space around him and amplifies these wonders as
fantasies emerge from his unconscious to supplement what he actually
sees. Such splendid but objectively existing solar spectacles as the Andromeda Spiral encourage him to muse: in this case over the nature of the more
than 100,000 million stars that constitute the Spiral—stars that were
known to astronomers more than one thousand years ago, and are so
distant that their light takes more than two million years to reach the
earth's atmosphere, even though light travels more than 186,000 miles per
second. Thinking upon this ancient light, Saint-Exupéry feels himself no
longer existing in the present, but linked to happenings occurring in the
last Ice Age. He feels *ekstasis*—that tremendous elation and sense of belonging known to mystics when undergoing an epiphanic encounter. As he
communes rhapsodically with the phenomena of outer space, he is simultaneously creating a myth with the collaboration of his own inner space—
his original experience emanating as archetypal images from within his
collective unconscious, that barrierless and suprapersonal sphere within
the psyche which is inaccessible to the conscious domain except in the
form of such images.

Spontaneous psychic phenomena, or the poetics of space, emerge in
Saint-Exupéry's unconscious as living stuff, arousing a whole world of
sensations, as well as an indescribable sense of liberation, endowing him
with a *raison d'être* not strictly empirical but also related to the Platonic
world of the *Ideal/Idea*. Thus it is not surprising that the more Saint-
Exupéry immerses himself in the elements, the more expansive are his
hallucinatory visions: optical illusions focusing on lunar surfaces with
mountainous and crater-scared areas and dark surfaces called "seas."[10]
Though they were inert long before earth's earliest civilizations and even
prior to the age of the dinosaurs, the constellations reveal their personalities to Saint-Exupéry: their "magnificent desolation."

The earth appears personified to Saint-Exupéry; its mounds and humps,
its flanks and plains, its mouths and gulleys, its "great subterranean organs," its fires, its "mute and abandoned" landscapes "strewn with black
glaciers," its turf and slope, its hillocks and austral ices fill him, strangely,
with a sense of security. He *knows* the earth; the atmosphere and what lies
beyond, the stratosphere and toposphere, are awesome and bewildering
powers. What he *marvels* at is "the rounded back of the planet, between
this magnetic sheet and those stars," and the human consciousness that
could assess these marvels.

Saint-Exupéry's return to earth—the Rio de Oro region in Spanish
Africa—does not prevent his adventurous musings from taking on a magi-

cal cast and arousing secrets kindling within his being. Again, while lying on the surface of seemingly endless miles of sand "composed of minute and distinct shells," he gazes upward to the infinite expanses, and suddenly, like Nietzsche's Zarathustra, is overcome with the necessity of knowing in those remote, icy regions far above the human world—the world of pure being. Rising from his recumbent position, he picks up a molded rock of lava on a bed of shells a thousand feet deep, and time is again foreshortened, as it had been when he observed the Andromeda Spiral from space. He feels himself embracing thousands of years—past, present, and future—fused in a single moment.

Like ascetics or anchorites who removed themselves from society, such as the fourth-century Saint Anthony, Saint-Exupéry luxuriates in visions that pursue their compensatory course. Like St. Anthony, who offset his solitude with visions of luscious meals to still his hunger and images of voluptuous maidens in response to his unfulfilled sexual desires, Saint-Exupéry peoples his solitude with hallucinatory and frequently numinous imaginings. Be they visions of the emptiness of the deserts, the remoteness of the seas, the primeval forests, or mountain heights, spontaneous psychic phenomena filled the inner void resulting from the intense feelings of divestiture which plagued Saint-Exupéry throughout his life—most particularly after lengthy periods on the ground.

The Desert Experience

Saint-Exupéry spent three years serving an airfield in a desert outpost where the Sahara meets the Atlantic. There he "succumbed" to the silence and solitude of the seemingly endless barren wasteland he encountered. After receiving his wings in 1926, he was transferred to the Dakar-Juby division, and thrilled at the prospect of flying from Agadir to Dakar and penetrating "the vast sandy void and the mystery" of this intensely occult and secretive area.

Although physically arduous—the heat and dryness at times reaching unbearable intensity—the desert experience, like his periods of flight, opened Saint-Exupéry up to new schemes. To linear time, which connected him with earthly endeavors, was added his understanding of cyclical time, unchanging and eternal. These broadening concepts helped him connect the measureless spaces above with timeless considerations concerning the aging of our planet. Such a time/space continuum triggered his subliminal spheres, enticing him into vastly incredible networks of unknowns. "A journey through time. Time was running through my fingers like the fine sand of the dunes; the poundings of my heart were bearing me onward toward an unknown future."

The desert years imbued Saint-Exupéry with a secret inner glow. At the crossroads of his earthly existence, he felt himself living alongside the charred remains of anterior civilizations, experiencing vicariously their gestation processes and his own. Like the prophets, monks, and holy men of old, who exiled themselves in vast oceanic deserts, unconsciously seeking communion with deity, so Saint-Exupéry awaited his revelation in the form of cataclysmic representations and signs. To disrupt the static and mundane life he could have led during this period, he divided his time between flights and days spent walking, touching, and counting infinite grains of sand. Under such circumstances, the utter *emptiness* of it all, which might have overwhelmed him, had the opposite effect: it churned unconscious contents. Remarkable visionary experiences emanated from remote and secret areas within his psyche.

Emptiness is an archetypal power which appears in almost all primitive and antique creation myths, according to which, at the beginning of the world, either emptiness or the godhead exists. Emptiness or the Void, as we understand it, means precreation or what is creative potentially. In that an archetypal image is a "mass of dynamic energy,"[11] when it is constellated, as it was during Saint-Exupéry's desert experience, the resulting inner tensions may reach a boiling point. In Saint-Exupéry's case, the compensatory forces that came into being prevented his ego from exploding, which would have led to an eclipse of consciousness.

Saint-Exupéry's desert years kindled within him a certain indescribable joy. Emptiness, though numbing, in his case had its productive side: it compelled him to inhale and exhale his own being—his needs and turmoil. On certain occasions it ignited an epiphanic experience: the manifestation of a god or other supernatural being. Outer and inner worlds seemed to coalesce as he faced the formless, unstructured, unrealized sands before him—a mirror reflection of his inner world—giving rise to a condition known as *metanoia:* the emergence of new values, or at least a shift in old ones. Such experiences—numinous in nature—occurred in Biblical and post-Biblical times: when the Hebrews spent forty years wandering in the wilderness after their flight from Egypt; during the forty days and nights Jesus spent in the desert after his baptism by John the Baptist. The desert experience, most poignantly after a plane crash, compelled Saint-Exupéry to struggle for survival against nearly insurmountable odds—testing his strength and faith in himself.

How does *metanoia* come about? When an individual withdraws from the company of others, libido (psychic energy), which would otherwise have been absorbed by daily activities is rechanneled inward, thus energizing unconscious contents and nourishing the inner world. When the Hebrews were exiled in the wilderness, hoping to reach the Promised Land, they nearly died of starvation, but "miraculously," at the last moment, were fed manna from heaven; Elijah, the prophet, as well as Saint Paul, were given food by ravens. The food or manna sent by God, which fed the Israelites, the prophets, and the apostles, may psychologically be looked upon as an aspect of the Self (total psyche), helping to rescue the weak ego, to strengthen and to water what has grown wan and sterile.

a. The desert and the numinosum: That the dry and barren landscape took on a cataclysmic dimension for Saint-Exupéry, thereby paving the way for increased awareness, allowed him to progress inwardly. He discovered hidden treasures, the secret source of his nourishment, that is, his *manna* or inner riches. His loneliness, reinforced by the remoteness of the desert regions, gave rise, in Saint-Exupéry's case, to hallucinations and mirages—archetypal fantasies and the *numinosum*. The influx of life at these junctures was so sudden and so forceful as to seemingly free the soul/psyche from the grip of fate. Vertigo ensued. So powerful were his feelings of displacement that he thought himself on the brink of madness.

When Saint-Exupéry's plane crashed in the desert and he discovered he was at the mercy not only of the elements, but also of fierce Arab tribes rebelling against European rule, not fear, but *mystery* took hold of him.

> The sea of sand bowled me over. Unquestionably it was filled with mystery and with danger. The silence that reigned over it was not the silence of emptiness but of plotting, of imminent enterprise. I sat still and stared into space. The end of the day was near. Something half revealed yet wholly unknown had bewitched me. The love of the Sahara, like love itself, is born of a face perceived and never really seen.

On another occasion, when concomitantly intoxicated and overwhelmed by a sudden sandstorm, he felt penetrated by sensations of terror. Coupled with these was the intense excitement of the empirical experience and the archetypal image which erupted into being. Although Saint-Exupéry knew what to expect and understood the very real dangers involved, he seemed unruffled by them. On the contrary, the cataclysmic energy which flooded his psyche activated his libido so intensely that, for the first time, he realized he was beginning to understand the *language* of the desert. This foreign discourse, eliciting in him a different sensual/sentient means of communication, invited him visually to palpate those strange expanses of sterile and indifferent primordial stuff. Until now exiled from this static, yet paradoxically fluid, granular dust power, Saint-Exupéry felt himself in touch with the *heart* of hermetic life.

Already its foam had touched me. I was the extreme edge lapped by the wave. Fifty feet behind me no sail would have flapped. Its flame wrapped me round once, only once, in a caress that seemed dead. But I knew, in the seconds that followed, that the Sahara was catching its breath and would send forth a second sigh. . . . What filled me with a barbaric joy was that I had understood a murmured monosyllable of this secret language, had sniffed the air and known what was coming, like one of those primitive men to whom the future is revealed in such faint rustlings; it was that I had been able to read the anger of the desert in the beating wings of a dragonfly.

The Sahara, for Saint-Exupéry, was an ever-unfolding and evolving mystery. Its history, both mythological and verifiable, the wonders associated with this time/space continuum, set off multitudes of abrasive embers within his psyche. So powerful were these energy-circuits that the rational world diminished in intensity, inviting feelings of belonging to overcome the previous sensations of alienation and exile. He felt at peace with the sand, those endlessly shifting autonomous mobile forms and currents, which molded their supple substances onto his soul and psyche. Such an experience, defined as a *regressus ad uterum*—a way of returning to the primordial bed: in this case, on the soft white sands or the angry tornadolike ones—invited him to bask in temporary repose. Making his way along this undefined *spiritus igneus*, he felt nourished and regenerated by the particles of glassy, shining, mirrorlike substances, each part of an endless tapestried structure—a complex of opposites. Parallels existed between such infinitesimal fragments of sand lying before him and his own psychological situation. His ego yearned for wholeness and for harmonious reintegration into the Self.

b. The desert's prisoner: To become the desert's prisoner, however, ushered into Saint-Exupéry's world a different set of values and sensations. Before taking his "ship," which he named the *Simoon*, on the Paris-Saigon flight (Dec. 29, 1935) that was to end in a desert crash, he had described the sensations elicited in him as he stroked "her wings" with his hand "in a caress" that he considered to be one of love. He had flown her eight thousand miles, "and her engines had not skipped a beat; not a bolt in her had loosened." Senegal. Morocco. Across two thousand miles of sand. Sardinia. Climbing to forty-five hundred feet. Tunis. Benghazi. Still, a sense of foreboding accompanied Saint-Exupéry's meditations: there was the chance factor—death.

In the morning, they realized that they had "run almost tangentially into a gentle slope at the top of a barren plateau." Saint-Exupéry understood that the plane "had run its course with the fury and tail-lashings of a reptile gliding on its belly at the rate of a hundred and seventy miles an hour." Miraculously, neither Saint-Exupéry nor his technician was harmed. Gas and oil tanks had been smashed. The drinking water was gone. A thermos with coffee and a pint of white wine was all that remained between them and two-hundred and fifty miles of desert.

Both men walked for six hours on the first day, carefully marking out their route so as to be able to return to the shelter of the plane. Saint-Exupéry's previous experiences with the Sahara had left him with an untroubling mind—reveling, in fact, "in the golden emptiness of the desert where the wind like a sea had raised sand-waves upon its surface." Now, however, things had changed. Suddenly he understood that his plane had crashed not in the warm and friendly sand of the Sahara that had been his home but in the Libyan desert. The contours, the mood, the aridity, the personality of the yellow dust was different. As he looked about at the shining black pebbles gleaming "like metal scales" around him, heightening the domelike mounds which "shone like coats of mail," feelings of alienation overcame him.

As the two men kept walking, "scourged by thirst," the sun beat down on the crystalline sands. Rivers of sand kept rising before them: sheets of watery particles materialized only to vanish seconds later, followed by green blotches of vegetation dazzling in their searing incandescence. Like the shadows of cumulus clouds dissolving into rain, mirage upon mirage poured forth. Disoriented. Lost. With no liquid remaining. Forty miles of wandering. No sign of life.

Mirages, autonomous manifestations of the senses influenced by the activity of the unconscious, seemed to generate endlessly. Antediluvian forests appeared before Saint-Exupéry's eyes, their broken limbs casting eerie glowings around him. A wooden cathedral, "its giant pillars" erect at his feet, like "steel, petrified and vitrified"—was the color of jet. Saint-Exupéry's psychic projections, based on omnipresent emotional foundations of personal distress and danger, activated relevant instincts which then predominated and determined the choice of images brought into consciousness as well as their interpretations. Such visualizations, like those of collective visions of crusaders or religious followers, excite the entire psyche as they give birth to images and symbols of all types.

As Saint-Exupéry strode ahead, calling out wildly and madly at phantasms he took to be real, he felt himself walking along a pathless sea, unable to weep. He forced himself on, his will dominating every facet of his being. At this juncture, the world took on the dimensions of "a gigantic anvil." Identified with the passive feminine principle, in contrast to the masculine blacksmith who pounds away in the symbolic inseminating process, Saint-Exupéry felt acted upon, helpless, and impotent.

Salvation lay in walking. The two men pursued their course, their eyes glued to the ground—thus no longer prey, they thought, to mirages. Because Saint-Exupéry was aware of the fact that a pilot's job was to "outwit the forces of nature" he forced himself to walk on—plagued by a hard dry cough, a tongue which had become more of a nuisance than anything else, and spots shining before his eyes. Then, incredibly, something inexplicable happened. The landscape had suddenly changed. There was hope. There was rescue.

What had Saint-Exupéry learned from his ordeal? The spirit of discipline and self-abnegation which had imbued him with the energy to struggle ahead, to fight for life, had also taught him to accept the peace which comes with death. This traumatic experience had paved the way for the discovery of a new factor buried deep within him: a sense of inner harmony and balance which had eluded him all these years. "Never shall I forget that, lying buried to the chin in sand, strangled slowly to death by thirst, my heart was infinitely warm beneath the desert stars."

When Saint-Exupéry came to realize that there were no answers to the mysteries of life, a *sense of deliverance* flooded his body and psyche. He questioned anew every facet of his earthly and spatial trajectories. What is truth? Faith? Values? Relationship? Life/Death? To rationalize, to build houses to deities and to adhere to organized religious groups, is to limit the unlimited, to translate into empirical terms what surpasses human comprehension, to evade the true enigma, which is infinite.

Likewise, the creative urge feeds on the transpersonal, bringing a poem, a musical composition, a painting into existence from some remote sphere of being. During the ordeal of the birth process, the artist learns to look out into and onto open seas and sands, astral and supernal spheres, or that infinite maw existing within and outside of being. Only then may the creative individual begin to tap that *unknown language*, that *sacred* neverending power that Saint-Exupéry refers to in *Wind, Sand, and Stars* and mystics allude to as *mysterious space*.

Christopher Columbus sailing away from Spain, astronauts landing on the moon, and space travelers wandering about alone or in groups through the stratosphere have searched out those incredibly marvelous and terrifying worlds that lie just beyond the known. Similar was the trajectory taken by Saint-Exupéry—seeking, as he did, to participate in and disclose in his writings the cryptic and baffling universe that filled him with *metaphysical anguish*.

6 Juan José Arreola's "The Switchman"—Life's Timeless/Timed Allegorical Train

Juan José Arreola's short story "The Switchman" (1951) uses the train as an allegorical device to underscore the dichotomies existing between such notions as deception and truth, capriciousness and constancy, eternality and linearity. In its machinelike capacity, the train also serves to heighten the feelings of alienation and powerlessness of finite beings living in the infinite vastness of an impersonal universe. These themes are surely not new. Indeed, they are commonplace today. What is surprisingly innovative, however, is the manner in which Arreola uses literary devices (pace, imagery, dialogue) to bring his philosophical ideas to the fore; he also skillfully uses satire to focus on the mundane matter of duplicity in the mismanagement of a national railroad.

A whole mysterious world lies hidden beneath Arreola's image of the train, which grows progressively in fascination, dimension, and impact, reaching virtually pyramidic proportions. The train as an object, however, never makes its presence known in Arreola's story. Doubt, for this reason, is cast in the reader's mind as to its reality. Is there a train in "The Switchman" or is it a figment of the protagonists' imaginations? Still, as George Berkeley stated, *Esse est percipi* ("to be is to be perceived"): material objects, a collection of sensations given a common name, do not exist apart from their perceptions in people's minds. The mechanical metaphor in "The Switchman," representative of industrial civilization, is ever-present—withdrawn, perhaps, and quiescent, but casting its somber shadow throughout. Arreola's style is elliptic and condensed; his economy of words suggests but never describes. Stark and incisive forms, both concrete and abstract, are imbricated into his visualizations, reminiscent in their simplicity and austerity of the canvases of Rufino Tamayo. Arreola's compatriot's paintings (e.g., *Woman with a Bird Cage*, 1941) accentuate the spirit of silent eloquence, solemnity, and extreme stasis by the minutest soupçon of movement. Analogously, Arreola's as yet nonexistent train accentuates the static pace of events in the uninhabited landscape in the middle of nowhere (or perhaps some desolate space in Mexico) in which his two protagonists are located. Like Tamayo's canvases, Arreola's tale discloses a surface atmosphere of uniformity, anonymity, and detachment. The electric charges lying repressed beneath its surface augment in intensity and drama in direct proportion to its exploration.

Comparisons between Tamayo's and Arreola's time sequences may also be made. While the painter experiences the passing of moments as a visceral and spiritual happening (*The Black Clocks*, 1945), Arreola measures time quintessentially via his photoscopic vision. Verbal brush strokes adorn Arreola's dimensionless horizons just as thickly pigmented objectifications in Tamayo's canvases revolve around one or more brilliantly lit forms at a time, generating, in both cases, increased emotional cravings. Such an approach not only seems to arrest the reader's apprehension of the passage of time, but also injects a cyclical mood—a mythic dimension—into the story itself.[1]

Arreola's verbal and visual meanderings reach deeply into a mythic universe, depicting a primordial experience, not necessarily personal but transcendental; not something invented for the sake of entertainment (though it may also be that) but a living and burning reality that exists in the psyche and culture of a people. The myth, as revealed in "The Switchman," is both ectypal (it deals with the existential world) and archetypal (it deals with eternal experience). Existence on these two levels contains past, present, and future within its structure.

Because a myth lives outside of temporal time, it is not bound within the limits of linear or historical time, but flows in a cyclical, sacred, or eternal dimension. Because myth-time is reversible, Arreola is able to interweave mysterious mutations of past religious traditions into his forms, verbs, and images, thereby removing himself and his readers from circumscribed and individual frames of reference and plunging them into a collective experience.

Arreola, born in Ciudad Guzman in the state of Jalisco, Mexico (1918), published his first short stories in the early 1940s in the magazine *Pan*. These were followed by *Various Inventions* (1949), *Confabulario* (1952), and *Punta de Plata* (1952). Arreola's *Confabulario*, in which "The Switchman" is included, is made up of fables, allegories, satires, vignettes, and parodies, each displaying a subtle wit, trenchant humor, and great reserve.

Well-versed in literature and history, Arreola frequently incorporates other disciplines into his tales: science, anthropology, psychology, and even esoteric subjects. His satire "Baby H. P." advertises an apparatus that will transform the energy of children into electricity capable of driving machines, thereby reducing their expense while increasing their productivity and efficiency.

Whether ancient or modern modes are generated in Arreola's tales, he digs deep into Mexican tradition—its magic and its arcana. At the same time he satirizes, in incisive and caustic terms, excessive commercialization and human deficiencies. Though frequently tempered with despair, his writings are never maudlin. His humor is too overt, his irony too biting and grating, his sense of the burlesque and his cynical outlook on life too sharp, his stoic approach to the world in general too strong, to allow himself to be overwhelmed by the universal flow at large. So powerful is the energy that inhabits his words that the sparks generated from them are continuously metamorphosized or analogized, injecting into his tales the very substance of life.

Perhaps two key words—*mute* and *voracious*—which Arreola himself used in his epigraph of *Confabulario*, serve best to state his message: ". . . mute I do my spying while someone voracious in turn watches me."[2] Both factors are used as technical and philosophical ways of increasing tension; both are highly controlled and disciplined throughout the tale—except for a single critical and shattering moment.

What is not said in Arreola's writings is sensed; what is not envisaged is experienced in the feeling realm; what is not heard is conveyed in prolonged and untenable silence.

"The Switchman" takes place outside of a "deserted station" in some unnamed expanse in Mexico. A stranger is waiting for a train to take him to T. The switchman, an old man, tells him the train rarely if ever makes its appearance at this station. The plot, if there is one, revolves around a brief exchange of words between the two men in connection with the probability of the train's arrival. The extreme immobility pervading the atmosphere ushers in a mood of stifling suspension.

The stranger is not only the victim of the chance factor—a puppet manipulated by unknown cosmic forces, as are all beings—he is also deceived by his own false values: the equating of continuous activity with personal and cultural progress. The tale's suspense is accentuated by Arreola's superb manipulation of space. Readers' eyes rove about the paradoxically vibrating/stilled images embedded in the discourse; their gaze gravitates magnetically to the figurations used to measure feeling, temper, and tone. Arreola's vision of space is both active and passive. Deserted distances, remote stretches, impassable terrain, and expectant stasis are juxtaposed with mobile intentions, such as the march of time, in discussions centering on timetables, days, months, years, tomorrows, and directions. Such tension reinforces the protagonists' sense of helplessness as well as their need to overcome their dependency upon those very forces which are out of their reach. It also intimates the necessity of integrating and accepting what remains uncontrollable and incomprehensible into their lives and psyches.

Archetypal Time: Rhythm and Repose

Because "The Switchman" is archetypal in dimension—dealing with suprapersonal universals and nonindividual images—a whole hidden domain may be unearthed and explored. Deposits of Aztec and Toltec heritage are alive and vital in Arreola's tale, though hidden beneath archetypal patterns of rhythm and repose. The burning sun, the incredible city of Tenochtitlán, with its canals and bridges, and the dazzling and harrowing drama experienced by the Aztec peoples during its destruction are all sensed by their unfathomable power, though never depicted by Arreola in his tale. Mystery and forboding reign, as ancient and modern, primitive and mechanical worlds, with their linear and cyclical time schemes, are fused and silhouetted one against the other in flawless narrative discourse.

Archetypal time, manifested in "The Switchman" by its mood of rhythm and repose, helplessness and dominance, alienation and belonging, may be regarded as "a structure which conditions certain probabilities" in the actions of the protagonists.[3] The primordial images used to make archetypal time manifest inhabit the collective unconscious of Arreola's protagonists (that is, the deepest layers of their subliminal psyches). What they observe and say throughout the tale, then, is to be understood in part as a projection of inborn characteristics or specific patterns of behavior. They are also to be experienced as universal and recurring motifs, accounting for both Aztec and the superimposed Christian religious concepts.

Let us recall that archetypal time, when constellated in early Aztec times, was so powerful a force that it was identified with Deity. Time did not flow forth continuously and linearly for the Aztecs; rather, it revolved around a complex of events that could be distinguished from one another both quantitatively and qualitatively. Time was a divine mystery.

The notion of passing time was worked out by the Aztecs, as well as among other peoples of Mexico and Central America, in complex chronological systems that involved number and sign, thereby helping them to regulate their empirical lives (plantings, seasons, rituals) and determine the destiny of individuals. Each day was ruled by a cardinal point, a sign, and a number. The Aztecs did not experience time or space as abstract notions, but rather as "concrete multiplicities of time and space, single points and happenings, disparate and unique." When certain forces determined that someone was to "come down" (*temo*), that person was inserted automatically into the order of things "and in the grasp of the omnipotent machine." Predestination and determinism governed an individual's personality, role in life, achievements or failures, until death completed his or her earthly trajectory.[4]

That a climate of moral pessimism dominates "The Switchman" is perfectly understandable, for the Aztec world was haunted with the notion of death and annihilation, with the feeling of humankind's helplessness and destiny's unrelenting harshness in a world beyond the control of mortals. What is impressive in both Arreola's tale and Aztec philosophical concepts is the dignity of comportment in the acceptance of an unrelentingly destructive and pitiless universe. That Arreola avails himself of this same illusionless outlook in "The Switchman" in order to satirize modern technological society—with its false values, superficial and complacent attitudes, arbitrary views of the human condition, and domination of humankind by the machine—is a fitting sequel to his ancient heritage.[5]

The opening paragraph of "The Switchman" sets the tone: rhythm and repose in the vastness of an impersonal universe that predetermines the fate of each mortal. A stranger arrives at a deserted railroad station; he is unaware of the fragility of his being and his powerlessness to rectify what he feels is askew. Like many Westerners, Arreola's stranger believes that everything must be carried out with clockwork precision and that industrial societies deserve to dominate the world. Such a person is ripe for the transformation ritual that will teach him to understand and accept his finitude and the infinity of the cosmos about him.

Arreola tells us nothing specific about the stranger. We do not know his age, background, nor even how he looks. We are told only that he has been walking briskly, that he has been carrying his large suitcase, that he is out of breath, that he shades his eyes, mops his sweaty face, and then gazes "at the tracks that melted away in the distance." Both "dejected and thoughtful," he glances at his watch, confirming the fact that the train is supposed to leave from the station at this very moment.

The tale's motif is interwoven into the discourse from the very outset: the stranger consults his watch, begins to broach the concept of archetypal time (the paradoxical notion of time and nontime). According to Einsteinian physics, such an enigma may be explained within a mathematical framework: time, as an energetic and dynamic principle, includes all opposites—change and stasis, good and evil, life and death.[6] Although the stranger is unaware of these antinomies as he makes his entrée into the story, he nevertheless penetrates into the readers' space, thereby descending into their present time, into the event. Hence the suprapersonal and nonindividual entity known as archetypal time, heretofore inaccessible to conscious awareness since it only exists inchoate in the collective unconscious (outside of time), will now function as a moral frame of reference and therefore participate in duration. In that the stranger becomes wedded to the event in the narrative discourse, he also takes on form and dimension.

The stranger's presence in Arreola's tale conforms not only to Einsteinian physics, but, interestingly enough, to the Aztecs' view of archetypal time. Omoteotl, identified with the creator of all things and both mother and father of four other Gods (the red Tezcatlipoca in the east, the black one in the north, the white one in the west, and the blue one in the south), is also known as Lord of Fire and of Time. That Omoteotl brought four Tezcatlipocas into being, each inhabiting one of the four corners of space, indicates that space and time were created at the same moment.

The stranger's arrival at the deserted train station paves the way for a similar birth process: the infinite withdraws as the flow of inner and outer events takes precedence, appearing both quantitatively and qualitatively as a substantive force. Henceforth time and space in "The Switchman" are inseparably connected, forming a four-dimensional continuum.[7]

Although not referred to specifically in "The Switchman," we can assume that the sun is shining strongly because the stranger shades his eyes as he peers down the tracks that "melted away in the distance." In keeping with Aztec belief, so powerful is the energy emanating from Omoteotl, Lord of Fire and of Time, that he not only obliterates all other thoughts but melts the tracks, or at least gives the illusion of doing so. In keeping with Einsteinian physics, the stranger, whose gaze is leveled exclusively on the distant tracks, sees them in a space/time continuum—i.e., as curving. Thus the geometry of space and time are affected—the latter being dependent upon the distribution of massive bodies.

All, then, is a blur; all has melted in the distance. Concretion seems remote and inaccessible. As feelings of dejection and frustration overcome the stranger, he becomes disoriented and, as previously mentioned, has recourse to the world of objects—in this case, his watch. By turning to a solid and concrete entity, he assuages his sense of disappointment and anxiety. Although he already understands that the train is overdue, once he verifies this by looking at his timepiece, he feels less vulnerable. He has framed his fears and limited his insecurities. Illusory methods, to be sure, but efficacious for the moment.

Unexpectedly, and as if from nowhere, the stranger feels someone tapping his shoulder gently from behind. He turns around and sees a little old man holding a *tiny red lantern* which is so small that it resembles a toy. Two factors are involved in this image: the old man's chance entrance into the event and the mention of his equipment. Like the Tezcatlipocas, the railroader in Arreola's tale represents transpersonal spheres: his conversation and his gestures embrace the cardinal points. Symbolizing age-old wisdom and thereby eliciting reverence and respect, it is he who, with the help of his little red lantern, will light the way. Also like the Tezcatlipocas, his presence indicates authority and domination. He seems to be unaffected by the limitations of time and space and divested of the tensions caused by linear schemes with their past, present, and future.

The archetypal little old man, existing in legends, myths, and fairy tales of all nations since time immemorial, is revered as a kind of unwizened ancestor, and like the dwarfs in Norse and Celtic sagas, he plays an ambivalent role in Arreola's tale. As an archetypal figure, he not only personifies those powers that transcend consciousness, but also plays the role of a mischievous being with childish characteristics. In Jungian psychology, the dwarf is a guardian who stands at the threshold of the unconscious, who provokes and triturates, always forcing new frames of reference upon those anchored in tradition. The same may be said of the little old man in Arreola's tale. It is he who tries to dissuade the stranger from being obsessed with linear time, with personal objectives, while attempting to teach him through dialogue to penetrate the larger scheme of things.

The lantern, which is described as a "toy," draws the reader into the child's world—the domain of play and fantasy where limitations are nonexistent and imagination and feelings are given free rein. As a toy, however, the lantern may also stand for regressive, puerile, or even infantile ways that do not conform to the demands of a mechanized consumer society.

The little old man, as we shall see, is antipodal to the stranger's obsession with linear time, order, and motivation. The stranger has but one goal: to get on the train, leave the station, and reach the T the following day, reintegrating himself into his organized world. That the old man tells him his goal is unrealizable at this moment creates anguish for the stranger. Alienated from himself and from society, his only frame of reference is his work: it alone gives him the structure and satisfaction he needs to pursue his linear course.

When the old man suggests that the stranger remain in the area longer, thereby disclosing the possibility that the train may never come to this no-man's-land, conflict between the two immediately becomes evident. As an archetypal figure of wisdom, the little old man, aware of the stranger's discomfiture and always in full control of the situation, advises him most calmly to ask for lodgings at the nearby inn—"an ash-colored building that looked more like a jail."

In a Kafkaesque turn, Arreola depicts the inn as both ash-colored and jail-like, thereby generating still greater feelings of pain and defeat for the stranger. Though Arreola is neither a Kafka nor a Poe, the mood of terror mounts, compelling the stranger, at least momentarily, to begin assessing the powers at work which prevent him from reaching his destination. Like the symbolic inn, he is paradoxically incarcerated in the emptiness of vast open spaces.

Significant as well for both Judeo-Christians and Aztecs, is the inn's ashen hue. For the former, it stands for penitence, renunciation, ascetic conduct, and awareness of one's helplessness vis-à-vis the Creator God (Gen. 18:27; Job 42:6). According to Aztec belief, the Sun God, Tezcatlipoca (Smoking Mirror), wanders alone at night in the shape of a giant wrapped in an ash-colored veil. Because of his continuous reemergence into view, he has come to represent eternal return. His magical qualities are linked with agricultural fertility rituals.[8]

The inn, an archetypal image because of its recurrence throughout religious and lay literature, may be considered a kind of house of worship. As such, it represents the center of the world and a sacred precinct within which transformation and sacrificial rituals are enacted. Comparable to Quetzalcoatl's pyramid temple at Teotihuacán, built by the gods at the outset of the world and standing as a reminder of a remote and fabulous past, the inn encloses arcana.[9] Let us recall that Quetzalcoatl, the Plumed Serpent, god of wind, creator of the calendar and patron of the arts, had been driven out of his sacred precincts by the machinations of Tezcatlipoca. Since that time the population has *awaited* his return.

The stranger, however, is unwilling to wait—to enter the inn, that inner sanctum where he could offer himself up to sacrificial ceremonies or transformation rituals. Like so many of his contemporaries, he seeks instant gratification and grows visibly annoyed when the old man tells him that to take a room by the month is cheaper than the daily rate. Has the old man gone crazy? the stranger wonders. Neither veers from his point of view—the stranger intent on instant departure, the other suggesting a more patient attitude and an acceptance of his mortal lot vis-à-vis the cosmic principle.

The old man decides to leave the stranger to his fate. Then he has a change of mind, deciding to release important information to the eager traveler and hoping to influence his way of thinking.

This country is famous for its railroads, as you know. Up to now it's been impossible to organize them properly, but great progress has been made in publishing timetables and issuing tickets. Railroad guides include and link all the towns in the country; they sell tickets for even the smallest and most remote villages. Now all that is needed is for the trains to follow what the guides indicate and really pass by the stations. The inhabitants of this country hope this will happen; meanwhile, they accept the service's irregularities and their patriotism keeps them from showing any displeasure.

On a mundane level, the old man has satirized an inefficient system; on a deeper level he has pointed to two ways of life: acceptance versus struggle. Having opted for the former, he indicates to the stranger that although he has been given a calendar, tickets, and timetables and lives in a mathematically organized universe, railroads do not function in such a routine manner. We may suggest that the two protagonists, and the old man's lantern, are mere toys or marionettes when faced with the ineffable.

The train in Arreola's tale not only represents a space/time continuum and the idea of communication in general, both on a material and an emotional level, but is also paradigmatic of cultural differences. Associated with extreme activity, rapidity, turmoil, and even chaos when not organized or functioning in an orderly manner, this machine is also symptomatic of the high-speed scientific factor implicit in an ever-expanding and ever more powerful mechanistic and technical civilization. Its functioning, regulated according to the split second via mechanical timepieces and encouraging punctuality and an impeccable and inflexible order, is geared to public and not individual needs. It represents universal life and social activity, as well as a determination to coordinate personal desires and needs to a collective performance.

But there are schedules and schedules. When the old man informs the stranger that the train follows *its own* schedule, which may not conform to the one he knows, the younger person is completely disoriented. Once again feelings of powerlessness, insecurity and confusion take hold. But then he begins to question. Are there universal truths? Is there such a notion as security in the world? a *modus vivendi?*

So perplexed has the stranger become that he begins to wonder whether or not the train really does come to this station. Like the prisoners in Plato's allegory of the cave, so the stranger may also be blind to *reality*, bound up as he is in his rational domain which posits that two and two make four. To the stranger's question as to the actual existence of the train, the old man answers ambiguously yes and no, leaving room for cogitation on the subject.

To say yes would not be accurate. As you can see, the rails exist, though they are in rather bad shape. In some towns they are simply marked on the ground by two chalk lines. Under the present conditions, no train is obliged to pass through here, but nothing keeps that from happening. I've seen lots of trains go by in my life and I've known some travelers who managed to board them. If you wait until the right moment, perhaps I myself will have the honor of helping you get on a nice comfortable coach.

The stranger does not seem to fathom the complexity of the old man's remark: the fact that the rail lines are present does not mean that the train is functioning, despite the fact that the contrary is indicated by their presence.

Train Tracks as "Mnemic Deposits"

Arreola's train tracks are like archetypal "mnemic deposits;" they are "fundamental forms of recurrent psychic experience."[10] Just as numbers emerge from the collective unconscious, spontaneously when the need arises, in the form of primordial images, the stranger's train tracks do the same.

The earlier and pre-Aztec races inhabiting Mexico based their philosophical and metaphysical arguments on astronomical, geometrical, and numerical calculations. Numbers helped them, as they help almost all cultures (and individuals) to bring order out of disorder since they fix the unpredictable and are based on space and time. They also have a numinous quality about them, appearing frequently in painting or literary narrative (as in Arreola's story) to compensate for some chaotic inner state.

The dual spheres inhabited by the train tracks (in the empirical domain and as an archetypal image) indicate the existence of conflictual binarism in the traveler's psychological makeup. He cannot seem to fathom what exists beyond his understanding, while attempting at the same time to dominate that which transcends it. If the stranger were not to rely so exclusively on the concrete, the phenomenological, and the objective world, he might be capable of freeing himself from his illusory trappings—his pacifiers—thus facing reality by experiencing his own insignificance and mortality. Unlike his creative ancestors, he has neither the courage nor the faith to accept himself and his place in the universal scheme of things.

The Mexican cultures antedating the Aztecs, preoccupied as they were with numerical calculations, had attained an extraordinarily high level of architectural expertise. Teotihuacán, with its 365 heads sculpted in high relief, its spatial arrangements exemplifying the strict enforcement of numerical law, its ceremonial centers with rectangles, triangles, squares, and courtyards, could have allowed monumental hubris to run wild, creating confusion on a grand scale, had there not been governing principles underlying all this construction.[11]

So, too, has modern civilization created a highly organized and incredibly complex railroad system with its tickets and timetables, its tracks and its stations. No matter how numerically perfect the calculations may be nor how modern and well-equipped the subsidiaries, each area functions without a central governing force, so nothing is predictable or efficacious. Such meaningful factors as the ancient Mexicans' predetermination of days, months, and years, each endowed with signs and indwelling qualitative/quantitative powers, are virtually absent today. The entire railroad system, a paradigm for industrial civilization in general, has fallen into confusion.

Still, the stranger does not understand why such a highly industrialized railway system functions so poorly. What is the mystery behind these trains? And the network of chalk lines representing tracks? Each time the old man endeavors to enlighten him by telling him that there are no guarantees as to the train's arrival, or whether or not it will take him to T, the stranger returns to his world of certainties, logic, and predetermined punctuality.

And the round continues: the stranger demanding logic, mechanical certainty, linear order, while the old man offers him cosmic consciousness, awareness of the whole rather than its parts, spiritual rather than material goals. One must look beyond the obvious, specific *tracks*, a metaphor for a spatial order, and try to detect inner organizational plans and structures in an archetypal network of coordinates. Certain meanings transcend articulation and logical explanation, and may be recognized only in terms of the effects they produce.

Be they real or traced in chalk, the tracks are comparable to hieroglyphs—food for speculation. Like the strange markings viewed on the Plain of Nazca in Peru, or the concrete constructions thought to have been ancient roads near Santa Cruz in Bolivia, the tracks in Arreola's story may be considered dynamic archetypal images. These entities within the psyche stand for a "preformed potentiality"—a bridge between consciousness and more spiritual domains. The physical facts viewed as tracks, like "mnemic deposits" or formative principles, are energetic centers upon which the psyche continues its transformation process, building its images.[12]

Had the stranger envisaged the tracks as living mementos of the cosmological lines upon which the Aztec capital city had been laid out—with its four quadrants divided by avenues, each leading into the four cardinal directions and centering upon the plaza with its temple to Quetzalcoatl—he might have been able to experience what has been referred to as cosmic consciousness.

Psychologically, we may suggest that because the stranger sees the railroad tracks only in terms of his reality, that is, his immediate needs, he is in effect projecting something definite onto objects existing outside of his understanding. Psychologically, his ego (the center of consciousness) alone guides him in his worldly encounters. Like symbols, however, these tracks transcend human understanding; they exist inchoate in the Self (the total psyche), outside of linear concepts of the space/time continuum.[13]

Quetzalcoatl's pyramid temple functioned in concord with the layout of Teotihuacán; the mortal sustained the divine. In psychological terms, we may say that the ego buttressed the Self. Such is not the stranger's case.

Despite the fact that the old man has informed him over and over again that there is no link between the stations, tunnels, bridges, and service, the stranger still remains adamant. He is intent upon using his ticket and his timetable. So preposterous is the entire system that railway managers, in their overeagerness to serve their customers, have resorted to "desperate measures," even bringing death to some passengers, particularly when passing through trackless stretches of land. The old man recalls that on one occasion, the tracks had been so "smoothed and polished by the sand" that "the wheels were worn away to their axles" and the train could go no further. The passengers, obliged to alight, so enjoyed each other's company that they founded a village in which their children played with the "rusty vestiges of the train."

Even if a train should begin its trajectory, the old man continues, it does not mean that it will arrive at the station indicated on the timetable. All is illusion. "There are stations that are for appearance only: they have been built right in the jungle and they bear the name of some important city. But you just need to pay a little attention to see through the deceit." These illusory stations are compared by the old man to stage sets: so extraordinarily well-constructed are the stations that they are indistinguishable from reality. People awaiting trains are like *dummies:* "Their faces bear the signs of infinite weariness." Still, the young and aggressive stranger does not see life as wearisome, but as bold and vibrant. He seeks to forge ahead and make something of himself during his earthly trajectory. He does not have the understanding necessary to realize the depth of the old man's comparisons of the stations to decors; the passengers to dummies. He looks upon them as clear-cut and simple; their *mystery* escapes him. Sacrality does not form part of his life, nor does he regulate his existence in keeping with aesthetic or cultural ceremonies. He believes what he sees.

Signs are not emblems for anything else, but are simply what fall into his frame of reference.

Although the old man does not negate the possibility of a train taking the stranger to T, he warns him that it may be filled with spies who might prevent him from reaching his desired goal. Indeed, he might spend the rest of his life in a prison car, lost someplace in a jungle. The spies and the prisons mentioned by the old man serve as warnings of physical and even spiritual incarceration. And, the old man finally warns, even if a train should stop at T, it may really be a test—a temptation set in the younger man's path. "If you look out the windows, you may fall into the trap of a mirage." Windows, he suggests, create "all kinds of illusions in the passengers' minds." So clever are these window displays—these fascinating facsimiles of landscapes—and the noises and sensations of movement generated by the engine, that these deceits are interpreted by the uninitiated as reality.

Like the soul, the window looks out on the world. Peering into external domains, one sees what cannot always be equated with reality and truth. If only an apprentice, one's receptivity may be faulty, one's awareness superficial, one's understanding chaotic and erroneous. It is a question of discernment.

When the stranger asks the little old man whether he has ever traveled, the answer is negative. His job as a switchman never necessitated displacements, nor does he have any desire to board a train.

A whistle is suddenly heard. Shocked, the switchman signals with his lantern, then starts to run down the track:

"You are lucky! Tomorrow you will arrive at your famous station. What did you say its name was?"

"X----!" answered the traveler.

The little old man "dissolved in the clear morning." The only visible sign of his reality emanates from the red lantern, which can be seen moving about in the distance as he runs "imprudently between the rails to meet the train." That the figure dissolves indicates the ephemerality of everything on earth and the reality of illusion, as long as it is needed to sustain an individual.

"The Switchman," satirizing false values and the mismanagement of a megalithic railroad company, also narrates a myth. Each image, form, and rhythmic pattern fits into a mosaic of universal dimension. Like the train and the tracks, human personality is fragmented, cut, sized, shaped into innumerable pieces. Arreola, godlike, weaves and arranges his patterns, unifying what is disparate, ordering the disordered, creating a complete and unified architectural construct out of the bits and scraps of conversations uttered by his two protagonists.

"The Switchman" is a meditation on the mechanics of truth and illusion, activity and repose. Like Tamayo's canvas *Man Contemplating the Firmament* it depicts fear and disquietude, but in a contemporary vein—in keeping with both artists' environments and their time. Arreola and Tamayo, each using his own medium, deal with anguish in personal and also universal terms. Each makes an immense effort to comprehend and transmute into art the enigma that is life. Carving out his verbal glyphs, as Tamayo his forms and pigments, the writer, like the painter, invokes true-to-life situations in their paradoxically magical presentations. When exploring the works of both these men, one discovers a line, an elliptical phrase, an energetic pattern, that suddenly explodes, destroying the well-knit boundaries of the rational world. The unreal and the fantastic erupt. Then the normal is transformed into the paranormal, the rational into the irrational.

Mystery cohabits with *machine!*

Perplexing questions raised in "The Switchman" are never explained, nor are the mysteries embedded in the fabric of the word or glyph disinterred. Absurd, perhaps, Arreola's allegory on the human condition elicits a rictus!

7 S. Yizhar's *Midnight Convoy*— Wheels, Circles, Eyes—The Dynamics of the Feminine Principle as Eros/Logos

The event narrated in S. Yizhar's novella *Midnight Convoy* takes place during one of Israel's many wars—it could even have been its War of Independence (1948), in which the author fought. Although the time span involved in the novella is short, from dusk to three in the morning, and the space traversed during the happenings is only three kilometers, the emotions experienced by the protagonists are intense.

The action revolves around the safe conduct of a convoy of trucks, half-tracks, and jeeps carrying crucial supplies to the army. The soldiers in the lead jeep, sent out to scout the territory in southern Israel, must keep an ever-vigilant eye to ferret out mines, snipers, or other dangers while also avoiding mechanical breakdowns as the vehicles make their way through ruts, slopes, hills, mounds, a sizeable wadi, and fields of sorghum and thistles. The drama involves the discovery of *the right path* over which the convoy can safely pass.

The quest for the *right path* entails the ingenuity, acumen, and courage of five soldiers at the outset of the novella, and the efforts of the entire convoy at the finale. Unlike the heroes of Biblical or medieval times (David, Saint George, Parsifal), the hero of Yizhar's novella is collective. Although individual names are mentioned, it is the group effort—its communal needs and desires—that are operational. Nor is it, thematically and philosophically, a question of reform, revolution, or martyrdom as in past Israeli history; rather, it is a question of *survival*.

Machines—namely the lead jeep, half-tracks, trucks, and other wheeled vehicles—make for the essence, pace, and symbology of Yizhar's novella. Along with machines, the constant interweaving of nature, mechanics, and what seems to be an all-observing eye—be it personal or impersonal, religious or psychological—provide the structure underpinning the novella's beauty, dynamics, and inspirational value.

The wheels of the machines involved represent both circularity and a circumambulatory process: the rise and fall of success and the concomitant tensions and anxieties with which the soldiers must contend. The rotational movement of the wheels, in a larger frame of reference, indicates the revolving, gyrating, cycling, and spinning nature of the universe, the year, the day: time and space. Their humanization suggests the volutes of the human personality.

The search or quest for the *right path*, along with Yizhar's use of such images as the wheel, the circle, the mandala, and the eye, necessitates crossings of all types and is archetypal in nature. It transforms the historical event into a rite of passage, thus marking a transitional stage of spiritual and psychological development for the group in general and for one soldier, Zvialeh, in particular. In Biblical literature, crossings, be they associated with Moses' crossing of the Red Sea (Exod. 14) or Joshua's of the Jordan (Josh. 5:12), reflect a stepping from one level of consciousness to another. Spiritually, such modifications imply an expansion and deepening of religious values: an ability to know both the individual and cosmic experience.

Dahlia, the single feminine force in *Midnight Convoy*, participates productively in the patriarchal event. Like the beloved Shulamite in the Song of Songs and the creative Divine Wisdom of Proverbs, Yizhar's Dahlia stands for both *Eros* (relatedness, feelings, and love) and *Logos* (Spirit). In her capacity as dual force in one, she brings wholeness to a previously one-sided existence. Psychologically, her presence reveals the need of the ego (center of consciousness) to relate to the Self (totality of the psyche; empirically, the God image in humankind). The ego's encounter with and activation of this central and comprehensive archetype increases its receptivity, inviting the ego to further expand its frame of reference, and thereby to discover how to experience the life principle as fully as possible.[1]

In that *Midnight Convoy* is archetypal in nature, the group of men and one woman making their way through time and space represent a mode of functioning as well as a living system of actions and aptitudes that determine their lives. Indeed, the happenings depicted take on a pneumatic or apocalyptic quality reminiscent at times of Elijah's and Ezekiel's visionary experiences.

Nor is the inclusion in literary or religious texts of such images as vehicles that ride, wheels, circles, or eyes a modern innovation. Elijah—the prophet who wandered incognito over the earth aiding those in danger or in distress—was borne to heaven in a chariot of fire. The prophet Ezekiel, who lived through the destruction of the Temple and of Jerusalem and was deported to Babylonia in one of the last convoys of exiles, experienced ecstatic visions of the *Ophanim* ("a wheel-like angelic creature") and of God's Throne-Chariot: a preexisting throne which embodies and exemplifies all forms of creation and, in another aspect, a "Chariot of Light" that ascends to supernal spheres.[2]

The mystical view of riding and of traveling alluded to in the Bible generally suggests a transformation from God's "unknowable and inconceivable" state to His perception by a prophet or some other worthy individual. "To ride" or the "riding vehicle" per se is associated with a "complete system and mechanism through which God 'leaves his place' and reveals Himself to those who are worthy."[3] For the Merkabah mystics—a group who based their school of thought on Ezekiel's vision of the Ophanim and of God's Throne Chariot, or Chariot of Light—journeying refers to the soul's trajectory through pleromatic spheres and its struggle against virtually insurmountable difficulties, including fire, vortices, storms, and angels. Once the soul begins its pilgrimage and beholds the realm of the Ophanim and God's Throne Chariot, the entire cosmos vibrates with divine energy.

Immutable Space: The Wheel, the Circle, the Quaternity, and the Eye

Elijah's and Ezekiel's visionary experiences, as well as the images conjured up in the minds and psyches of Yizhar's characters, may be viewed as symptomatic of a struggle between a traumatic empirical condition and a need for a well-ordered, well-rounded, relatively harmonious world. The appearance of the Chariot and the four wheels in the writings of the two prophets, and the four-wheeled vehicles in Yizhar's novella, indicate a quaternity. Psychologically, such fourfoldedness comes into being in dreams, religious experiences, and literary works to compensate for the lack of cohesion and balance in the real world. The function of the quaternity, as it emerges from the unconscious into consciousness, is to make the individual aware of the existing imbalance, and thereby help to redress what is unsteady, disoriented, and conflicting in the psyche.[4]

The quaternity, or number four, as viewed in the wheel and circle images used throughout *Midnight Convoy*, is a living symbol, and as such a catalytic force. "Symbols," writes Jung, "are images of contents which for the most part transcend consciousness." They are therefore replete with potential and hidden meanings, factors with which the individual in question must come to terms. As an earthly visualization, a wheel or circle divided into quadrants represents terrestrial direction. Representations of undivided circles, as in the novella's opening image with its gusts of wind, stand for pneumatic spiritual powers. In both cases, the flow of energy (riding on land or through the heavens) activates what is a *massa confusa*, an initial state of chaos, in an attempt to find an order.[5]

That the image of the wheel, circle, and quaternity is imbricated so pervasively throughout Yizhar's novella suggests the psychological image of the *Self*. In that the Self transcends the ego and is identified empirically with the image of God, the writer is suggesting a need to expand consciousness, to deepen insights and understanding so that each and all of his dramatis personae will be able to cope with the anguish they face. The search for *the right path* is living out or reliving a collective ordeal: the survival of catastrophic happenings which have taken place almost continuously since ancient times (the destruction of Jerusalem, the Babylonian exile, the captivity, the burnings at the stake during the Inquisition, the slaughter of six million Jews during the Holocaust, to mention just a few examples). The intensity of the suffering endured by Jews throughout history has left deep psychological scars.

The soldiers in *Midnight Convoy* know, therefore, that they must complete their mission: it is a question of survival. They also know that the *eye* must forever be awake and observant, ferreting out any and all dangers. As an instrument of perception, the eye is the source of light, intelligence, and spirit. It is also the window of the soul. As the soldiers in Yizhar's novella gaze into the vastness of the landscape and attempt to spot the enemy, night begins to fall and darkness slowly invades the atmosphere. Not only do the soldiers *see out*, but the enemy *sees in*. Throughout the novella, therefore, horizontal and vertical eye movements are nearly continuous. In that both the terrestrial and the cosmic eye are at work here, each in its own way encountering the unknown and immutable infinite expanses, the unfolding visualizations at times take on apocalyptic dimensions.

Let us attempt to decode the multiple signs (wheel, circle, quaternity, and the dynamics of the eye) in the opening image of *Midnight Convoy*. The pneumatic and terrestrial event is introduced as immutable, infinite, and awesome space becoming visible in masses of whirling, wheeling, and circular images.

> The shawls of dust, twisted tight to the rear in a grappling coil, went forward on an occasional dare and knotted up the front view as well. At once everything was dimmed and greyed, walled up in a ball, thickened with dusty spinning, a choked and blinded enclosure— except when the wind gave in, not a minute too soon, and slackened a bit, venting the rest of its rage on that gigantic whirl of wake in

back, waving and tearing at it, scattering it furiously to the sides of the road and deep into the fields, which were already as blanched as could be; for stubble and summer grasses, great clods and minute granules, had long since been entirely levelled into grey lumps, nameless and formless in the scorn of uniformity, fainting under this floury, weighty, compulsory veil.

The above cataclysmic natural event, with its violent and blinding helicoidal movements, is a manifestation of uncontrollable powers directed by superior ascensional forces. The cosmic wind described in the above quotation is indicative of extreme spiritual and psychological turmoil. Although such a wind ravages everything in its wake, it also paves the way for renewal, as attested to by the Hebrew word for wind (*Ruach*), which is synonymous with *breath:* Spirit of God. In both the Old and New Testaments, among other religious works, winds are identified with divine messengers: the Great Wind that parted the Red Sea, the one that took Elijah up to heaven (2 Kings 2:11), that was seen by Ezekiel (Ezek. 1:4), that brought the Tongues of Fire of the Holy Ghost to the Apostles, that was the Hindu God, Vayu, who is Cosmic breath and the Verb, the Chinese *k'i* (breath) that fills space. Winds, manifestations of both inner and exterior happenings, pave the way for a *hierophany:* the dialectical process that transforms profane objects or events into something sacred.

To search for *the right path* in the midst of the chaos brought on by the storm of military events and their emotional aftermath is not an easy task. Without the central and comprehensive archetype of the Self, as viewed in the image of the swirling and circular winds, the ability to sublimate or to rise above the world of contingencies into aerated spheres would be virtually impossible. On the other hand, to confront the Self in sublimated domains, which invites an atomization of the previous solid and secure ruling principle, requires a highly developed ego-consciousness: an ability to deal with reality. If the ego is weakly structured, it may be drowned or buried by the onslaught. During the transformation process, earth is transmuted into spirit, the coarse into the refined, the liquid into the evaporated and distilled. Psychologically, sublimation—which implies height, flight, and an amorphous condition—suggests an ability to abstract and conceptualize problems, thereby divesting them of their strictly earthly accoutrements and entanglements.

As the knots, dust, coils, rage, and whirling granules in the opening paragraph kick up continuous clouds of formless matter, these opaque mobile forms, viewed psychologically, are like so many obstacles impeding the protagonists from making the necessary split-second decisions demanded to assure the convoy's safe passage. Where sight is needed, opacities exist; where clarity of vision and singleness of purpose should be envisaged, diffused and fragmented approaches to empirical problems pave the way.

Circling and circular images also come to the fore in the opening whirlwind image. Circular movement around a center not only focuses energy, but relates to the idea of "circulation," thereby generating energy and activity and beginning a course of action. Let us recall that Yahweh directed Joshua, in his conquest of Jericho, to "compass the city . . . and go round about the city . . ." (Josh. 6:3).

The circle, as it appears and disappears amid the swirling winds, the coiling eddies, and the particles of sand, also has a mandala effect. Because of its motility in this instance, it cannot serve as a meditative device nor foster a unitive experience. Only when the turbulence dies down can energy be concentrated on a given area and fragmentation cease, thereby divesting the brain of extraneous matter, idle thoughts, and random feelings. Since a mandala actualizes cosmic energy, it may also be looked upon as a microcosm of divine power, thereby taking on the contours of a sacred space and interiorizing the energies within its sphere.[6]

The mandala, circle, and wheel, all of which appear in one form or another in the opening image of Yizhar's tale, are synecdoches for the jeeps (the lead jeep in particular) and the trucks making up the convoy. Because they are associated with both celestial and terrestrial mobility, displacements, and journeys, they are also linked to the notion of ascension and descension as well as horizontality. The continuously rapid eye movement in the opening apocalyptic vision spells a crucial psychological need for *oneness*. Dualities must be embraced. And so they are when members of the group live out their separate existences, each individual experiences disparate yearnings but functioning as a single body when participating in their earthly drama.

As the soldiers eye sorghum fields, thorns, shrubs, wadi, hills, and the mountains in the distance, a mist of sadness hangs over them, "unclear, indefinite, like the end of the Sabbath gazing down at the coming week of toil." Such a premonitory image encapsulates both the reality of the situation and the psychological condition of the group. In that the word "Sabbath" is used, meaning a brief period of repose after which travail begins anew, their mission spells the end of an epoch, an era, a journey. In that each Sabbath marks an ascensional progression—a sacred as contrasted to a profane time—the end of this period, in the above metaphor, indicates the emergence of its opposite: a differentiated, time-laden world. The eyes of these five soldiers know the task that lies before them. Their gaze sweeps the whole vista; all is still yet all moves. As the reality of their mission descends upon them, feelings of isolation, alienation, awe, and fear mount at the awareness that just as they see out, so an invisible enemy in an unfathomable wilderness targets them.

The jeep starts up again, the wheels turn, more land is traversed. Then it stops. Personified, it waits "silently by the crossroads, as if restraining itself from another burst of motion and at the same time as if in a daydream." Referred to at times as modest, faithful, devouring, wailing, blinding, or leaping about as it climbs ravines and slopes, the jeep takes on the role of a protagonist; its wheeling and rolling generate cumulative tension. Circling again through the wasteland, the wheels pulverize clods of dirt and sand, kicking up clouds of dust as they grip the parched, calcareous soil, as had the whirlwind storm in the opening image. Vision is once again barred as curtains of particles encircle the soldiers and their vehicle. Floury and powdery, these dustlike elements create dizzying opacities: mounds of white emerge as if from nowhere or everywhere, then swell to inordinate size. Suddenly movement subsides. The jeep halts. The rotating wheels of the jeep start up once again, as if transcending their earthly functions and inviting the soldiers to view these circular forces cosmically as an earthly manifestation of the immobile sun. Like so many energy centers—be it as envisaged in Ezekiel's "throne chariot borne by the four cherubim with the four faces;" or as in Psalm eighty-three, "O my God, make them like a wheel; as in the stubble before the wind;" or as the *chakra* of Tantric Buddhism which represents subtle centers traversed by energy, so, too, is the wheel by its axle. The soldiers feel fired by the dimming but still incandescent circular golden rays of the sun.

Lost tracks of an ancient path are found. Confidence is renewed as the soldiers revert to the security of a sacred past time. With the incisive descent of night, shapes and shadows take on greater eeriness, their enigmatic meanings fusing a pre-Christian era with a present reality. Imagination knows no bounds as a new universe is born in the mind's eye of the soldiers, each feeling transfigured, virtually sanctified, with every step he takes on the ground walked upon by the prophets of old.

The question of life and death and the cyclicality of this cosmic circularity manifests itself in representations of stones: when the jeep halts, the soldiers get out and pile up small mounds of stones on the side of the road as markers to show the convoy the way.

Stones, which figure in Biblical images and those of other religious tracts, are identified with regeneration and eternality. In Greek mythology, Deucalion and Pyrrha threw stones behind them, which were transformed into people. As opposed to sand, stones represent solid mass, or a cohesive whole. Durable, stable, and hard, they are antipodal to the diffused and splintered particles of the previous images, always subject to immediate and constant change.

On the human plane, stones stand for stability rather than nomadism, the lot of the Jews since the Diaspora which began with the Babylonian exile (586 B.C.). As a symbol of strength and unity, stone possesses spiritual qualities: the ancient Greek *omphalos*, according to Pausanius, was a white stone which marked the center of the earth; the Muslims venerate a precious reddish black meteorite housed in the Kaaba; the Hebrew *Beith-El* means the House of God, and refers to the stone pillar in Genesis 28:22. In Matthew 4:3, we read that when the tempter came to Christ he said: "If thou be the Son of God, command that these stones be made of bread."

Not surprisingly, then, the soldiers in *Midnight Convoy* consider the miniature pillars they erect to point the way to the convoy as sacred markers, pneumatic centers which see to the safety and thereby the strength and long life of those traversing the area.

The jeep starts up again, jolts, and slips down to the gully at the foot of the hill, butts its way through the sorghum, reaches an open field, and picks up speed now that the furrows run "in the same direction as their wheels." An obstacle is encountered: a large wadi, capable of halting the wheels of the five- and ten-ton trucks making up the convoy. Biblical time once again emerges into present reality, inspiring the soldiers to struggle on, as Joshua had when crossing the waters of the Jordan with his precious cargo. "And the priests that bore the ark of the covenant of the Lord stood firm on dry ground in the midst of the Jordan, and all the Israelites passed over on dry ground, until all the people were passed clean over Jordan" (Josh. 3:17).

Calling upon an historical or mythical past in moments of crisis, bringing timeless and spaceless dimensions into consciousness, implies a rejection of the rational approach and the choice of irrational guidance. Such regression, as in the case of the scouts in *Midnight Convoy* is salutary. Energies formerly directed outward are now turned inward. The ensuing concentration of thought acts as a stimulant, renewing activity within the unconscious. As its dynamism increases, so does its turbulence, bringing about a kind of "reshuffling" of contents, pushing forth into the conscious mind what had previously existed inchoate, thereby paving the way for a different attitude and approach to the empirical domain.

Rather than feeling depressed by the magnitude of their responsibilities, the soldiers are energized. They are like the pioneers, navigators, architects, and road builders of old, endowed with the fire and energy that comes with the need to survive. The detour is found, the wadi is crossed, and the jeep starts off again. One kilometer and a half to the main road. But where is *the path?* One of the soldiers looks around. He loses his way in a field of sorghum. Standing alone in silence and wonderment, he is held by this single instant, concretizing and securing some intangible power. He feels a new and never-before experienced force within him: "the presence of some thing or feeling, a wonderful sensation, spreading and moving, and at the same time so warm."

The numinosity of the sensation experienced is so powerful that he feels as if he has penetrated a new land, some inexplicable sphere for which he has always longed. "This was something of his own, hoped for. He shivered with the strength of a new vision suddenly perceived, and loneliness emerged from all sides to embrace him." This altered state of consciousness has expanded his feeling realm, encouraging something within him to begin singing out. Calmly and clearly he realizes he has been *away*, both empirically and psychologically. He tells the others of the new path.

The Radio Operator: The Feminine Logos/Eros Factor

Dahlia arrives in one of the vehicles of the convoy with its cargo of oil, spare parts, and ammunition. Her function as radio operator also determines the psychological role she will play in *Midnight Convoy*. A mediating force, she is capable, like the radio, of putting individuals in touch with each other or with themselves. Similarity also exists between the radio—which converts sounds or signals into electromagnetic waves, then transmits these directly through space, without connecting wires, to a receiving set that changes them into sounds—and Dahlia's presence on the scene, as *Eros/Logos*, effecting a similar transformation within the psyche of the collective, but mostly of one soldier in particular.

Dahlia is that *Eros* factor which stands for relatedness, connecting outer and inner worlds within an individual and feelings within a group. In that she is given an important task to fulfill as radio operator, she is *Logos*, equated with reason and intellect, but also with spirit in the energy she sends out in waves at assigned frequencies. Dahlia answers the need of those seeking a higher form of consciousness which transcends that of the ego. Reminiscent psychologically of the "Bride of God," "Divine Wisdom," and the "Wisdom of God" in the Song of Songs, Proverbs, and Esther, Dahlia, for Zvialeh, represents that feminine creative factor within the Godhead. She, too, has taken on the contours of the Logos, God's preexistent helper in the creation of the world (Prov. 8:22–31). Psychologically, logos as a creative factor appears after the ego discovers the unconscious, and in so doing begins the process of individualizing itself, that is, perceiving its objective as well as subjective nature.

That Dahlia appears in the novella as the last glimmers of the sun are visible and the moon is born underscores still more overtly her interconnecting quality. *Eros*, usually associated with the moon, has in times past been considered a feminine attribute, whereas *Logos*, associated with the sun, has been identified with the masculine. Psychologically, we may suggest that Dahlia is androgynous, answering the needs of the military in general, but of one soldier—Zvialeh—in particular.

When Zvialeh first sees her she is "shapeless in her baggy trousers and leather jacket," yet the radiance of her presence, bathed in moonrays, bewitches him. She is glamour personified in his eyes, but also a warm, soft, loving individual who answers both sexual and spiritual needs. What he looks upon as her gentle presence tempers the hazards involved in the work he and his fellow soldiers must accomplish. As *Eros*, she gives him what he lacks, sustains him with what he views as tenderness, which is in no way to be confused with weakness. Representative of *Logos*, she anticipates the spiritual or love-related thoughts in the masculine consciousness.[7]

As a communicating force not to be confused with verbal impartment alone, though this, too, is of import, Dahlia and Zvialeh speak a language of their own, of sensation and intuition. Until Zvialeh met Dahlia he had not listened to his feeling world, which was so repressed as to be virtually nonexistent. The emotions her presence engenders in him reshuffle subliminal contents. The energy aroused in the process ushers into being a broader emotional view.[8]

The energy Dahlia projects into Zvialeh's psyche as *Eros/Logos* is not fossilized nor unpleasant, but clear, workable, and directed. She aims her psychological power toward Zvialeh's weak spots not by assaulting him with pointers or precepts, but through gentle verbal and feeling interchange, her goal being to bring conscious and unconscious needs and traumas together in a *coniunctio:* a fusion of opposites within the personality.

Although Dahlia is *Eros* and triggers the feeling function in Zvialeh, she is in no way a weak individual. Nor is she authoritarian because *Logos* is implicit in her personality. She is strong and has a mission to fulfill, and in this regard is not unlike Esther or other courageous Biblical women. Reminiscent of Esther, she is a transpersonal and guiding principle occupied with the mysteries involved in saving her people from slaughter. Impregnated with that divine spark, she, like Esther, is also very much of this earth, involved in the world of reality. Nor do either of the women actually fight; rather, they participate in a collective effort, thus ensuring the survival of their people. Although courage in the face of danger is displayed by both women, neither is divested of her femininity.

As interwoven in Yizhar's narrative, Dahlia's character is a positive, fecundating, and nourishing force. Unlike the Biblical Delilah (an anagram for Dahlia), she is not the woman who enslaves the man, the demon-woman, who performed a symbolic castration when she cut off Samson's hair. On the contrary, as *Eros/Logos*, Dahlia is an archetypal woman of a kind that has appeared frequently throughout the ages in the dreams of young men at crucial moments in their lives: the comforting, understanding, and loving young wife/mother—psychologically, a soul force or anima figure. Dahlia's floral name suggests a combination of Mother Earth, since the roots of this annual dig into the soil, and spirit, and its blossoms look up toward the heavens for nourishment.

That Dahlia functions effectively as *Eros/Logos* in the patriarchal environment of war suggests an ability on the part of the military to relate to women. Neither resentful nor fearful of the "castrating" power of the feminine principle, as was the case with the ruling consciousness in Persia at the time of Esther, the Israeli soldiers—and Zvialeh in particular—are comfortable with an interplay of opposites.

Nevertheless, Zvialeh's relationship with Dahlia is very special on both verbal and feeling planes. He glows when explaining his method of celestial navigation to Dahlia—and understandably so, since the energy her presence triggers in him has opened him up to his feelings, that lifeline to his inner world which has been closed and stifled until now.

Feeling is a subjective process and not an intellectual value. It is a way of judging and reacting which may activate bodily innervations and sensations. As related to Zvialeh's experience, the libido aroused during the verbal/emotional interchange attracts his feelings and compels them to participate in his acts and thinking processes, valuating them not according to intellectual intent or content alone, but also through bodily consciousness or bodily awareness, that is, emotionally and sensitively. This impression-like reaction, which gives rise to a new susceptibility, invites Zvialeh to endow every day of his existence, hazardous as it is, with those tender, warm, and beautiful feelings which Dahlia's presence generates in him.[9]

> A special channel of awareness was opening up within him, a silent cry of adoration, a dark yearning which needed no eyes to guide its object. It was she who possessed the creamy warmth, hidden and fragrant, which should be held and caressed, with a murmur in her ear, until you were hers, and you could sing to her of an end to all wars and dust and noisy crowds of packed and pushing soldiers, you could sing of something else, broad fields and hills, that would be given to those who had such a Dahlia, who adored her just for being as she was—a world of true peace and beauty, rich as fertile, rain-soaked soil, of fresh, peaceful verdance, and the little things in life that, having neither tongue nor time, sing a ceaseless praise of their own.

The same feeling world is manifested semiotically, when an "unoppressive silence quivered in the space of night," and Dahlia and Zvialeh seemed enclosed in a circle, set apart from the others.

Although there is nothing traumatic in Dahlia's entrée into Yizhar's novella—it could even be called perfunctory—its effect on Zvialeh is crucial to his spiritual and emotional growth. As for her presence on the scene, it is unexpected, and from this point of view may be looked upon as a synchronistic event, "a coincidence in time of two or more causally unrelated events which have a similar meaning."[10] Viewed in ancient times, and perhaps even today, as miraculous happenings, such unexpected encounters or events depend not on rational but irrational factors. Because the unconscious is in some unknown way connected to outer forces, and the tendency for things to happen together—be it in the empirical or psychological domain—occurs for some inexplicable reason, it is at this juncture that the acausality and space-time relativity of the unconscious acts upon the field of consciousness, linking events.[11]

Nor is Zvialeh—as was expected of heroes in past times—obliged to fight against the dominion of the previous patriarchal order and conventional standards in order to embrace a new approach to life. He has been yearning unconsciously for the warmth and gentleness, strength and sobriety, that Dahlia has brought to him; it is she who has paved the way for his psychological wholeness and completion, thereby helping to reconcile opposites as well as develop his potential. No longer will polarities such as masculine and feminine, law and love, conscious and unconscious, encourage him to repress one or the other factors in his personality. In her capacity as *Eros/Logos*, or as a unifying and ordering symbol, Dahlia is instrumental in drawing both aspects of Zvialeh's psyche together in the individuation process: the circular or wheel-like course of cooperation between the Self and the ego needed to form an all-inclusive psychic entity.

Although a *modus vivendi* with the world in general and his military mission in particular has been reached after Zvialeh's interlude with Dahlia, fear has not been banished, nor the harrowing moments and difficulties awaiting him. Henceforth, they will be approached archetypally, as part of a destiny that has to be fulfilled.

The first platoon arrives, machine gunners and riflemen, another unit, then another. Perhaps two hundred or four hundred. "A human chain setting out in the darkness," diligent, silent, and momentous as they pass on into the night. The safety of the convoy is the sole concern. Advance. Damaged trucks are abandoned, their contents unloaded, carried if need be. Time is of the essence. Silence. Flares. The convoy pursues its course, its winding journey, relentless, seemingly endless. Not all will come through alive. A mine will blow up, killing some of the soldiers, wounding others. Still the lads arrive—on and on.

Convoys with their machines cannot occupy territories, nor can they break a siege or win peace. Nevertheless, the surviving scouts and the members of the convoy learn from the experience: greater perception of the meaning of death and therefore life, of the nature of open fields, hills, slopes, wadies—"the truth of existence." For Zvialeh, though anchored in his machine and focused on accomplishing his task, Dahlia's presence, like that of the Shulamite in the Song of Songs, taught him love and relatedness—and also that Divine Wisdom which directs one toward *the right path*, not without ruts or wadis, but a path that teaches each individual the significance of the gift of life.

The driver starts up the *engine of the jeep*. As it purrs and roars, he knows that energy is being transformed from one form to another: physically by making the concrete machine go and abstractly, that is, in the psychological domain, as new energy centers build up within him.

> It was life, the movement of life . . . Breathing very deeply he gained speed and drove up the road, and the jeep's power was awakening and flowing through it. And now you, son of man, pay heed to these hills, let your gaze extend till the very boundaries of the skies and the further expanses, until the limits of all life in this night world . . .

8 Jiro Osaragi's *The Journey*—The Semiology of Transformation

Jiro Osaragi's novel *The Journey* (1960) reveals a complex network of displacements and equivocations involved in the semiology of transformation. The outer signs of this activity are manifested in the constant use by Osaragi's protagonists of trains, cars, buses, and boats during their multiple trajectories. The various vehicles not only allow them to shift perpetually from one area of Japan to another, but the velocities of the machines used reflect inner frenetic, anguished, or serene psychological conditions.

The conveyances in question signal yet another theme in *The Journey:* the dichotomy between pre- and post-World War II Japan. Perhaps more than any other country in the world after the war, Japan was forced to undergo an enormous spiritual and psychological uprooting. Values as well as living conditions had suffered an upheaval. The underpinnings of the virtually feudal and relatively closed society that had existed prior to 1945, when the Emperor assumed the power of deity, women were considered inferior to men, and class distinctions were sharp, suddenly were swept away after 1945—at least legally. The void that came into being after the cessation of conflict and the American occupation of Japan was, to some extent, filled, and incredibly swiftly. The *new way* sprang forth from the highly industrious and compulsive nature of the Japanese personality. An ingrained work ethic and an intensely disciplined nature gave birth in the space of a few decades to one of the most highly industrialized societies in the world. The psychological price paid for the replenishing of the vacuum, however, was high, as we shall see. It was higher, perhaps, for the older generation, such as Osaragi's, than for youth.

The perpetual displacement of vehicles (trains, cars, buses, ships), while signaling distress on the part of the characters, also marks a directional shift and a split between young and old in Japanese culture. Despite the fact that the new generation takes advantage, outwardly at least, of the society's mechanized instruments and tries, as best it can, to integrate these with tradition, this generation is inwardly torn, struggling between two points of view. The morals and ideals of the generation's ancestors clash with the new ones initiated by the war. The fathers and grandfathers in Osaragi's novel find themselves at a loss, so violent and heartrending has the transformation been for them. The changing of their set ways is a crushing dispossession which is not only unacceptable, but leaves them without identity, empty, unsettled, and confused, resulting at times in suicide or withdrawal into an inner world. As for the younger generation, some forget the very meaning of morality in their endeavor to make money, while others attempt to find some kind of balance in their lives.

In all cases—and this is characteristically Japanese—the protagonists relate intimately to the moods of nature: its transcendental oneness and aloofness, experienced in seemingly infinite multiplicity in the everyday world. The power of mystical contemplation of nature helps the individual feel at home with the temporal and atemporal world; the innate simplicity of natural settings encourages a breakthrough from the artifice of the world of contingencies to the mysterious realm that lies behind it.[1] An autumnal evening, for example, may stimulate feelings of aloneness; it may also uplift. A tree, a patch of grass, a bird perched on a branch—all manifestations of nature's infinite forms, shifting colors and variously sounding tonalities—may produce feelings of belonging and serenity.

Unlike Westerners, the Japanese neither identify with Nature nor look upon this continuously mobile force as an opponent, as an entity to conquer, dominate, or violate for selfish purposes. Nature is considered a friend and companion whose grandeur and aloofness—when "the sublime morning sun" rises in the heavens—bedazzle and are cause to marvel.[2]

One may well ask how the Japanese developed their most special relationship with Nature. How is it that emotional, aesthetic, and spiritual feelings, triggered, for example, by the presence of a single flower in a vase, are so all-encompassing? A partial answer may lie in the religious practices of the Japanese. They are the only nation in the world in which two religions are observed, each working in harmony with the other: the animism of Shintoism and the spirituality of Zen Buddhism. Nature, like the individual, is destined for Buddhahood; and human "nature is one with objective Nature."[3]

Shinto ("The Way of the Gods") is a religion with no official scriptures. It teaches that a life force exists in all things, animate or inanimate. Everything in the phenomenological world has a soul or spirit within it;

each entity is in a state of becoming. Shinto deities (*kami*) are many. They include spirits of trees, mountains, and flowers; the sun and moon; deified ancestors, heroes, and emperors, among others. Human beings approach the kami without fear and in friendship. Before doing so, however, they must purify themselvs by washing and taking part in devotions, such as standing within a sacred enclosure or in a certain area on a mountain. Shinto shrines are usually very simple. They include a symbolic representation of a kami or a substitute spirit in the form of a stone or a mirror. No image exists in ancient Shinto ritual.

Buddhism, founded by the Indian S'akyamu Gautama (566–485 B.C.), preached the doctrine of Buddha, the Enlightened One. Happiness and salvation result from inwardness and are not dependent upon transitory exterior phenomena; life on earth is characterized by imperfection and sorrow; the annihilation of desire leads to salvation and "perpetual enlightenment" (nirvana). Following the introduction of Buddhism in Japan in the sixth century A.D., the doctrine was modified by the Japanese and divested of most of its theology. It became a philosophy. Zen Buddhism, which follows the teachings of the monk Eisai and became popular in the twelfth century, was one of several Buddhist sects flourishing in Japan. Zen Buddhism, according to the twentieth-century monk Suzuki, is the result of the Chinese pragmatic mind coming into contact with Indian philosophy.[4]

Zen Buddhism seeks to transmit the Buddha Essence, or Buddha Mind, to humankind through silent meditation and abstract contemplation. If these are properly experienced, enlightenment may result. The aesthetic perception of reality takes place through flashes of intuition which reveal the truth about the universe. During such moments acolytes may transcend their individuality (their self-consciousness, or personal ego) and know oneness with the universe. Unity of existence underlies all meditative practices. The mind becomes vacant and detached from worldly problems, while at the same time the individual slowly absorbs the universe into himself.

In accordance with Zen Buddhist doctrine, the protagonists in Osaragi's novel attempt to relate to, as well as transcend, the world of particulars, the world of contingencies, via their approach to nature and the machine. Journeys are particularly meaningful to these personages. Indeed, journeys have been and still are a way of life for the Japanese. Rooted in the Japanese psyche and culture since ancient times, displacements, many and frequent, are of two types: empirical and spiritual. The former used to be made by foot, by carriage, or on four-legged animals. In Osaragi's work, as expected, emphasis is placed on high-speed and ultramodern conveyances. Spiritual journeys are more difficult and complex than empirical ones.

They can be engaged in only by free spirits—those who have succeeded in opening themselves up to the timeless world of pre-creation or to the one existing prior to manifestation. Only when the spirit has been unshackled from the dross of the world of particulars can the *journey of life* be lived cosmically. Expressed psychologically, such a quest conveys the need of the ego (the center of consciousness) to experience the Self (the total psyche).

No one has depicted more superbly this desire to shift, to see, to experience nature's multiple and continuously altering images and feelings than Basho (1644–94). His haiku-poems—referred to throughout Osaragi's novel by one of the older protagonists, a professor, who like Basho is trying to conform to the modern way—convey the feelings experienced with the sudden glow of enlightenment. The haiku form, with its three lines containing five, seven, and five syllables, respectively, is particularly apt in expressing the meteoric nature of his perceptions "into the life of things."[5]

Basho, who spent much of his life traveling from one part of Japan to another, succeeded in deflecting his anxieties and self-doubts by conveying his needs in imagistic gnomic poems. A lonely explorer, he walked through the rugged northern provinces of Japan in search of aesthetic and moral values which he felt had been lost in his day. So, too, do some of Osaragi's protagonists engage in a similar quest—not on foot, but by swift, sleek, and highly mechanized vehicles.

The theme of *The Journey* revolves around young and old, each individual steeped in tradition of his or her own way, but nevertheless at loose ends in the new, high-paced, glittering consumer society. Some are drawn into shady business deals, such as buying automobiles from Americans and selling them illegally to the *nouveau riche* Japanese whose moral values have vanished. Others attempt pathetically to find an answer for themselves. The central narrative events occur during the characters' trajectories on trains, buses, cars, and boats. Such enclosed spaces signal a concentration of psychic energy (*libido*), paving the way, in some cases, for greater understanding of situations and relationships. The mechanical devices used to transport the protagonists here and there may be envisaged as symbolic codes bringing momentary equilibrium to the unsettling psychological and spiritual mixture which is their lives.

Jiro Osaragi (1898–1973) was the author of successful plays, novels, and travel books. His themes revolve around feelings of loneliness, love, fear, and greed, as well as the problems brought about by the sudden changes occurring in the lives of individuals and Japanese society generally, after World War II and the American Occupation.

A graduate of the Imperial University of Tokyo, where he concentrated on political science and French law and literature, Osaragi worked for three years, at his father's insistence, in the Treaty Bureau of the Foreign Office. During this period, he was forbidden to publish anything under his own name. In 1924, when he could no longer repress his urge to write, he took a pen name and started on a literary career. Since he lived in Kamakura, near the Great Buddha, he chose the very suitable pseudonym of "Jiro Osaragi:" *Jiro*, translated as "second son" or "next to," combined with *Osaragi*, a variant reading of the characters for the Great Buddha.

Although he was the vanguard of the literary movements during the time of his youth, Osaragi felt isolated after the war. He refused to follow the trend set by so many contemporary writers who tried to emulate the French novelists. To ape the style of others was inauthentic and dangerous, in his opinion. "Nor can a way of thinking be imported intact. But it can be useful to study foreign literature if you absorb its ideas. Even then, in the long run, one should accept only those ideas that really fit into Japanese culture. In Japan there is no abstract philosophy or religious dogma. We are unable to acquire thought as such."[6] The young who rejected their heritage, overtly or covertly, were, Osaragi wrote with melancholy, "in too much of a hurry either to write well or to read well."[7]

The Train

The train, the first of several mechanical vehicles alluded to in *The Journey*, sets the tone of the novel. Modern, rapid, and sleek, the train symbolizes displacement and evolution in *time* and *space*. Because this conveyance adheres to specific time schedules, it compels riders to follow strict disciplines, and the riders are confined to specific areas. In that the train complies with certain spatial organizational patterns and directional goals, marked out by a network of tracks in various topographical regions, and depends upon a complex of public transportational devices, it makes for better communication between individuals and society. Because of both its individual and collective aspect, the train may take on cosmic impersonality, imposing its law and rhythms on certain persons, while for others it may fill a pragmatic need.

In that the train has its temporal and spatial destiny marked out in advance and is an impersonal functioning organism, it may be viewed, psychologically, as a coordinating power within the psyche. Linking the disparate, setting standards and goals in keeping with certain rigorous rational and subliminal disciplines, the train may be viewed as a centering and coordinating power, an archetypal image with its own patterning devices and modes of behavior.[8]

For the Japanese, as previously mentioned, modes of transportation, on foot, by cart, on horseback, or by mechanical means, imply an inherently wandering spirit as well as a sense of loneliness. Although traveling encourages one to view new vistas, it also triggers reflections about life, such as the need to accept one's isolation as part of an ever-unfolding mystery. Considered as a journey, life leads the wayfarer from one imponderable to another. Individuals—in Japanese terms—see themselves as "eternal wayfarers," who spend their lives roving about in a peripatetic quest for truth, and greater spirituality—Buddhahood.

The train taking Osaragi's protagonist, the young and most attractive Taeko Okamoto, from North Kamakura station to Kamakura proper, where she will visit her aged uncle, Soroku Okamoto, suggests a sharp and definite directional image within her mind. She gives the impression of having chosen her path in life and of understanding the complex network making up her feeling world. She looks out the train's window and sees a cedar forest, a cluster of hills, the roofs of the temples, and "peaceful looking houses." These enable her to define her feelings in terms of the natural surroundings encapsulated in her mind's eye, with their concomitant spiritual and psychological implications.[9]

Kamakura is an ancient city known for its magnificent temples and its colossal thirteenth-century bronze statue of the Great Buddha (Daibutsu), forty-three feet high and weighing ninety-four tons. It sits in meditation on a lotus throne with arms outstretched and thumbs joined.[10]

Taeko calls upon her widower uncle, only to discover that he is away on a trip. She then makes a traditional visit to the cemetery, where she visits the grave of her uncle's only son, Akira, who lost his life in the war in southern China.

Kamakura's patriarchal Buddhist background is momentarily transformed with Taeko's visit to the cemetery, since cemeteries and tombs are identified with the feminine archetype: Mother Earth envelops and embraces those returning to her. The power of the archetype works its wonders on Taeko. Feelings of grief but also serenity intrude. The religious sensations emerging within her psyche, as she enters the precinct reserved for the dead, create a link with a personal and collective past. Her thoughts of her cousin, and also of her ancestors, fill her with secure and nurturing sensations, like the ones she enjoyed as a child, when life seemed to open up in all of its beauteous harmonies.

In keeping with Shinto custom, Taeko sprinkles some water on Akira's grave and then puts the flowers she had brought with her into a vase. Partaking in the religious ritual stirs unconscious contents within her which then help her unblock repressed desires and emotions, while ushering in sensations of renewal. These are concretized by a visit to the cemetery by Akira's old friend, Ryosuké Tsugawa. The two meet and a relationship between them begins. Nor is it surprising to learn that, almost immediately, fundamental spiritual and psychological differences arise as well. While she loves flowers and reacts with joy to the white and dark purple clematis she brought to her cousin's grave, Ryosuké, whose feelings for nature have remained relatively undeveloped, brings a cup of saké to honor his cousin's spirit. Saké, the antithesis of the tea ceremony, stands for sociability, conviviality, and frequently for boisterousness.[11]

On another train—taking passengers from Tokyo to Kyoto and Nara—we meet a fashionable and successful businesswoman, the Baroness Kaoruko Iwamuro, who in time becomes Taeko's rival for Ryosuké's affections. Estranged from her husband, the baroness has made her own way in life. At present, she is traveling with a party of businessmen, including the president of an American company, his wife, and subordinates.

Seated in the spacious observation car of "The Dove" at the far end of the train, Mrs. Iwamuro has full visibility into the world outside, in all directions. That Mrs. Iwamuro chose to be seated in this most expensive first-class section of the train, with its comfortable sofas and armchairs, indicates a need on her part to reveal the material success she has achieved, and to display her feelings of superiority. Economic independence has imbued her with power. It has given her the right to detach herself from her financially unsuccessful husband, to see to the support and upbringing of their child, and to feel free to experience the attentions of other men. Unwilling to remain subservient to a husband for whom she feels nothing and who treats her like an object—as was customary in prewar Japan and has continued to some extent, even after the war—Mrs. Iwamuro can free herself from what she considers marital bondage. She seeks to enjoy herself, as men had for centuries in Japan, and for the same reason, since they were the money earners. Why "begrudge women the privilege, now that their roles were so often reversed"?

The observation car in the train, like the symbol of the tower, or the medieval fortress, encourages the clever Mrs. Iwamuro to peer into the vastness of the world and view it panoramically—that is, above and beyond its fragmented aspects. To see life as a panoply of infinite possibilities is to experience it as a *whole* in its collective and social aspects. Such a broad spectrum view gives the baroness additional insight as to how she can better handle her own destiny. As a businesswoman, she understands the necessity of farsightedness when trying to assess the negative and positive factors in monetary transactions.

That her business dealings revolve around machines—the very modern and evolving aspect of Japanese society—is not surprising. This new type of woman makes her money buying cars from Americans and selling them to wealthy Japanese on the black market. Such transactions not only require great audacity and a gambling spirit, but also expertise and sophistication. Mrs. Iwamuro has to have financial acumen and the ability to spot danger: to discover the weak links in the chain of transactions she directs. Unlike the sacred towers of past times, which projected believers towards heaven, thereby increasing their wisdom and spirituality, Mrs. Iwamuro's observation car encourages her to pursue her material needs and increase her worldly power and prestige.

Beautiful, subtle, and infinitely clever, Mrs. Iwamuro knows how to make the most of her body—an important factor in her business dealings. Walking into the observation car, she knows instantly that all eyes concentrate their gaze on her. Self-possessed and controlled in every way, Mrs. Iwamuro is one of those women prepared to confront any type of person or situation. If she does not approve of certain people or if she feels snubbed or looked down upon for providing what some could consider dishonest services, she smiles to hide her annoyance or even turns her back to the offensive party. Because her countrymen judge her negatively, this *femme fatale* prefers, understandably, to work for foreign clients.

During the train's high-speed trajectory, Osaragi cleverly intersperses into the narrative sequences featuring Mrs. Iwamuro followed by others in which Taeko's image takes precedence. One replaces the other as the train moves along the rain-drenched tracks; glides down the long platform; and leaves the Tokyo station, which grows smaller and finally vanishes from view.

Unlike Mrs. Iwamuro, whose existence revolves around business and the sense of power it brings her, Taeko, more reflective, seeks harmony and equilibrium. Despite the fact that Taeko has lived away from her family for several years and has been economically self-sufficient, until she met Ryosuké she lived a somewhat sheltered existence. That she has devoted all her energies to finding an unobtrusive niche for herself may account in part for the fact that her experience with young men is very limited. Nor has she evolved psychologically. Indeed, she is unable to see behind Ryosuké's *persona*, to discern his subtle motivations and manipulations, which are so different from her own. Unlike Mrs. Iwamuro, Taeko's heart rather than her mind guides her. A *puella*, she trusts Ryosuké naively, and this places her almost immediately in a difficult and painful situation.

As Taeko peers into nature's patterns, so as better to understand the world at large and her own place within it, the speeding train gives her the impression that time and space are being conpressed. She feels suddenly anxious, as if she were participating in a continuous and progressive ephemerality. Significant as well are the colorations and levels of moisture in the fleeting world she observes: the gray sky pours out its rain and even the hills seem to flow along as if they, too, have turned to water.

That water not only pours from the heavens, but everything Taeko views assumes a fluid condition. This may be seen as a premonitory indication of her *karma*—the tears she will shed in her distressing love relationship. Her problems, we learn later on, are not of a sexual nature. She has no difficulty in enjoying a physical relationship with Ryosuké. Her anxieties are psychological. She seeks what Ryosuké is incapable of giving her: fidelity, along with a modest but financially secure existence. Energetic and excited at the thought of making a fortune, pragmatic and amoral when it comes to achieving his ends, Ryosuké reacts negatively to what he considers to be Taeko's demanding and possessive nature. The more secret he keeps his whereabouts and the more freedom he demands in his relationship with Taeko, the greater is her need for a hold on his body and soul.

Ryosuké's relationship with Mrs. Iwamuro is, at the outset, strictly commercial. When, however, the seductive businesswoman finds herself alone with Ryosuké one evening in a hotel in Kyoto, he succumbs to her charms. Unaware of the liaison, but noting a change in Ryosuké's schedule and activities and in what she believes to be his previously forthright attitude toward her, Taeko saddens. She realizes that he is *slipping* through her fingers, always *flowing* or *gliding* away. Solidity and tangibility are not in his nature. He is made of a *watery* substance, like the landscape she sees from her train window. Fluid, mobile, unstable, intangible, and always streaming along, he has come to be an unsettling force in Taeko's life. Will he change? she wonders. Will he fit into the mold she has created for him and give up his gambling instincts, his lust for money?

That Taeko also muses on the dahlias and cornflowers she sees from the train window once again underscores the disparities between her and Ryosuké's views of life. Flowers, which she loves, though representing ephemeral and passive worlds, are creations of beauty and purity, reflecting nature as a whole. As in the art of *ikebana*, Taeko's view of a flower, in its ternary arrangement (including superior, median, and lower branches, representing heaven, earth, and the inferior world), implies an ever-continuing cyclical development toward enlightenment and perfection. The dahlias and cornflowers viewed from her window, though multiple rather than single, unplanned and in disarray instead of arranged and unified, may be looked upon as mediating instruments, linking heaven and earth, harmonizing and balancing what is in disequilibrium in the universe and the psyche.

The Car

The car differs from the train in that it has freedom of direction and does not have to adhere to a schedule. Needful of a road, to be sure, it can nevertheless trace its own complex routes. Because the automobilist can set his own pace and goal, he holds a somewhat autonomous position. Like the medieval knight, who was trained to become "master of his horse" (instinctual world), the driver of today's car is in charge of his mechanical device.

The type of car driven, and the driver's ability to maneuver this frequently perilous machine at high and low speeds, reveals, to a certain extent, his subjective and objective adaptation to life. The outer mechanism and its functioning, therefore, may be looked upon as a mirror image of the individual's inner structure.

The automobile is first encountered in *The Journey* during the brief holiday Taeko and Ryosuké spend on the Izu Peninsula. Seated next to Ryosuké in the car he has borrowed from a friend, Taeko, preoccupied in thought, looks "absently like a doll." Once the car takes on speed, however, things change. Ryosuké reveals his domination of the machine, and, by extension, of himself. Taeko notices his "strong arms holding the wheel," symptomatic of his mastery of the vehicle's velocity and direction. His driving is "macho," to be sure. It also reveals a certain determination—that of a man fully aware of the world around him and the path he has set out for himself. The question remains as to whether his destiny in life is compatible with Taeko's.

As the car speeds down a hill and rounds a curve, leaving behind the parched land, the dusty road, and the grass which yearns for rain, the island of Oshima comes into view, and then a sea from which "a sort of blurred purple color" radiates. This dark hue represents life's deepest tinctures, its energy and its dynamic qualities.

Clusters of ambivalent sensations stimulate Taeko. "Overcome by temptation," she is dazzled by feelings of liberation as well as a kind of "suffocation in her heart" at the thought of her deepening involvement with Ryosuké. That neither she nor Ryosuké knows at this point what road they are taking or where they are to spend the night opens her up to a world of possibilities which makes her feel giddy.

Recalling their disagreement concerning the value of money suddenly causes her sense of well-being to vanish. "I hate to be poor," Ryosuké had told her. Because Taeko cannot understand his tremendous drive, determination, and unalterable desire for success, she cannot fathom his words. From the time she had started living on her own, she was perfectly content with the little she earned.

While she is musing about their different outlooks upon life, the scenery changes abruptly: "The lush trees that covered the hill on their left looked as if they had burst into a flame of green. There was a wonderful energy about these trees as they clustered thickly together, jostling each other all the way up the distant hilltop." The image of the hill in its semiotic verticality encapsulates Ryosuké's need to ascend, to climb to the top. For the Japanese, mountains—particularly the Fuji range, which such artists as Hokusai and Hiroshige re-created in their wood blocks—stand for immutability and permanence. They represent the *yang* principle in all of its energy. The struggle involved in the ascension of a mountain has its psychological and spiritual parallels in Ryosuké. He feels impelled to go on.

Taeko's needs are less high-flown. Although she is pragmatic, there is room in her personality for the dream. It helps her to escape with Ryosuké "deep in the woods" or "somewhere by a lake," to live out "some mythlike" existence. In this regard, we may suggest that she is trying as best she can to prolong the experience of the previous night: the "misty scenery" with the "delicious" feelings it conveyed—particularly when obliterating all sense of distance and time.

When Ryosuké stops the car unexpectedly to go bathing in the clear waters, Taeko follows suit, and, although shy at first about taking off her clothes, she feels so attuned to nature and to her own physical being that she does so, enjoying the cleansing quality of the seawater coupled with the warmth of the sun's rays beating down upon her.

> She was conscious of this happiness within her body, and it filled her with an ecstasy as though she had been overcome by the fragrance of the lilies she now held in her hand. She had passed through a gate in her own life. . . . Although in one way she felt as if she were wandering through a mist, she was strongly aware of Ryosuké's guiding hand, and her eyes were bright and open.

Whatever constraints she had felt prior to this incident have "loosened." She understands now that something has opened up within her body and psyche, and that this day has special significance for her. With every passing moment, it gains in extent and depth.

Ryosuké, nevertheless, sounds a warning that takes her out of her intoxicating reverie: "Be careful as you walk. It's full of rocks here," introducing a premonitory note. That night, upon reaching a modern, Western-style hotel, Taeko sees the Mihara-yama volcano in the distance and understands that she may have to deal with *fire* directly.

What Taeko does not know is that Ryosuké has arranged a business rendezvous at the hotel with Mrs. Iwamuro and an American automobile buyer. When Taeko sees her rival in the dining room, "wearing a conspicuous red jacket, gay and so bright that it seemed to be on fire," she understandably feels very distressed. We learn later that Mrs. Iwamuro has always loved the color red, and fire itself. An incendiary personality, flamboyant, exciting, and dynamic, she is well suited to such a fulgurating hue. That she will have an injurious effect on Taeko is predictable. She stands for conflict and struggle; her personality engenders pain and hurt.

Taeko begins to understand that Ryosuké and Mrs. Iwamuro have much in common: a gambling spirit and an intense need for financial success. Will these factors and their secret lovemaking destroy Taeko? She wonders whether she is to be burned to "ashes" in the forthcoming melee.

Mrs. Iwamuro thrives on displacements; they excite her. On one occasion, a luxurious car belonging to one of her business clients takes her to the Great Buddha in the Todai Temple, to the Kasuga Shrine, the deer park, the Chion Temple, and other Japanese sites of artistic wonders. Interestingly enough, she understands why the Americans with whom she is traveling are unable to understand the artistic and spiritual principles that prompted the creation of these works of art.

Westerners, for the most part, cannot possibly experience Buddhist thought, particularly Zen, which teaches how to see directly "into the mystery" of life and not to "believe in a higher being other than oneself."[12] Eschewing western logic and discursiveness, Zen Buddhism is concerned with experiencing *satori*—that which does not rely upon concepts in order to reach the truth of things, but rather upon intuition. This larger frame of reference suggests a spiritual relationship between the human being and the mysteries inherent in the work of art.

Psychologically, satori may be looked upon as that "supreme moment" in the life of a human being or artist when he or she becomes conscious of the Unconscious (*mushin*-no-mind).[13] If a Zen Buddhist writes a poem, creates a sculpture or drawing, or simply admires or meditates upon a monument, such as the Great Buddha (Daibutsu), which sits cross-legged on a lotus pedestal in the imposing Todai Temple, satori may break through with such power as to put the individual in touch with his transcendence and arcane nature. That such moments of extraordinary enlightenment have been experienced reveals the importance of the unconscious factor—that transpersonal power implicit in the creative process.[14]

Zen Buddhism, so foreign to the Western extroverted mind, seeks to transmit the Buddha Essence, or Buddha Mind, to humankind through silent meditation and abstract contemplation. If these are properly experienced, enlightenment may result. Reality is aesthetically perceived through flashes of intuition, which reveal the truth about the universe. During such moments, the acolyte may transcend individuality (self-consciousness, personal ego) and know oneness with the universe. C. G. Jung calls the experience of enlightenment (satori) a *mysterium ineffable*, when the ego is released into the Self. Unity of existence underlies all meditative practices: the mind becomes vacant and detached from worldly problems, while the individual slowly absorbs the universe into himself. The hierophant is no longer disturbed by the vicissitudes of daily life; he remains serene when faced with adversity.[15]

The Japanese psyche can combine inwardness with a highly technical and industrial existence. Because Zen is based on the intuitive experience and cannot be taught, it is neither intellectual nor considered an accomplishment. It is a way of life which, unlike the Western, allows the world of particulars to be experienced in daily activities simultaneously with the "original mind," or cosmic consciousness. Such an interchange between the personal and the collective strengthens the Japanese psyche, making it capable of living harmoniously in both worlds at the same time. Zen Buddhists cannot be destroyed by outside events nor be disconcerted by the effects which plague most individuals. Suzuki, the twentieth-century Zen philosopher, explained the Zen Buddhist mind in the following manner:

> It is always flowing, it never halts, nor does it turn into a solid. As it has no discrimination to make, no affective preference to follow, it fills the whole body, pervading every part of the body, and nowhere standing still. It is never like a stone or a piece of wood. . . . If it should find a resting place anywhere, it is not a mind of no-mind. A no-mind keeps nothing in it. . . . [T]he mind moves from one object to another, flowing like a stream of water, filling every possible corner. For this reason the mind fulfills every function required of it.[16]

Great Japanese architecture, sculpture, and painting permit transcendence of the multiple world and the experience of timelessness and inwardness; they encourage compression of feelings and expressions of them through symbols, a word, a brush stroke, an image, a color, a mood. Westerners, who live in the rational and intellectual realms—or their opposites—find it difficult to experience the inwardness and dimensionless universe of the Zen Buddhists, and the sense of incompleteness implicit in their artistic arrangements. What is visible for the Japanese in an incomplete and imperfect state is only an aspect of the life process and an example of an object in a state of repose. Rather than revealing the outer world in detail, the Japanese artist focuses on the inner domain. The artist's emotions are awakened by the vast emptiness of a landscape or the excitement and dynamism of a mechanical instument, be it a train, car, or ship, that makes its way along in its individuality and collectivity.

The Bus

Like the train, the bus makes set stops, following a preestablished schedule. Unlike the car, it is a collective vehicle, transporting groups rather
than individuals. Bus riders may experience social anonymity as well as a
certain protection afforded by group situations. Because the driver of the
bus, train, and car is responsible for his passengers, he must follow a code
of ethics, a set of road rules, and conventions of all types. Unlike the driver
of the car, who feels a certain amount of empirical and psychological
autonomy, the bus driver is constrained, adhering as he must to certain
strictures.

Taeko's bus ride, which will play an important revelatory part, takes her
to Sangen Bridge. After walking through the murky streets to Ryosuké's
office and discovering that he is not there, she continues to the Nikkatsu
Hotel, where he has gone many times before. It is there that she spies the
beautiful Mrs. Iwamuro, more stunning on that night than ever before.
Taeko cannot help but be in awe of this woman, standing motionless
staring at a *red* Chinese vase. She is struck by the breathtaking magnifi-
cence of her kimono, decorated in gold patterns, which look like white silk
from the distance, in sharp contrast to the black *obi* splashed with great
red leaves wrapped around her waist. Ryosuké is there, with others. Seeing
Mrs. Iwamuro surreptitiously give Ryosuké a small glittering object—the
key to her room—Taeko feels a lacerating pain in her heart.

Mrs. Iwamuro is fire—a catalyst that sparks change. Understood symbolically, the whiteness of her kimono and the blackness of her obi, noncolors or
the sum of all colors, are instrumental in activating the beginning of a new
existence and the demise or *putrefactio* of a former relationship. Listless and
weak, "ineluctably sunk in misery," Taeko is no longer herself; she feels a
prey to outside forces. The incident in the hotel has so shocked and dis-
mayed her that she is traumatized. Sorrow dominates.

Nature mirrors her feelings: it is autumn, preluding winter and desolation; the trees in the city's garden are denuded. Now that the glow of Taeko's
passion for Ryosuké has dimmed, she reveals herself *plain:* her *persona,* or
outer covering, is removed. Yet this same autumnal day is clear and bright;
its light—will help her better discern and face her bleak situation. Her
dreams, she will eventually accept, are antithetical to reality.

A chrysanthemum coming into view at this particular time imbues
Taeko with strength. She is energized by its regularly placed and radiant
petals, symbolizing solar luminosities, and identified by many Japanese
with the resplendent Sun Goddess, Amaterasu. As a solar image, the
chrysanthemum may be looked upon as a mediator between earth and
heaven, consciousness and the unconscious, plenitude and divestiture. For

the Chinese philosopher Tcheou T'ouen-yi, the chrysanthemum is the flower that hides and flees the world, while for the Taoists it represents spontaneity and discretion, all of which are essentially Taeko's qualities.[17]

Although she loves Ryosuké, she understands that his desire for freedom, in business and personal life, revolves around his need to make something of himself and is symbolized by his quest for money. The simple but honorable life she seeks to live is unacceptable to him; nor can he fit into the image she expects of him. Their relationship has turned into a double-edged sword. The more uncertain she is of his love for her, the more possessive she becomes, until her possessiveness virtually takes on stranglehold proportions. Indeed, she is truly robbing him of his freedom and he resents it. Under such conditions, should they marry, the inner rage seething in both of them would bring out their most destructive and vitriolic characteristics.

Some time later, on a bus trip along the Japanese coast, Taeko passes stiff and dangerous cliffs, a lighthouse, and hamayu trees with their beautiful summer flowers. The sharp, menacing rocks; the beacon, an observation post which gives warning and guides those who live a tenebrous existence; the hamayu trees, manifestations of the living cosmos in that they partake of the celestial (branches), the terrestrial (trunk), and the infernal (roots)—all these may be understood as premonitory *signs*.

By the time the bus trip comes to an end, Taeko has made up her mind to break off her liaison with Ryosuké—no matter the pain. Her "first consideration was life itself and the process of living"—always a fluid and evolving operation for her. To stand still, to extract from her lover promises that he remain close to her and lead a conventional life would be counterproductive. She understands at this point that she must make this choice or else stagnation will force her and Ryosuké to live out a putrescent torment.

As she waits for Ryosuké on the beach, she sees a *shadow* move across the sand. It is Ryosuké advancing toward her. That she associates him with a shadow is, psychologically, a perfect definition of the role he plays in her life. Not only does he represent a destructive element within her unconscious, but were she to pursue this relationship, this most charming young girl would be transformed into a virago.

As Taeko and Ryosuké ride back together in the bus to the train station, where she has planned to part with him, their eyes focus first on a pine grove of Enju Beach, beyond the rice fields, and then on the famous eighth-century Dojo Temple. A fortuitous image, since the legend associated with this house of worship invites troubled lovers and happily married couples to make pilgrimages there to heal and renew love bonds. The legend, so popular with the Japanese, had become the source of a fifteenth-century No play, *Dojoji*, and was adapted in 1753 for Kabuki (*Musume Dojoji*, "The Maiden of the Dojo Temple"). The story tells of the beautiful and seductive Kiyohime, who, having fallen in love with the monk Anchin, implores him to renounce his vows of celibacy for her. Unwilling to acquiesce to her demands, the virtuous monk hides from his passionate admirer under the bell of the Dojo Temple. In a rage, Kiyohime transforms herself into a snake and coils herself around the bell. Buddha intervenes to rescue his faithful servant.[18] The other, perhaps more dramatic version of this same play ends differently: Kiyohime, in the heat of anger, causes the bell to become red and then white-hot.[19] The monk is burned to death; his bones alone remain. As for the monster, she escapes in a cloud of steam in the Hitaka River.

The evocation of the *Dojoji* legend confirms Taeko's decision as to her future course. Neither she nor Ryosuké is sufficiently mature to marry. If they were to do so, Ryosuké could not but grow increasingly resentful of her constraining ways and she would become more hostile and embittered over his gambling instinct and his amorous interludes with Mrs. Iwamuro. Like Kiyohime, Taeko realizes, she wants Ryosuké only on her terms.

What has brought Taeko sudden enlightenment (satori)? What has made her cognizant of her problem and its solution? Her religious feelings and the Buddha Essence which exist within her have erupted in flashes of insight. Psychologically, we may say that the intuitive experience has aroused memories, feelings, and sensations that live inchoate in Taeko's collective unconscious. For the Buddhist, this suprapersonal sphere corresponds to a certain extent to the idea of *alayavijnana*, or the "all-conserving consciousness."[20] Only with the flush and upsurge of these never-before-experienced energetic powers could Taeko have come to understand the meaning of real freedom. In tune with her inner world, in harmony with the empirical domain, she opens up to new dimensions— that Cosmic Consciousness that encourages her to pursue her own way.

Taeko is ready to examine her *living* feelings and to separate these from the *dead matter* encrusted in her psyche. The latter feelings, which do not pass directly into life's experience, are the fruit of conceptualizations and therefore cut off from the living roots of being. Her intuitive experience has awakened her to multiple personal and nonindividual levels within her psyche. Zen pedagogy underscores the individual's need for self-reliance in the following saying: "Do not rely on others, nor on the reading of the sutras and sastras. Be your own lamp."

Both Taeko and Ryosuké understand that the breaking up of their relationship is not an end to life but "simply one stage of a journey—a journey that would in all likelihood continue for a long time."

As the train for Tokyo roars out of the station and the winter afternoon grows dimmer, Taeko again looks out of the window at Ryosuké, who has remained behind in the train station. "There was something unmistakably military about his bearing. . . . In the failing light of the winter afternoon his face became smaller and smaller in the distance until he looked like a little dark statue." No longer only an empirical power in Taeko's life, Ryosuké remains imprinted in her psyche as a work of art, "a little dark statue," a living and continuous memento of her own creative powers—those which safeguard the destinies of families and peoples.

The Ship

The ship, like the train, follows a scheduled route. As it makes its way through water, passengers may be affected by its lilting or harsh rhythms and the fleeting and floating feelings these arouse in both body and psyche.

The words "floating world" are used by the Japanese when referring to a ship, and also as an image basic to their cosmogony, art, and literature. A "floating world" suggests feelings of impermanence, buoyancy, unsteadiness, that which is unfixed, fluctuating—the drifting nature of the life experience.

According to the Japanese creation myth, Izanagi and his sister, Izanami (the last divine couple of the seven generations of Gods), were ordered to consolidate and fertilize the moving or "floating" earth. The "floating bridge" upon which they stood enabled Izanagi to stir the waters of the sea with his celestial lance. No sooner had the waters begun to coagulate than the lance formed the island of Onokoro (meaning to "coagulate"). The two Gods then descended to the island and, together, created a column and a home, after which they engendered the islands of Japan. Izanagi started to walk around the column from the left; and Izanami, from the right. As they met, Izanami said, "What a pleasure to meet such a handsome young man!" Izanagi was angered because she had spoken first, rather than allowing him to do so since he was a man. Because of his anger, a "leech-child" was born from their primordial union. Rejected by both parents, he was placed in a raft of reeds and set adrift. More fortunate was Prince Ninigi, grandson of the Sun Goddess, Amaterasu, for he descended from the "floating bridge of heaven" in a ship, bringing with him the sword, the heavenly jewels, and the mirror, later to be identified with Japanese Imperial power.[21]

The ship may also be associated with Buddhist philosophy. Indeed, Buddha himself is called "The Great Navigator" since he is the one who helps people cross the river of life, guiding them from one bank to the other. Because of the great use made of water in purification rituals, Zen

Buddhists have been called "masters of consecrated waters." For Lao-tzu, the sixth-century B.C. philosopher and author of the *Tao Te Ching*, water was the emblem of supreme virtue, spelling wisdom. It was free and unattached, and flowed according to the lay of the land: with nature and not against it.

Literary and poetic examples of sailing ships and floating worlds abound, which arouse regret for a past that has been left behind or for feelings that exist no longer. The T'ang poet Li Shang-yin wrote of the nostalgia involved in the unfixed, migratory sensations he felt when sailing on the waters, which for him were implicit in the life principle: "In this floating world there are many meetings and partings." The seventeenth-century Japanese poet and novelist Saikaku added an erotic note to the notion of the "floating world" and its emphasis on sadness.[22]

The ship, as a reality and as a metaphor for Osaragi, is like a home, a place of pleasurable escape. Its upper decks represent spirituality and intellectuality; its lower areas, including the hold beneath the waterline, stand for the whole subliminal world of prenatal and pre-conscious existence. It is in this undifferentiated and inchoate sphere, unconcerned with rational notions of time and space, that problems may be shorn down to their essentials and examined from multiple vantage points. Like circulating air within a ship, unconscious contents in the psyche also surface from the plunge back into invisible and unknowable substrata, protected from the vagaries of the outer world by the ship's shell.

Because water has the power to *dissolve* hard matter, it may be looked upon, psychologically, as an agent capable of liquefying solid problematic conditions. It can *solve* otherwise impossible quandaries by breaking them up into their component parts, so that they may be viewed from different angles. As the ancient alchemists believed: *solve et coagula.* Ships, be they celestial or earthly, metaphoric or real, may imply humankind's victory over dangerous waters. When, concomitantly, waters are identified with the unconscious, these same oceangoing entities, sailing through fluid realms, may be said to dominate or be on top of them.

That we first encounter a ship in *The Journey* as it moves out of Ryozu Bay, with the corpulent Professor Yoshitaka Segi in his luxurious first-class cabin, and his secretary, Sutekichi Ata, suggests an unsolved and problematic emotional situation.

Professor Segi is returning from an excursion to the unspoiled island of Sado, thirty-two nautical miles west of Niigate. Interestingly enough, he refers to Basho, from the very start of his conversation with his secretary, and throughout the novel. For Professor Segi, haiku, the succinct and elliptical seventeen-syllable poetic form used by Basho, makes manifest a world that lies beyond the visible. Its intuitive images nourish his soul and psyche with fresh and ever-renewed perceptions concerning the nature of reality. Basho's haiku, conveying sudden and fleeting flashes of enlightenment, stir a whole world of wonderment in Professor Segi.

Professor Segi recites Basho's lines on shipboard. The images, rhythms, gentle pulsations, and emotions that lie embedded in the haiku universalize the overly specific, producing a broader vision of the whole.

> The sea of Spring
> Rising and falling
> All the day long.

What was fragmented, dissociated, and conflicting in Professor Segi's psyche, underscored by Basho's references to linear time ("Spring" and "day"), seems to give way to a holistic vision of life. Indeed, we might suggest that Basho's haiku enables Professor Segi to experience "the mystery of being-becoming and becoming-being."

Sado Island, from which Professor Segi and his secretary are returning, was once known as a place of exile as well as an artistic and intellectual center. The thirteenth-century Emperor Jintoku, who had rebelled against the Kamakura shogunate, was sentenced to spend twenty-two years there for his crime. Here, too, dwelled the Buddhist religious reformer Nichiren, the founder of the Jokke sect.

Perhaps Professor Segi also feels himself returning from exile. A pariah of sorts, he differs from his colleagues. As a youth, he had indulged his bent for amusement; later he worked on his own pet research projects which, for the most part, did not meet with the approval of his associates. A surprising incident which takes place during the sea journey serves to flesh out a latent or dormant aspect of his personality, which will, in time, help him find certain fulfillment.

Although the waters are far from turbulent—indeed, they are "completely still," like a "glazed mirror"—Professor Segi is surprised when the ship suddenly stops. What has happened? Moments later, he notices some divers bringing up the nearly lifeless body of an old man (Soroku Okamoto, the uncle whom Taeko had gone to visit); the professor subsequently learns that this man had attempted suicide. Because Professor Segi's stateroom is the most comfortable one on shipboard, the captain decides that once the old man returns to consciousness, he will be taken there.

When the old man is finally brought to Professor Segi's stateroom, his "painful gasps," his "vacant look," and his "deep agonized wrinkles" suggest excoriating anguish. When, a bit later, Professor Segi, with great compassion and understanding, suggests that he call a member of Okamoto's family, the old man seems utterly distraught.

Okamoto, a widower and childless now (since his only son had been killed during the war), felt no reason to go on living. He plunged into the waters to end his suffering—there to *dissolve.* That he failed in his endeavor enclothed him in even greater loneliness—in the meagerness of life.

Once Professor Segi is on land, his eyes focus on a dark canal and the one cherry tree still in bloom. As previously suggested, when preoccupied with problems, rather than having recourse to abstract discussions, the Japanese frequently use small things in nature as a reference point: a cherry tree or a flower in bloom. Although such images may seem insignificant to Westerners, they are deeply moving to Orientals, opening them up to a transcendental level.

> Some petals also lay on the somber ground. . . . And no doubt the pink petals were floating along the stagnant waters of the canal.
> "Stubborn things, these cherry blossoms!" commented the professor. "Blooming this late in the season . . . [t]hese blossoms are like elderly women who remain amorous beyond their time. Heavily rouged, you know, to disguise the encroachments of age."

Professor Segi's framed image encapsulates his hitherto repressed world of feeling. As for the utter isolation of the flowers, the only ones remaining in the entire vicinity, they mirror his covert but painful loneliness. Quivering and unsure, these images of beauty look as if they were at the end of their resources and out of touch with the present world. That Professor Segi associates the cherry blossoms with older women who remain "amorous beyond their time" reflects the grotesque nature of his own persistent sexual desires. For he, like Okamoto, is an old man. Like the lonely petals, both men have outlived their time, both are out of tune with contemporary society.

Okamoto, the more severely stricken of the two, lives in benumbing loneliness, unable to communicate his feelings to anyone. His universe has been divested of all living matter; and he is exiled from the world at large—similar to those sent to Sado Island as punishment for their crimes. Weaker and more passive on his journey back to the mainland because of his failed suicide, he feels like a leaf cast here and there by the wind. Okamoto is "a man whose spirit had slipped away, leaving only an empty husk."

Because Okamoto fails to recall his address, Professor Segi takes him into his home. He can look after his grandson, Taro, he reasons. Instinctively, he knows that the old man and the young child will get along well. They do. What Professor Segi fails to understand is why Okamoto calls Taro "Akira."

Okamoto cannot recall his past because it is unbearable to him. He has blocked it out—first, by an unsuccessful attempt at *dissolutio* through the water element, now via amnesia. When, some time later, he suddenly recovers his memory through association, he returns to his home in Kamakura. Loneliness and restlessness force him on another journey—in search of serenity—just as bereaved parents of past generations used to make pilgrimages. Okamoto deals with grief by journeying to unknown parts of the country, exposing himself to wind and rain, dragging his body to the most desolate and wretched places, hoping eventually to find "peace and a surcease" of his sorrow. Finally, he understands that loneliness has become "an essential condition of his life" and that the constant activity triggered by his *journeys* has taken on the ritualistic and powerful force of a prayer.

Okamoto decides to climb Ozawa mountain, at the entrance of the Harinoki Pass on the Shinshu side of the Japanese Alps. He knows this undertaking to be difficult and hazardous; nevertheless, he feels compelled to carry it out in order to feel nearer his son, who had accomplished it years before. But Okamoto, unlike his son at the time, is too feeble to drag his frail body to the top. He stops, exhausted, but when he rises to wash his face in the clear mountain waters, a refreshing feeling passes over him. As the songs of the early birds fill the crisp air, Okamoto feels sudden attunement to nature's tones and rhythms. Stillness sets in. Okamoto, inexplicably, hears the echo of unspoken words. His son is calling to him: "Father, Father!" An entire past surges forth, possesses, then overwhelms him. He feels himself fusing mysteriously with the mountainous slopes, as if participating in the earth's configurations.

The mountain experience, though it reinforces his sense of utter aloneness, also teaches Okamoto that he is part of the larger sphere of Cosmic Consciousness. It encourages him to turn toward others—outside of himself—for an exchange of ideas. When he again sees Professor Segi, he understands that he, too, suffers from his own brand of sorrow, which is different from Okamoto's, yet glacial in its power. Okamoto comments on his friend's continuously cheerful smile; there are multiple ways of handling sorrow, the Professor answers. Tradition wills that there are certain patterns of behavior that must be adhered to in the respectable society to which he belongs. "It doesn't matter so much when you're alone, but in the company of other people it's a good policy never to show that one feels gloomy. That's something we can learn from the old *samurai* tradition. It's a sort of courtesy toward the people we happen to be living with."

Professor Segi's reference to the *samurai* (the warrior class in premodern Japan), requires an explanation of the relationship between the doctrines of the samurai and those of Zen. The members of the warrior class (considered guardians of dignity) based their lives on loyalty, filial piety, and benevolence. Like Zen monks, they required great training in asceticism. To become a samurai involved not only physical but philosophical preparations. The ability to face death at any time was imperative, implying a willingness, even an eagerness, to sacrifice oneself for a higher cause. According to Zen doctrine, no great work has been accomplished without adherence to the notion of self-sacrifice.

Psychologically, the samurai's sense of abnegation required him to break through ordinary levels of consciousness and allow the mysterious or hidden powers existing inchoate in his collective unconscious to emerge, thereby encouraging his ego to immerse itself in the waters of transpersonal spheres, with a resulting diminution of consciousness. When the ego makes such a trajectory, latent contents within the suprapersonal sphere are tapped, then released. As these energetic factors and their corresponding emotions pour out from subliminal areas, the individual's previous outlook may be sharply altered. No longer existing in a world of diversities or of particulars, he transcends his own limiting and perhaps even stultifying views. In Zen Buddhist terms, when an individual intuits feelings of Universal Oneness, sacrifice and even death lose their fearsomeness.[23]

The samurai's spirit of personal divestiture has also made itself felt in Okamoto's psyche. No longer does he seek personal serenity; instead, he looks toward larger principles. He confesses to Professor Segi that ever since he was a boy he has longed to walk and to travel *without a particular destination.*

> Someday I'd like to undertake a real journey in the same spirit . . . Of course, it can be fun to travel with a fixed destination in mind, but even if it is fun it's a fixed kind of fun. To travel, not in order to arrive, but for the sake of the journey itself—what a delight that must be! For that is the sort of journey in which the real humanity of a human being can come into its own.

The solitary wanderings of the Buddhist priests throughout Japanese history indicate an ability on their part to surpass the world of particulars, a world which encourages acquisitiveness and possessiveness. Only when finite beings become conscious of the infinite residing within and outside of them, can they appreciate the mysteries of life—and of art.

For the Oriental, the condition of transcendence implies bathing in what has been termed the "utter darkness" of mystery. The presence of the arcane is intuited, as previously mentioned, appearing in flashes of enlightenment (*satori*). Satori breaks occur, most particularly, when one has reached the end of one's resources—as is the case of Okamoto and also of

Professor Segi. The professor's reputation as a failure in the eyes of his colleagues, and his inability to become the great innovator he once dreamed of being, have eaten away at his insides. Although he gives the impression of being at ease, joking, smiling, making light of things, and chatting away, as he does with friends and acquaintances, feelings of anguish lurk behind each word, facial expression, and gesture.

Basho has shown the way to satori, pointing out the importance of divesting oneself of the fragmentary and fixed in the journey that is life's. Although Basho's works—*The Narrow Road of Oku* and *Journey to Yoshino*—Professor Segi suggests, give the misleading impression that he knew where he was going as he walked on and on, the truth is that he "walked in order to walk. Arrival was never his objective." Basho was a committed person, but consigned to a higher principle. His entire existence was therefore without reason and destination. Not only was he "unshackled," but he lived the deepest and fullest experience of a truly free man, divested of materialistic goals and ego-driven needs.

Okamoto and Professor Segi understand that for so many people in postwar Japan, "*destination has become everything*." Goals, programs, and systems of all types have been set up in order to control and determine people's lives, whereas the opposite should be the case. Neither of the two men is blind to the necessity of earning a living, but to go through life absorbed in this single aim is to limit one's *way*. It suggest that people are born merely to "scurry about and fill" their rice bowls.

Basho's dreams, transcribed in his haiku, filled his universe, as did the barren fields in which he wandered and became absorbed and into which he effaced himself. The transient and the contingent were superseded by a state of *absolute annihilation*. Although Basho was present in the empirical world, he experienced his existence in keeping with the mystery of "being-becoming and becoming-being." For Basho, however, this paradox existed only in the empirical world; it did not take on reality in transpersonal spheres—where all existed in a state of transparency.[24]

Basho's poetic expression of his feelings of imminent death, in his farewell poem, encapsulates his outlook upon life.

> Fallen ill on a journey,
> In my dreams I run about
> Over the barren fields.

Because the world is forever "floating," Osaragi refrains from providing his readers with either a happy or a tragic conclusion to his novel. He merely suggests that Okamoto and Professor Segi will pursue their discussions; and that Taeko and Ryosuké will learn to determine their own direction, each at his or her pace, thereby experiencing a freedom concomitant with their personalities.

The world of the machine in Osaragi's novel, coupled with the traditions of Shinto and Zen Buddhism, invites protagonists and readers alike to correlate impersonal situations and images with intimate feelings. It permits the intertwining of the wisdom of the ancients with the innovations of the modern era, the intuitive with the rational, the fragmented with the transpersonal, the ego with the Self—thereby expanding reality and cosmicity.

9 R. K. Narayan's *The Man-Eater of Malgudi*—The Printing Press and a Secret Initiatory Language

The Man-Eater of Malgudi (1961), by R. K. Narayan, focuses on the printing process. The novel's protagonist owns a primitive hand press, and from it he earns his livelihood. The letters, syllables, words, sentences, paragraphs, and pages he sets down in type may also be viewed as factors in activating and actualizing a secret initiatory language. As he contemplates or meditates upon the signs or glyphs that come into view on the blank page, *libido* (psychic energy) flows inward, catalyzing his subliminal spheres. Although it is impossible to disclose and certainly to develop an epistemology of meditation, the machine's visual output does become the object of contemplation which triggers sequences of altered states of consciousness while disclosing fascinating psychological activity.

The Man-Eater of Malgudi, narrated in the first-person singular, is more than a confessional novel. What is essential for Narayan, and Hindu novelists in general, is neither the story line nor the suspense engendered by the events. Uppermost are the emotions these embody—which the writer tries to communicate to the reader through suggestion. Narayan, like his literary forebears, universalizes the feelings conveyed and in the process abstracts them, detaching emotions from their particular form and situations from their settings. He transfers each to a supramundane plane and evokes a unique experience for the reader.

Narayan's presentation infuses a condition of serenity in the reader, dissipating, as if by a feat of magic, the cumulative restlessness implicit in mundane activities. The philosophical and religious discourses which are interwoven in the happenings of *The Man-Eater of Malgudi* are at the very heart of such Hindu religious works as the *Bhagavad-Gita* and the *Mahabharata*. Indeed, events veer from circumscribed to atemporal spheres, using the metaphor of the press as a filtering mechanism. For Narayan, the printing machine is a paradigm for the cosmic process of creation and dissolution. The blank page is suddenly filled with forms and patterns, or divested of these, and represents the very life process.

Psychologically, *The Man-Eater of Malgudi* dramatizes the protagonist's attempts to deal with an evil that comes to plague him, which may also be viewed as a projection and transference of his own hitherto dormant *shadow*. As defined by C. G. Jung, the shadow is made up of those characteristics within the unconscious that the ego considers unacceptable and therefore labels negative and destructive. How the protagonist deals with such a force not only enhances the novel's fascinating occurrences and denouement, but also serves to underscore the great differences that exist between Hindu and Western psychological conditioning.

R. K. Narayan was born in Madras, South India. While attending the Christian missionary school there, he became fascinated with Hinduism, defying the school chaplain, who derided Indian religion. Narayan pursued his studies, becoming a diplomate of the Maharaja's College in Mysore.

Narayan was a Hindu who remarked that he couldn't "write a novel without Krishna, Ganesha, Hanuman, astrologers, pundits, temples and devadasis, or temple prostitutes." He attributed the literary success of his first book, *Swami and Friends* (1935), to Graham Greene's encouragement and friendship. His novel *The Guide* won the National Prize of the Indian Literary Academy in 1958. Prime Minister Nehru awarded him the Padma Bhushan honor for distinguished service in 1964. The author of numerous novels and short stories, Narayan has also published his version of the *Ramayana*, a book of "perennial philosophy;" as well as *Gods, Demons, and Others*, which deals with Indian legend.

The Man-Eater of Malgudi takes place in a fictional town, Malgudi, perhaps in the environs of Madras. The narrator, Nataraj, lives with his wife and young son in the house he inherited from his parents. His printing press, which permits him to earn his modest living, is kept in a *separate* part of the house, right under the attic. One day Nataraj decides to clear the attic of its clutter of old papers. A taxidermist, Vasu, happens along at this very time and asks if he can move into the attic temporarily. Nataraj's acquiescence nurtures the seed from which no end of problems will grow.

The Archetypal Printing Press

The printing process, as depicted in *The Man-Eater of Malgudi*, aside from being a business enterprise, takes on the stature of a religious act. While working the machine, the protagonist not only feels attuned to the spiritual powers which flow through him, but the birth of each letter or word, like an act of faith, reinforces his belief in Divinity's omnipotence, omnipresence, and omniscience.

Though the printing process insures Nataraj's livelihood by printing bill forms, visiting cards, wedding invitations, and the like, it is also an emanation or postulation of his personal sphere. As a meditative device, it summons up both the personal and collective unconscious. The former is made up of forgotten and repressed matters that arise from situations in daily life, the latter is composed of a "phylogenetic substratum" which follows the schemes, systems, and behavioral structures formed and reformed during the process of evolution.[1] The visual patterns or archetypal images (letters, syllables, words) that surface from Nataraj's collective unconscious during the printing process, usually inaccessible to awareness, he experiences as signs—mysterious glyphs. Each energy charge—a nodal point in a complex of semiotic networks—is the center of a magnetic field which confronts and aggresses against the pristine purity of the uncreated, leaving in its stead a splintered vision of a psychological inner climate: blackened forms alongside empty white spaces.

Printing, then, may be looked upon as both a rational and an irrational act. As a rational act, it is pragmatic, earthly, functional, and comprehensible. As an irrational act, with each glyph as a primary force, it links the individual to the collective, the mortal to the immortal, the temporal to the cosmic. Letters, syllables, and words become *manna*: holy forces hidden within form that guide and rule the protagonist's course in their own special and frequently indiscernible way. Vigilance, therefore, must accompany each act and each reading, for printing, a way of bringing the indeterminate into the determinate world, also has its pitfalls. If overly involved, the practitioner may be caught up in a web of illusion: *maya*, the fleeting and deceptive finite sphere. Therefore the printing process may act as a lure, a snare, an entrapment which imprisons the naive in a world of desire, multiplicity, and separateness.

Although the printing press in Narayan's novel functions within a variety of parameters, the area is always bounded by a Hindu ethic and framework. Thus even mundane activities are considered both from a personal and impersonal point of view: the former as a way of earning money, the latter as a metaphysical obligation in life (*dharma*).

That Nataraj's printing press fulfills a spiritual necessity endows it with the characteristics of an altar. Its operation at certain times becomes a sacred act. Because of its virtual sacrality, it occupies a very special area in the house. Not only is it located directly beneath the attic, thereby set apart from the living quarters, but it is further cut off from mundane activities by a blue curtain. "Between my parlour and the press hung a blue curtain. No one tried to peer through it." Indeed, no one is allowed beyond the blue curtain except for Nataraj and his helper, Sastri, so everyone imagines that Nataraj has modern equipment capable of printing the most difficult works. No other eyes are permitted to watch the process or observe the "special colour effects" used or discern the manner in which these are achieved.

To open up a sanctuary—such as the space in which Nataraj's printing machine is located—to the general public is to corrupt its essential sacrality and invade the privacy needed to come to terms with disturbing philosophical and psychological factors. Nataraj's private and remote world—the cavelike area closed to the sun and to the world at large where he does his printing—may be looked upon psychologically as a gigantic receptacle for energy or a spiritual center: a microcosm of the macrocosm. That his cavernlike space is right beneath the roof rather than beneath the ground or close to it, the usual locus for such retreats, indicates other factors to be subsumed, directly related to the architectural metaphor. Upper floors of a building are identified with the head and stand for wisdom, mind, thought, and consciousness; lower floors, or basements correspond to unconscious or instinctual spheres. The enclosed sacred space, or *temenos* that contains Nataraj's press, then, is devoted to intellectual and spiritual spheres conducive to the smooth functioning of the printing machine. However, it is also endowed with the energy necessary to create and to destroy: an avatar of Shiva's *lingam*. The blue curtain which seals off the sacred space to everyone except Nataraj and Sastri sets the demarcation line.

That the color blue was chosen for the curtain, veiling the inner from the outer sphere, increases the arcane nature of the enclosure and the machine it holds. The curtain's hue, the most immaterial of colors and identified with aerial spheres, invites those working within its reflected tones to become absorbed in the infinite, thereby liberating them from worldly ties.

As a holy force, the printing press, set apart from the profane world, at times takes on the characteristics of a *hierophany:* a sacred power existing and becoming manifest within an object. It invites Nataraj to experience altered states of consciousness, and deeper levels of being. A new world radiates before him: one of dazzling beauty, as if self-generating in its perpetual transformations. As letters, syllables, and words emanate into the phenomenal world (*prakrit*), they arouse strong emotional reactions in Nataraj. Such psychic activity occurs particularly when he prints religious texts. At such times, a sense of the divine takes on such overwhelming force that the ego (the center of consciousness) may become alienated, triggering libido, which in turn motivates the psyche in positive or negative ways.[2]

Nataraj's personality, it must be observed, is basically harmonious and balanced. He accepts only certain printing jobs—those he enjoys fulfilling or feels equipped to complete. The others, for one reason or another, he gives to his neighbor, the Star Press. Its owner has an original Heidelberg printer with a double cylinder, and a whole staff to man the complicated machine. Nataraj is not driven by an ambition for success or financial gain. To earn enough money to support his wife and son and to print the sacred text of his poet friend, who is writing the life of the Lord Krishna in monosyllabic verse, gives him sufficient satisfaction.[3]

Printing as a Meditative Device

Meditation, a philosophical discipline that requires periods of introversion, is also a psychological mechanism. It allows the conscious mind to burrow within and, in so doing, to imbue itself with its own personal and mythological substratum: the collective unconscious made up of what Jung calls "mnemic deposits"[4] which are the common sharing of humanity. During these periods of meditation/introversion, Nataraj's powers of concentration leave his mind undisturbed, unbound, liberated from the torment of existence, from the transient world of contingencies.

Letters, syllables, and words are *signs* for Nataraj: meditative devices. These points of reference (concrete forms or symptoms of an invisible inner reality) are brought first into Nataraj's visual field, and then into his mind's eye. In Hindu tradition, such glyphs are inert, as is all nature, until Shiva wills them into activity. Printing, then, is both a latent and an overt visual expression of Divinity. The letters emerging into view also have tonal value, the universe being "sonorous" as well as "chromatic." Whatever form nature adopts, be it visual (*mandala* or *yantra*), or a tonality (*mantra*), an occult correspondence exists betweeen the world of signs and the subtle organs of the human body and the cosmos as a whole.[5]

Each time a sign is awakened within an individual, the forces associated with it trigger various levels of being, as if every cell in the brain had been catalyzed and tuned into experiencing a sphere beyond the rational. Like the blind person who compensates for his handicap by developing his tactile, auditory, and olfactory senses, the meditator compensates for not being able to reach his subliminal sphere directly: Nataraj contemplates all the more sensitively the letters, syllables, and words before him in order to detect more accurately the subliminal reverberations they arouse. In so doing, he finds himself able to turn off all extraneous thoughts and sensations.[6]

When Nataraj meditates on a glyph, therefore, be it imagistic or tonal, he is slowly drawn into a trancelike state. He absorbs and is absorbed into a variety of planes of existence as is a yogi. The deeper his sense of continuity with the macrocosm, the more he will be able to divest himself "of that mental static" which impedes awareness and of that insurgence and confluence of images and thoughts which the mind ejaculates when under conscious control.[7] When such bombardment diminishes in intensity, primordial spheres seem to reawaken, ushering in a sense of *completeness*. While Nataraj, psychologically, opens up to the infinite suprapersonal sphere within himself, he is better able to revalorize his secular experience when coping with problems in the mundane world.

That Nataraj needs an inner sanctum within which to place his holy press suggests his deeply religious nature. Daily, before four o'clock in the morning, he sets out for the river to perform his ablutions. Attuned to the universe around him, Nataraj lives his life in keeping with the essential truths of Hinduism. He experiences the magical powers inherent in prayers, be they from the *Upanishads* or the Vedic hymns, as regenerative forces that allow him to regress to the very source of life—to past incarnations. Prayer, like the informal solvent, water, invites him to disintegrate, so to speak, to an embryonic state, to feel that dazzling sense of liberation as he penetrates the very heart of mystery. In the *Rig-Veda* we read: "Waters, you are the ones who bring us the life force. Help us to find nourishment so that we may look upon great joy. Let us go straight to the house of the one for whom your waters give us life and give us birth."[8]

On certain days, it is Sastri who sits at the type-board and the treadle, not only working for Nataraj, but guiding his course.[9] What he is *imprinting* or making manifest via recurring letters (to be understood as underlying energetic primordial forms) may be regarded in the psychological sphere as "forces" and "tendencies" that reveal patterns of behavior in the empirical world.[10]

That Sastri, a male figure, is Nataraj's psychopomp is not surprising, since the Indian Trinity is preeminently masculine: Vishnu, Shiva, and Brahma.[11] As a positive father image for Nataraj, he teaches him how to channel energy and transform the *prima materia* from an invisible to a visible world of spiritual spheres. When using the treadle, the swiveling or lever device pressed by the foot to drive the printing machine, he also keeps contact with earth through the network of rhythms resulting from the constant foot motion.

When Nataraj takes over the printer's work, he fixes his gaze on the letters before him, which then become the center of his attention, excluding all else from his field of vision. When he presses the pedal, his footwork seems to be at one with his own and the universe's pulse beat. His body and soul flow in tune with cosmic rhythms and their subtle variations. The energy generated by the mental and physical activity is heat-producing; it is Nataraj's way of calling upon Agni, the Vedic God of fire and divine mediator between temporal and atemporal spheres.

Fire may be looked upon, psychologically, as an emanation of libido in that it arouses a whole emotional system; the same is true of language. To think in words is an instrument of culture, resulting from the long development of subjective mentation. It is also a reflection of religious consciousness, the Word having been accorded supreme position in mythical cosmogonies. In Egypt, for example, the primary force, "the heart and the tongue," was attributed to the Creation God Ptah; consider also the Ten Commandments, in Exodus (20), and in John the phrase "In the beginning was the Word" (1:1).

The addition of colors to the printing labors—"pale orange" and "a sort of violet"—increases Nataraj's absorption in the entire process. Minutes later, he feels himself hypnotized "by the sound of the wheel and the dozen kinks that were set in motion by the pressure I put on the pedals." Pale orange, a kind of saffron color, may be looked upon as a compromise between red and yellow or celestial gold. It is the most actinic of hues; it exercises chemical action on certain substances. In view of these associations, we may suggest, psychologically, that orange symbolizes the fire of energy which stands midway between spirit and libido. As such, it is a catalytic force. In that violet, a color midway between red and blue, is imposed upon the orange, the power of reflection is invited to come forth.

Colors, words, and rhythms, like the geometric designs in *yantras* and *mandalas* and the auditory tones and rhythms of *mantra*, transform sense experience by channeling the powers inherent in the energy centers created during the meditative process. So, too, does the sound and rhythm of the wheel. Like the Tantric *chakras*, the wheel creates a circle of warmth or fire around Nataraj which sweeps him *out of himself*. As the irrational sphere takes over progressively, ego-consciousness diminishes in intensity, and the worlds of differentiation and bodily functions merge with and interpenetrate each other.

Although Nataraj uses the word "hypnosis" to describe his condition, a "trance" state associated with a religious experience seems more appropriate here. As his ego is momentarily eclipsed by the Self, it paves the way for a union of opposites. Envisaged as the total psyche, the Self is considered, psychologically, as God.

During Nataraj's trance state, then, the mental and emotional tensions or obstructions to which he had been prey fall by the wayside as he experiences images, rhythms, and tones—subtler vibratory sound patterns—through the letters, colors, and rhythms in higher frequencies. A realigning of the energy flow through his body and psyche invites a reattunement within himself as well as within the environment. So open does he become to cosmic consciousness that what the mystic terms "silent sound" is perceptible to him.

Nor is it surprising, then, that immediately following Nataraj's trance episode he should become more vulnerable to happenings in the empirical world. When someone intrudes into his secret room where his holy printer is located, he regards the act as a violation of his inner sanctum.

The Violation of the Inner Sanctum

When the poet who is writing a life of Lord Krishna in monosyllables lifts the edge of the blue curtain leading to Nataraj's arcane sphere, the printer does not feel disturbed, for the poet is one of the elect or elite. He understands the religious role the machine plays in Nataraj's life. When, however, Vasu, a six-foot-tall man with "thick eyebrows, a large forehead and a shock of unkempt hair like a black halo," intrudes by "tearing aside the curtain," Nataraj looks upon it as an act that violates the "sacred traditions" of his press.

Such an infraction is a sacrilegious act or a rejection of those forces dedicated to the service of Deity. To discount what is venerated by others is to look down upon what is holy and thereby promote what is secular and mundane. Vasu, then, is an *aggressive* power or an eruptive force that progressively impinges and encroaches upon Nataraj's way of life.

Vasu, the "intruder," is a taxidermist. He learned the art of stuffing animals from a master who could make lions and tigers look more terrifying dead than they did when roaming the jungle. He is proud of his profession and tells Nataraj: "After all, we are civilized human beings, educated and cultured, and it is up to us to prove our superiority to nature. Science conquers nature in a new way each day; why not in creation also."

From the very outset, we learn that Vasu's philosophical and psychological attitudes toward life are antithetical to Nataraj's. Vasu knows only one way of dealing with people and animals: dominating the former and killing the later. His training as a strong man, prior to his study of taxidermy, had developed these characteristics. He tells Nataraj that he can snap steel chains, hit a block of hard granite with his fist and pulverize it. Years before, when Vasu's master had decided to get rid of him, the younger man was in such a rage that he killed him by hitting him with the edge of his palm in a chopping movement. Nataraj is shocked when Vasu tells him that he walked away from the dead man. "I helped him," Vasu remarked, "by leaving him there, instead of holding him upside down and rattling the teeth out of his head."

Philosophically and psychologically, Vasu represents Evil for Nataraj. How the printer will deal with this force remains to be seen. A relatively passive person, he will have to firm up his ways if he intends to cope with this titanic power that imposes itself on his life and household. The question remains as to whether Nataraj will be able to transform his passive ways sufficiently to rid himself and the community of this progressively dangerous enemy.

Difficulties begin the moment Vasu informs Nataraj that he intends to move into his attic. Although annoyed at the thought of having a stranger in his own home, Nataraj, in keeping with his imperturbable ways, says nothing, preferring to resign himself to the intruder's presence rather than to alter his unassertive course. Nearly immediately after moving in, Vasu begins bullying everyone in sight; he even usurps the chair reserved for the poet in Nataraj's parlor. This would be important enough to warrant a call to arms for a Westerner, but is met with submissiveness by the printer and his friend. Nataraj does call Vasu a veritable *man-eater* who "sniveled and purred, and tried to be agreeable only in the presence of an official."

During the days and weeks that follow, every time Nataraj attempts to confront Vasu, the strength necessary to perpetrate such an overt act fails him. Nataraj backs away, withdraws into his cavernlike space behind the blue curtain. There, in peace, he works his machine, producing letters, syllables, and words. The rhythmic patterns that the archetypal images arouse in his unconscious as they emerge into view lull him into another dimension: the collective unconscious. In this immense reservoir of latencies exists a preprogrammed "phylogenetic substratum" to which Nataraj has direct access. When the mental residues of previous existences are actualized, they can again emerge into consciousness during periods of meditation.[12]

Vasu's presence indicates that Nataraj is being put to the test: he has to learn to transcend the dichotomies that plague him. His meditation is unlike that of the Buddhists, which releases a person from the bondage of existence with all its spiritual and physical desires. His interiorization resembles in part the happenings depicted in the *Katha Upanishad*: the intellect, which understands the situation, controls the mind, which in turn dominates the senses. But even when Nataraj is experiencing such a state of superconsciousness through the printing process, knowledge and a guiding principle may activate the pulsions in Nataraj's collective unconscious, accounting for an increase in his malaise. However, once these are sorted, a greater harmony may be forthcoming. He simply has to endure turmoil until such time as a sense of order and justice inhabits his being.

That Vasu brings an enormous dead tiger into his attic room is troubling to Nataraj, but when the stench of the decaying animal permeates his workroom after a few days, it becomes unbearable. The odor, however, is not really the culprit. What it stands for torments Nataraj deeply: it is a constant reminder that death stalks his house; that a human being is taking life into his own hands.

The tiger is particularly important in Hindu iconography. Its skin represents Shiva's trophy; the animal itself is Shakti's mount, nature's energy. Because of the tiger's power and ferocity, it is looked upon as a warrior: an active principle in nature. Since energy may be used for both positive and negative purposes, Vasu, Nataraj believes, has appropriated for himself the tiger's killer instinct: he is a *man-eater*. Vasu's physical strength and his highly developed intelligence serve destructive ends. Intent on personal aggrandizement and power, he is at the mercy of his own hubris: he vies, perhaps unconsciously, with Divinity in his desire to create, to destroy, and to restore. That a human being appropriates such powers unto himself is untenable to Nataraj.

When, some days later, Nataraj sees a stuffed crow, a golden eagle, and a cat on Vasu's workbench, he is dumbfounded. Why has he shot these animals? Nataraj questions. His sensate world, so attuned to every aspect of nature, enables him to actually hear the cat's soft "mew" and to see the crow and eagle fly high in infinite aerial spheres.

But "rivaling" or "dominating" nature is not Nataraj's way; he wishes to work in harmony with this sacred force. To do away with an animal, like the crow or the eagle, is to destroy a positive power—a divinity—like the "sacred *Garuda*," Vishnu's mount.

Nataraj is mortified by the turn of events. His press has been converted into a "charnel house," he confesses. Everything about Vasu infers killing—a repugnant act for Nataraj, since from early childhood he has been taught never to hurt anything in God's created world. Even swatting flies has been ruled out. Like the Jains, Nataraj believes in the doctrine of nonviolence; in study; in the preservation of important ancient texts whose wisdom in so many fields, be it mathematics, astronomy, philosophy, or science, can always be imparted to human beings the world over. Mahatma Gandhi, whose ways Nataraj and his friends admire and follow, was born in Porbandar, a part of India where Jainism was widespread. The sage admitted many a time that the Jains' philosophy had made a profound impression upon him.

The world is a living entity, the Jains believe. Every stone has a soul, as does every drop of rain, every breath of wind, every lump of clay. Acts of violence against animate or inanimate entities are looked upon as inviting an influx of heavy and deleterious *karma:* unhappy rebirths.[13] Liberation from worldly existence will therefore not be forthcoming: "If a man kills living things, or slays by the hand of another, or consents to another slaying, his sin goes on increasing."[14]

Such will be Vasu's fate, Nataraj thinks. Every time this man returns to his attic, he becomes more and more of a *killer* in Nataraj's view. "I would see some bloody object, small or big, brought in, if I cared to peep out. But nowadays, as far as possible, I tried to shut my *eyes.*" That Nataraj shuts his eyes does not disculpate him; on the contrary, such an act increases his complicity.

The eye, the organ of sensible perception, represents illumination by spiritual light. In both the *Bhagavad-Gita* and the *Upanishads*, Shiva's two physical eyes correspond to the sun and moon, while his third frontal eye (located on his forehead) is identified with fire. Everything that comes within its orbit may, if he wills it so, be reduced to cinders; thus he is capable of destroying the world of manifestation. That Nataraj closes his eyes indicates his inability at this juncture to deal with the problem at hand, to try to actively eradicate or diffuse its troubling effects. Not only does Nataraj close his eyes to the problem, but he mounts a physical barrier: he puts up a steel mesh beyond the blue curtain so as to prevent anyone from passing into his inner sanctum.

One afternoon, while working his treadle and printing his forms in his private quarters, he comes to a great decision: he will ask Vasu to leave the premises. Whether he will have the moral fiber to carry out his plan remains to be seen. When the chance to act on his decision occurs a few days later, after Vasu verbally accosts him, Nataraj remains silent. Had not Mahatma Gandhi said, Nataraj thinks back, that "aggressive words only generate more aggressive words" and that nonviolence includes both thought and speech, and not only deeds.

Overt or Passive Resistance in the Struggle Against Evil

Nataraj *knows* he has to deal with the problem of Evil and cannot withdraw from or reject overt confrontation. Conflicting needs and ideations intensify his problems. As a follower of Gandhi and his nonviolent attitude, he is devoted to passive resistance. By the same token, he is also drawn to the teachings of the *Bhagavad-Gita.* When Lord Krishna enlightened Prince Arjuna, he advised him as to his duties and obligations (*dharma*): he had to take up arms to help his brothers fight the enemy. Not to take action when necessary is to wallow in selfishness and egocentricity. Whenever worldly righteousness declines, Krishna's mysterious power (*maya*) allows him to create a form for himself (out of *prakriti*, thus making himself manifest and able to guide the person in need. "For the preservation of the righteous, the destruction of the wicked, /And the establishment of *dharma*, I come into being from age to age."[15] One must act, Lord Krishna continues, but never be motivated by the fruits one hopes to gain: "You have a right to action alone, never to its fruits"[16]

Although Nataraj understands that he must protect both his family and the community from the encroachment of Evil, and he understands the profound lessons taught in the *Bhagavad-Gita* and in Jainism, his course is still conflictual. In keeping with the teachings of Krishna, he must act overtly, yet he cannot. Unlike the Jains he tries to emulate (they feel no anger and strive always for complete calmness and patience), Nataraj experiences intense contention. The times of inner serenity during his periods of withdrawal behind the blue curtain are no longer his. Nor is his life rooted in fellowship, sympathy, and love for all beings.

The Jain *Quatrains*, which also appeal to Hindus, incorporate the doctrine of nonviolence and Krishna's teachings to Arjuna in the *Bhagavad-Gita*.

> When men rise up in enmity and wish to fight
> It is not cowardice, say the wise, to refuse the challenge.
> Even when your enemies do the utmost evil,
> It is right to do no evil in return.[17]

Nataraj's philosophical and psychological dilemma can therefore be solved to a great extent if he demonstrates the stamina and strength to act overtly. He must speak out to his enemy. His inability to do so thus far stems from his home life during his formative years. Nataraj tells his readers that even as a child, he worried about offending others and arousing enmity in friends or even strangers. The highly sensitive and intuitive lad had, interestingly enough, always made it his obligation to dissipate bad feelings by seeking out and speaking directly to the persons who might, for one reason or another, feel hate or hostility toward him. "I felt acutely uneasy as long as our enmity lasted," he thought. It "bothered me like a toothache."

Nataraj even hesitates to take action in an analogous but less dangerous situation, when Sastri informs him that a hyena—already dead—is lying at the foot of the stairs. Nataraj's immediate desire to confront the intruder is stifled by second thoughts. Is it prudent to act overtly? he wonders.

That a hyena has been shot is significant to our story. A nocturnal carrion animal, known for its voracity, it has powerful jaws which are capable of crushing the hardest of bones. Because of the hyena's extraordinary faculties for assimilation, it is associated with purely terrestrial and mortal domains. Its powers and knowledge focus solely on functional, material, and gross matter. The hyena could be looked upon as Vasu's animal avatar: his fetish. Like the hyena's, Vasu's tremendous strength (as well as his intelligence, scientific acumen, business sense, and other qualities) has been misdirected to destructive and cruel ends. The same may be said of his human relationships: kindness, a sense of fair play, and compassion are nowhere to be found in his makeup. Just as hyenas are dangerous, particularly when hungry, so, too, is Vasu when intent upon achieving a goal. Both must be approached in a very special way.

Sastri, whom Nataraj alludes to frequently as the "Sanskrit semischolar," calls Vasu a *rakshasa:* a demon, according to Hindu belief. Most appropriately, he quotes a verse suggesting ways of dealing with such powers: "one must possess the marksmanship of a hunter, the wit of a pundit, and the guile of a harlot."

Rakshasas, malignant beings, are capable of transmuting themselves into all types of horrendous shapes; of disturbing religious rites; and of acting in a hostile and abhorrent manner. In the *Ramayana*, the hero Rama, his brother, friends, and the Garuda bird attack and annihilate the *rakshasas*—but only temporarily. Unlike Westerners, who believe Evil can be annihilated permanently, the Hindu understands that such a negative force is implicit in the life experience and can only be shunted aside for short periods of time.

The Hindu looks upon the *rakshasas* as the prototype of negative powers, eternal opponents of what is generally considered righteousness. When such powers, in the psychology of individuals—and collectively, in nations and cultures—are rejected and repressed rather than brought out into the open, aerated, and integrated into the personality or the community at large, results may be dire. If the shadow is repressed (as in a hermetically sealed jar), it tends to gather more and more libido unto itself. Such concentration of psychic energy in an individual or group may under certain circumstances explode with violence.

Vasu, the *rakshasa*, is Nataraj's enemy. A shadow figure, psychologically, he lives forcefully within him as the "dark side" of his personality. Understandably, the locked-in or repressed libido implicit in the shadow archetype grows more and more powerful, disturbing the individual's sense of well-being. That Nataraj can no longer work in peace in his inner sanctum indicates the strength of the seething, pulsating forces sealed within him: it is as if he were sitting on a keg of dynamite.

Nataraj's first step in breaking away from his negative shadow's domination is to transfer the very qualities which he despises and are his, unconsciously, onto an outerworldly creature. Such a shift or relocation enables him to live his own life as best he can while also seeing it in projection in another: Vasu. Once the shadow is projected outside of himself, he can pinpoint the problems with which he has to deal in his own way. Let us recall that in the *Ramayana*, one of the *rakshasas* took the form of a ten-headed and twenty-armed Ravana, whose physical powers, although enormous, were finally vanquished.

Until now, Nataraj has not acted overtly, even though Vasu's tyrannical ways have made his life unpleasant. When he learns that Vasu is entertaining all sorts of women of ill repute in his attic room—"He had turned his tracking instincts in another direction"—fuel is added to the fire. One woman in particular visits Vasu more frequently than the others: Rangi, a dancer attached to the nearby temple of Lord Krishna.

Let us recall that temple dances for the Hindu are religious in nature. Shiva, it is believed, danced the world into existence by uniting space and time within evolution. As the incarnation of eternal energy, dance incorporates the timely and the timeless, the mortal and the immortal, the rational and the irrational, the individual and the collective. Since dance is pantomimic and conveys a metamorphosis, usually changing a dancer into a God, or a demon into something else, it is cosmogonic in nature. Hindu dance, whatever its function, uses a complex system of mobile hieroglyphics to disclose its spiritual message: eyes, brows, chin, forehead, cheeks, lips, legs, fingers, hands, arms—each is endowed with its own finite and infinite movement, expression and meaning. Because temple dancing combines faith, thought, emotion, and sensation, as well as imaginative qualities, body and mind must become a single harmonious unit.

Because of the discipline and study required to perform before a God, not everyone is capable of becoming a temple dancer. Rangi, although a prostitute, is someone very special. Her spiritual devotion to Divinity (since she is attached to a temple of Krishna) is complete. There are precedents in Hindu belief for the paradoxical alliance of immorality and religion. In the *Rig-Veda* we are told that Usa, the Goddess of dawn, was a gorgeous dancing girl who donned bright ornaments and uncovered her breasts while performing her pantomimic ovations to her Lord.[18] Prostitutes whose lives are dedicated to Divinity are not necessarily looked upon with disfavor in the male-oriented Hindu society. In fact, many temple prostitutes are kept women, their holiness enhancing their allurement; others, perhaps overly promiscuous, may be endowed with negative attributes.

That Rangi has devoted her services to Krishna (an incarnation of Vishnu, the merciful aspect of God) is significant in Narayan's tale. Lord Krishna, looked upon as the inspiration for poets, dancers, feasters, and celebrants, is also identified with love. When dancing with his beloved Radha and the *Gopis* (divine cowherds and milkmaids) under the autumnal full moon against a background of flower-filled bowers and blossoming trees, he lives a great passion. The *Gopis* represent the countless souls in search of the divine or universal soul symbolized by Krishna. In that Divinity manifests himself in all beings and in the whole universe, the singers and dancers participating in the celebration experience themselves transcending their mortal state (their ego consciousness) and merging with the cosmos (the Self). Released from the sensate world, they come to know a world of inner bliss.

The love motif represented by Krishna and Radha's marriage not only symbolizes a play of emotions, but a philosophic concept: the need for relatedness, for the coming together of disparities in life and within the psyche. The flowing together of informal fluid relationships paves the way for a richer *feeling experience.* Although dancers such as Rangi and individuals such as Nataraj's poet friend know that the celebrants identify with the infinite during the creative process, they are also aware of the momentary nature of such fusion of disparate sensations. Nevertheless, the very experience of true reality, as opposed to human ignorance, which is the lot of those identified with the transient world of illusion, serves to ennoble individuals and alter and expand their understanding of their place within the cosmos. As for the moon rays which flow forth during the dance period, they represent growing enlightenment emerging from a world of darkness—not the brash luminosities of the sun, identified with the rational sphere, but rather the dimmer, more subtle illuminations associated with the unconscious.

The Word Is Holy

Understandably, the poet who has completed the *Radha Kalyan*, Krishna's marriage ceremony in monosyllabic verse, feels "exalted." His "crystal clear" stanzas are not only a feat of the imagination and discipline, but examples of an evolving personal prosody. He has achieved originality by "ruthlessly carving up a polysyllable." Once this was accomplished, "the most familiar term took on the mysterious quality of a private code."

To print such a sacred work entails both emotional and spiritual difficulties. Everything has to be just perfect: worthy of Deity. After its completion, a celebration, according to Hindu tradition, is required: "When a poet has arrived at the stage of the marriage of a god, it would be auspicious to celebrate the occasion." Nataraj has to gather funds for the great festivities, and he takes his task to heart as he does everything else in life.

Because Nataraj is printing a sacred work endowed with its own "private code" and "mysterious quality," he takes additional steps to insure the privacy and purity of his inner sanctum. A thickly woven bamboo mat is hung to screen off the room from the outside world. Interestingly enough, he leaves a pinhole in the bamboo grill to peek through.

Vasu alone does not respect the sanctity of the new curtain any more than he had the blue one. He "pierced its privacy." Nor does Nataraj reprimand him for his intrusion, wanting nothing at this juncture to interfere with his main consideration: the printing of Krishna's life. The act of transforming the sublime deeds of Divinity into glyphs, verbal pictures, and thoughts absorbs him completely.

The evocative powers of the archetypal images implicit in the monosyllabic work, and their related rhythmic resonances made manifest during the printing process, usher in a tapestry of complex undercurrents. These seem in turn to weave strange melodic and magnetic sonorities and patterned undulations into Nataraj's very spirit and psyche.

That *monosyllables* have been chosen to depict Krishna's life is particularly significant for the Hindu. The monosyllabic *OM*, an all-containing sound and an object of contemplation, has been compared to a "carrier wave" throughout the universe. Human ears experience its modulations in frequencies or amplitudes as sounds which anchor meditators while they perform their spiritual disciplines.[19]

The iconographic description of the syllable OM may also be identified with Brahma, the Supreme Being, the God of Gods, as One and implicit in the Trinity of Brahma, Vishnu, and Shiva. Its letters are endowed with mystical colors, tones, and pulsations. OM is also homologized with four states of consciousness, the deepest being "undifferentiated cognition" or the "invisible, ineffable, intangible, indefinable, inconceivable, which is beyond diversity, the Self." Such unity, however, or reintegration into the *Whole*, can be realized by the practitioner of spiritual disciplines only—if ever—before creation or after time.[20]

The printing process, such as Nataraj experiences it, may be understood, therefore, as a *transformation ritual*. The letters come into view progressively, destroying the preceding empty or blank spaces and silent sounds. Such an act, though cruel and conflictual, invites Nataraj to gain access to transpersonal and undifferentiated spheres. In so doing, however, he is uprooted—through form—from his previous condition; he is constantly torn away from one state as he makes his way to the next. Words function as mediating devices. Given specific characteristics and meanings, they link Nataraj to both personal and collective spheres, temporal and atemporal domains, depending upon the manner in which they are approached. As Nataraj prints a sacred work, concentrating on a word or non-word, language takes on the power of a secret initiatory ritual, transcending its usual empirical purpose of communicating with others in the mundane world.

That a link exists between linguistic and religious consciousness dates back to Vedic times (1500–1200 B.C.). For the people who lived in those times—Aryans who invaded India from the northwest—words were holy, as was everything in nature. Magical power was believed to be embedded in the sacrificial prayers chanted by the established priesthood. When these took on the power of spells (termed *brahman*), the person reciting them was alluded to as a "pray-er" (a *brahman*). This accounts for the origin of the name for the priestly caste (Brahman). With the writing of the *Upanishads* (600 B.C.), "wind" or "air" (Vayu), referring to human "breath," added a cosmological and spiritual power to prayer. Vedic poets divinized such forces in their invocations and a Lord of Prayer (Brahmanaspati), derived in part from Vach, the Goddess of speech or holy word, came into being.[21] In the *Rig-Veda* we read about mystical speech associated with Vach: "I am the queen, the confluence of riches, the skillful one who is first among those worthy of sacrifice. The gods divided me up into various parts, for I dwell in many places and enter into many forms."[22]

Understandably, as Nataraj prints the poet's monosyllabic work on Krishna, he is imbued semiotically, aurally, and rhythmically with the power of the Holy Word. He feels exalted by the *manna* embedded in the letters and syllables that the printing machine brings forth. He senses their minutest alterations in meter and amplitude. Their potencies and rhythms affect his inner ear, strengthening or weakening his mode of feeling and thinking—his very approach to the fullness of life.

The Lysis: Krishna, Radha, Ganesha

When Rangi informs Nataraj in great secret that Vasu is going to shoot the sacred elephant, Kumar, on the day of the great celebration, he is dumbfounded. It has all been planned: Vasu is going to hire someone to make the elephant mad just as he passes in front of his window; at that point, he will shoot Kumar, thus earning the gratitude of the crowd that might otherwise be trampled by the animal. Vasu will sell the elephant's various parts, particularly its tusks, which will bring a high price.

For the Hindu, elephants are manifestations of the sacred elephant-faced God, Ganesha, the son of Shiva and Parvati. The God of wisdom and prudence, he is also looked upon as the legendary scribe of Vasya's epic, the *Mahabharata*. It is customary for anyone beginning an important work, such as sacred writing, to venerate Ganesha. It must also be noted that Ganesha is one of the most popular Hindu deities. Children love to watch elephants parade about, bathe, or ask for sugar cane and other goodies.

What to do? If Nataraj informs the police of Vasu's plan, they will demand proof. Nataraj has to act rapidly because the decorations for the celebration are already being gathered. The day of the celebration arrives and Nataraj has still not acted. Kumar, chained to a peg at the end of the temple corridor, is scrubbed and clean. On his back he wears a seat for a mahout; his forehead has been painted in white, red, and green floral patterns; his ivory tusks, decorated with bronze bands and rings, gleam in the sun. Nataraj marvels at the animal's joy, at the fuss made by the children gathered around him. What a "happy animal," Nataraj thinks, his heart sinking at the possibility of its demise.

The priest begins making his offerings at the feet of Lord Krishna, "draped in silk and gold lace, and he held a flute in his hand; and his little bride [Radha], a golden image draped in blue silk and sparkling with diamonds, was at his side, the shy bride." Rangi, who has begun her undulations before the God—arms, torso, and feet swaying and gesticulating in traditional rhythms—is bedecked in glittering tinsel ornaments.

Relaxed, Nataraj's mind is free to drift where it will—into suprapersonal spheres where myths are born. Almost immediately a myth does emerge into consciousness: the tale of the elephant, Gajendra, whose foot, after stepping into a lake, was caught in the jaws of a crocodile. The elephant's struggle and trumpeting was to no avail. In desperation, he called upon Vishnu, "who immediately appeared and gave him the strength to come ashore out of the jaws of the crocodile." The synchronistic summoning into consciousness of this myth enlightens Nataraj's heart.

Psychologically, we might say that Nataraj's ego has begun to indwell. Relaxed and off-guard as it is, it penetrates the irrational sphere—the timeless and spaceless collective unconscious. The inner tensions plaguing him are constellated in the form of a particular myth that will—if perceived and intuited correctly—liberate him from his limited ego-dominated world. That an archetypal story like the one recounting Gajendra's ordeal should have emerged into consciousness above the myriad myths existing inchoate within his psyche suggest the dynamic intensity of the problem plaguing him at this juncture—making the advent of a synchronistic happening possible.

A *synchronistic* (acausal) experience may be looked upon as a creative act—an event which constellates the unknown and the unpredictable. We may suggest when an individual cannot seem to cope with a situation, the archetype that might help the person resolve the quandary may be constellated in the unconscious. If properly understood by the conscious mind, the "mobilization of unusual superhuman 'capacities of the psyche' " may be put to good use.[23]

Nataraj's profound faith in the Gods (or Self) has triggered the energy necessary to arouse the archetypal myth that will indicate *the right course to take*—given the personalities involved. When the myth erupts into consciousness and libido gushes from his subliminal to his conscious sphere, Nataraj lets out a "terrific cry" as he sounds out his prayer: "Oh, Vishnu! Save our elephant, and save all the innocent men and women who are going to pull the chariot. You must come to our rescue now." So powerful is the cry that it stuns the crowd into silence. No one budges—not even Rangi.

Understandably, once the episode is over, Nataraj feels faint. Choking sensations overwhelm him. When reaching down to his archaic depths, as he had done when extricating his prayer to Vishnu, the energy which poured out of him broke through layers and layers of matter which had settled in on him from years of disuse or inaction. No longer ego-bound, Nataraj had entered the sanctuary of the undifferentiated sphere, where creation and dissolution cohabit and inner and outer states are integrated. Only then did he feel his wholeness, his Self—Divinity.

What had been fragmented and disruptive within his psyche had erupted with the force of a thunderbolt, like an immense flow of lava. By the same token, he had destroyed the fabric of the life he had been living and shed the web of illusion which had veiled his inner vision. The psyche's own dynamic and magnetic forces, which had united what was chaotic and turbulent, had in the process successively stripped away the sheaths of diverse densities and vibratory rates which had imprisoned him until now in his false conceptions and perceptions.

When returning to consciousness from the vantage point of an infinitely expanding world, Nataraj notes expressions of concern on the faces of his friends. After carrying him to the veranda, they began fanning his face, and a doctor gives him an injection to soothe his nerves. Oddly enough, though Nataraj's strength has left him, he feels in such command of the situation that he expresses his fears for Kumar's life to the chairman of the Municipal Council. No longer is he fearful of approaching the highest of dignitaries if it means saving Kumar's life. Since concern for Nataraj's well-being is important to those in charge, as well as to his friends, they decide he should be taken home to rest, after which they will investigate the situation.

Although Nataraj resents being treated like a baby, he yields to his wife's wish that he rest. Soon an onrush of unconscious material flooding his psyche suspends his outward orientation; he falls into a deep sleep and feels himself descending once again to the deepest layers of the psyche. There, as he reaches back into the space/time continuum, he experiences past incarnations, his embryonic nature. Is it any wonder that Nataraj should remark, after awakening, that he has "never felt better"?

The dreamless sleep from which he has just awakened continues to actualize the latencies stirred up so powerfully when he howled his prayer to Vishnu. Embarrassed, particularly when the elephant's owner compares Nataraj's sudden outburst of prayer to a dog that howls or to an elephant that trumpets for no apparent cause, Nataraj finally understands that the same mechanism exists in all creatures: "Only the stimuli and medicinal doses differ between human beings and animals."

A plethora of analogies to animals, avatars of deities, are implicit in *The Man-Eater of Malgudi*. They are part of Hindu culture, as they were and are of many others. The ancient Egyptians worshipped theriomorphic deities; each of the Christian Evangelists has his animal form; the signs of the zodiac take on the forms of fish, bears, dogs, etc. Animals may evoke instinctual and/or cosmic energies; psychologically, they may be regarded as projections of an individual's or a group's inner climate. Because the elephant symbolizes stability and immutability, and is an avatar of Shiva's and Parvati's son, Ganesha, as previously mentioned, his well-being is of particular importance to the Hindus. In that he is endowed with a human body, representing the microcosm, and an elephant's head, symbolizing the macrocosm, he is regarded as a link to the ineffable. As such, he transcends time and space, and is therefore looked upon as the *beginning and the end*; the child and the adult; the Christian alpha and omega; everything that takes place from the non-manifested OM to its manifestation.

Nataraj's thoughts center on the very real danger facing Kumar. He knows that it does not take much to arouse an elephant: a needle stuck in a banana which someone gives him to eat, an ant dropped in his ear, a grain of sand falling into his eye—and the elephant will go mad and trample hundreds of people. In such a situation, the multitude would be grateful to the elephant's killer.

As Nataraj muses, his gaze fixes on the moonlit street, and he falls into another deep sleep. The moon, representing indirect knowledge, is a reflection of conscious life. Looked upon as a container for immortality or for life-sap, it symbolizes cyclical rebirth: the fulfillment of ancestral ways (*piri-yana*). Shiva, the eternal cosmic force of creation and destruction, wears the moon in his hair. (In classical Hinduism, both the moon and the sun are masculine. In the *Upanishads*, the sun is masculine and the moon is feminine. The sun leads to release from one's *karma*, while the moon leads to rebirth.)

The moonbeams lull Nataraj into a state of dreamless sleep, inviting him once again to descend into the deep, but he cannot relax. He lies on his mat tossing and turning, and when he awakens about midnight, the procession has already started. As he hears the piper's music from the distance, the drummer's harsher sounds, and the more elaborate and intricate melodies which follow, he visualizes the crowd gathering around the musicians, the chariot in which Lord Krishna reposes, and Kumar standing at the head of the procession. It will take about an hour, Nataraj calculates, for the group to reach the market fountain, the danger point. Here the elephant is to be maddened and Vasu is to shoot him. Until that time, Kumar is safe and Nataraj can rest.

Meanwhile, the melodies the musicians play—Nataraj's favorites—bring back memories of his childhood and of his father, who loved music and had so many instrumentalist friends. The serenity of these thoughts induces him into another sleep; when he awakens this time, however, it is to a different tune. The procession is nearing the danger point.

Sleep has strengthened Nataraj—or so he thinks. His way seems clear to him; his mind is made up. He will join the procession and divert it away from the fountain into a side street. Upon second thought, he realizes that any change of direction will create a panic. Precious moments pass while he cogitates. Suddenly, just as his prayer to Vishnu has erupted into consciousness, he understands that only one road is open to him. All others were and are escape mechanisms, leading him away from the source of the Evil. Vasu has to be confronted directly: open dialogue has to take place. Nataraj's timorousness has vanished. He is prepared to stand up to the formidable rakshasa, to deal with "the prince of darkness . . . in darkness"—cleverly and with an understanding of the forces at stake.

Nataraj's prayer to Vishnu, his two periods of deep sleep, and the archetypal image of the elephant have catapulted him into that inner sea where the energy necessary to *act* has been summoned. There, paradoxically, his mind has quieted, making perceptible certain forms and sensations existing beyond the rational domain—discerned during certain altered states of consciousness. His potential is actualizing itself through his psyche. He rises, squeezes himself past the little grill between his press and the staircase leading to Vasu's room, and climbs the flight of stairs silently, *determined* to stop Evil from disrupting the worship of Divinity.

Despite the fact that Vasu's door is slightly ajar, which augurs something out of the ordinary, Nataraj pushes it open gently, peeps in and sees his enemy sitting at the window in his easy chair. The strangeness of the luminosities and the stillness of the moment transform an otherwise mundane image into an apocalyptic vision.

> The lights, the Kitson vapour lamps and the torches of the procession were already illuminating the walls of the room, and there were moving shadows on them. The band and the pipe and the shouts of the men pulling the chariot could be heard from below. I could see his silhouette at the window, where he seemed to have made himself comfortable, with a pillow under his head. . . . Other

silhouettes, of the small tiger cub and a few animals, stood out in the semi-darkness.

With cunning and trepidation, Nataraj crawls to where a gun lies on the floor, within Vasu's reach, and grabs it. The very touch of the killer instrument stuns Nataraj: never has he held such a weapon in his hands. Despite his nonviolent approach to life he *knows* deep down that he is prepared to use the weapon, should Kumar's life be threatened. Nataraj waits patiently in utter silence and complete immobility, aiming the muzzle of the gun directly at Vasu's head.

The drumming grows louder and louder. Nataraj is certain that as the procession passes beneath Vasu's window, it will awaken him. Vasu does not move. Nataraj stands motionless. Stasis. So confident is Nataraj as to the course of his action that he even looks away from his enemy for a moment, toward the window, and sees "the flower-decked top of the chariot and the little bulbs sparkling on it, the head of the elephant brilliant with the gold plates. . . ." Once the procession has passed, "the reflections on the wall vanished and the drums and pipes sounded far away, leaving a faint aroma of jasmine and roses in their wake." Kumar's life has been saved.

Suddenly, the alarm clock goes off. Now that the danger is over, the power summoned from Nataraj's subliminal sphere—the energy which catalyzes him—has dissipated, flowing back into the collective unconscious. Fear overcomes him. Nataraj jumps and runs from the room—out of Vasu's reach.

The following day, life seems to resume its usual course, with one exception: Nataraj is told that Vasu is dead. How had it happened? Who has murdered him? The pathologist's report states that Vasu has "died of a concussion received on the right temple on the frontal bone delivered by a blunt instrument."

Everything has changed. Nataraj's friends avoid him. He is thought to be Vasu's killer and therefore no one visits the "murderer's press." Days of isolation and cogitation follow. Only when Rangi comes to see Nataraj is the secret of Vasu's death finally unraveled. She had visited Vasu on the night of the procession and had mixed a narcotic in the food she has prepared for him, hoping he would sleep through the event. But he refused to touch a thing. When he was informed that the procession might be delayed, she saw him set his alarm clock, then sit down in his chair, after which he ordered her to fan the hated mosquitoes away from him. He dozed off for a while, as did Rangi. Once the fanning had ceased, however, the mosquitoes returned in battalion force. "Damn these mosquitoes!" he yelled. Awakening with a start, Rangi saw him fight them off; seconds later, she "heard a sharp noise like a thunder-clap." Unthinkingly, he has slapped his forehead with the palm of his hand. Such an act was surprising in view of the fact that after he had given up his work as a strong man, he had taken great care *never* to hit anyone with his hand, even if provoked, knowing that such a blow would be fatal. It was Vasu who had struck himself unconsciously, thereby ending his earthly existence. Why Vasu had never struck anyone with his hand was explained otherwise by Sastri, the *wise old man*.

> Because he had to conserve all that might for his own destruction. Every demon appears in the world with a special boon of indestructibility. Yet the universe has survived all the *rakshasas* that were ever born. Every demon carries within him, unknown to himself, a tiny seed of self-destruction, and goes up in thin air at the most unexpected moment. Otherwise what is to happen to humanity?

Time and time again have Hindu demons used their divinely given powers to destroy themselves.

Only when the tyrannical force of Evil was beyond endurance did Nataraj act. There are times during life when overt action must be taken and to refrain from such a course is to wallow in selfishness, inertia, and darkness—to allow the demonic within the individual and the culture to take hold. Because Nataraj has lived the experience and understood it only intellectually, as an abstract notion, he now *really* understands the lesson Lord Krishna taught Arjuna when he spoke as follows:

> Now give ear to my supreme utterance. Because thou art dear to Me, I will proclaim it to thee for thy good. Neither the hosts of the gods nor the great seers know My source. Altogether more ancient than they am I. He who knows Me as the Unborn, the Beginningless, the Great Lord of the World, he among mortals, free from delusion, is released from sins. From me alone arise the manifold states of mind of created beings: power of judgment, knowledge, purity of spirit, forbearance, true insight, discipline, serenity, pleasure and pain, well-being and distress, fear and reliance, compassion, equanimity, contentment, self-control, benevolence, glory and infamy. . . . He who knows in truth this manifestation of My might and My creative power is armed with unshakable constancy. I am the Source of all, from Me everything arises. Whosoever has insight, knows this. And with this insight the wise worship Me, overwhelmed by awe. . . .[24]

For the Hindu, Evil is implicit in the manifest world. It can never be eradicated any more than can duality; it can only be held in check. Only after one ceases to be held in bondage on earth can the beginning of the great *initiatory* process—in keeping with the law of *karma*—lead to the cessation of duality (the struggle of Good versus Evil) and the reign of *Absolute Reality.*

For Nataraj and his community, Vasu's death puts Evil temporarily in abeyance. Krishna, "the dark one," an avatar of Vishnu, thus "a divine particle of the holy supramundane essence, who had descended to earth for the salvation of mankind," is celebrated by the community in peace.

Nataraj's periods of meditation during the printing process—particularly when attending to the monosyllabic celebration of the nuptials of Krishna and Radha—as well as the printer's eruption into prayer and his episodes of dreamless sleep, called forth latent energies within his collective unconscious. Then the unfalsified voice of *nature* itself was catalyzed and came forth to help him, first in adjusting to his situation, and then in confronting that destructive *shadow* figure within his being concretized in the form of Vasu: a potential scourge to him as well as to the community.

Nataraj's periods of indwelling allowed him to suspend outward orientation and to sense *a center* within himself, a kind of inner point within the psyche. The fragmentation, dispersion, and confusion he had felt in his daily life was transformed by the strange language of the unconscious, giving him entrée to the affective components of the collective unconscious. In so doing, a fertile field for the *numinosum* was created—opening him up to eternity. As Jung wrote:

> Insofar as tomorrow is already contained in today, and all the threads of the future are already laid down, a deeper knowledge of the present might render possible a moderately farsighted prognosis of the future. . . . Just as memories that have long since fallen below the threshold are still accessible to the unconscious, so also are certain very fine subliminal combinations that point forward, and these are of the greatest significance for the future events insofar as the latter are conditioned by our psychology. . . .[25]

10 Peter Handke's *Kaspar*—The Mechanics of Language: A Fractionating Schizophrenic Theatrical Event

Peter Handke's play *Kaspar* (1968) is an example of neither the Theatre of the Absurd nor Anti-Theatre; nor does it follow traditional concepts of this art form since it is neither representational nor descriptive. Absent as well are plot, characters, tension, coherence, connecting processes, or meanings of words as we understand them. A spectator therefore must not compare stage reality with the reality he or she knows. Events represent themselves—no more, no less.

Theatre, for Handke, has neither object nor subject. Concepts, values, functional systems of signification, verifiable contents are non-existent in *Kaspar*. Words alone are of import; they alone create reality. The *signifying* (word) assumes a life outside of the *signified* (object). Handke writes: "The play *Kaspar* does not show how IT REALLY IS OR REALLY WAS with Kaspar Hauser. It shows what is POSSIBLE with someone. It shows how someone can be made to speak through speaking. The play could be called *Speech-Torture.*"[1]

Words, therefore, and not subjective evaluations of them, are acceptable to Handke. Comparisons, associations, metaphors, or referents, he suggests, prevent people from dealing directly with the object itself (the *signified*), inviting them to have recourse to a "system of differences," to use Derrida's expression, thus contrasting or modifying one with the other. Evaluation breeds buffers and hierarchies; it encourages people to rank or compute ideas, notions or feelings, and therefore prolong illusionism. Reality is not approached in a forthright manner, but rather experienced through a *system of signs*—a cultural product.[2]

Kaspar is innovative and challenging because it subverts the conventional system of relationships and comparisons. Words and figures of speech, as used in *Kaspar*, have become mechanical devices endowed with concretion. Hard, unyielding, feelingless, these *machinelike abstractions* bludgeon into submission, cutting and dismantling well-worn responses to old ways of thinking and understanding. New dimensions are opened up for the protagonist in Handke's drama, but they also undermine his security and create a climate of malaise. Feelings of oneness and cohesion are transformed into *fractionality*, triggering havoc in mind and psyche and ushering in a schizophrenic condition.

Handke—like the Cubists, who split objects and figures and reduced them to their basic geometric forms—dichotomizes both language and protagonist in *Kaspar*. The breakdown of traditional verbal sequences, the severing of the conventional word-feeling dialectic, endows each morpheme with its own identity and independent value. Like the Cubists, Handke is an artist in control of his material: the chaos or disorder implicit in his play is willed and directly distilled from the expressions he chooses to use.

That Handke looks upon the word as a *thing in and of itself* liberates it from a central consciousness but, by the same token, also invites it to develop its own potential. Its direction, then, is its own and not dependent upon something else. Because there is no supreme guiding principle, no dictatorial force, to show the words their way, a point of focus, in keeping with our logo-centered Western concepts, may be lacking.

The passage from *oneness*, or traditional use of language, to *dispersion*, freeing the word from former definitions, has significant psychological ramifications. Just as the once *whole* and coherent sentence has been broken down syntactically into disparate and frequently unrelated parts, so, too, has the personality. Once functioning under the aegis of an ego-complex, considered the "seat of an individual's experience of subjective identity," the personality was related to its parts through a central consciousness. Such *self-containedness* becomes fractured in *Kaspar*.[3] The word, considered as a thing in and of itself, abolishes its once sacrosanct associational meaning with the other morphemes in the clause or sentence. Likewise, the authority of the supreme consciousness or transcendent order within the psyche is broken down. The formerly all-powerful ego-complex has yielded its powers to individual egos; as autonomous entities, they live out their existence as each sees fit. Such split-offs from the ego dynamic can only encourage psychological fractionalization and ensuing schizophrenia.

The *problem of the mechanics of language* and its manipulative powers hold Handke in thrall, melding into the very framework of the play: it becomes its *prima materia*. Influenced by the Viennese-born Ludwig Wittgenstein, who suggested that people's problems usually begin and end with language, Handke focuses on *language as a system* and as a mechanical power. Instrumental in *creating order* or arrangements, language as an automating force has the capacity to dominate, dictate, and more frequently than not, destroy, individuals and societies.[4]

Handke tells us that his character's name, Kaspar, is based on a historical figure, Kaspar Hauser, who arrived in Nuremberg in 1828 at the age of sixteen. At first no one knew where he came from or anything about him. In time, it was discovered that he had been raised in a closet, far from human contact. He spoke only one sentence: "I would like to become a rider like my father once was." Although incoherent to the outsider, his single sentence was seemingly meaningful to him. Understandably, when transplanted, he feared everything and everyone with whom he came into contact.

Peter Handke was born during World War II (in 1942) to an unwed mother living in Griffin, a province in southern Austria. To legitimize her son, she married a German sergeant stationed in Austria. The family then moved to Berlin, but returned to Griffin once the Allied bombings started. Returning to Berlin in 1944, mother and son remained there until 1948, leaving the capital only after the city was divided into sectors. The year 1961 saw Handke enroll at the university in Graz, where he studied law for four years. During this period, he also wrote and published *Salutation of the Board of Directors* (1963) and *The Hornets* (1966).

Handke was in the process of formulating a new and innovative aesthetic, about which he spoke at Princeton University at a meeting of Group 47. He derided postwar literature in Germany: castigating the writings of such pillars of literature as Günter Grass and Heinrich Böll for their standardization of language and their insistence upon pursuing illusionism, representationalism, and realism—when these approaches to life were passé. If the link to reality becomes routine and "the words for the objects are taken for the objects themselves," one merely repeats through identification what has been said. Handke went on to remark: "People fail to recognize that literature is made with language and not with the things that are described with language," which cause literature to lose its *raison d'être*.[5]

Handke's fame began to spread far and wide. His first play, *Offending the Audience* (1966), was said to be the fifth most performed work in German-speaking theatres in Europe. Stressing his point of view, he suggested that one must face the question of language outright and no longer withdraw or hide behind masks or veils. He acted on his principles when invited to be a juror for *Commended*, a film entered at the Oberhausen Short Film Festival (1968). When an image of male genitals was flashed on the screen and created great embarrassment, he noted that had it been viewed symbolically, metaphorically, surrealistically, satirically, ironically, or in any other referential manner, it would have been called art. "But if [the penis] is shown in one of its real functions, with a nonsymbolic hand included, one has to look on, uneasy and embarrassed, without the release of laughter or artistic appreciation of surrealism."[6]

Handke, who despised illusionism, mannerism, and so-called representationalism, had taken Samuel Beckett's statement, referring to Joyce's *Finnegans Wake*, seriously: "His writing is not *about* something; *it is that something itself*."[7] In addition, Wittgenstein's notion that to understand a sentence necessitates the understanding of language led Handke to banish conventional reactions and psychological probings from his writings. "Narratives and novels really have no story," he remarked. "What is 'story' or 'fiction' is really always only the point of intersection between individual daily events."[8]

Handke referred to his nonrepresentational and nonfigurative play, *Offending the Audience*, as a *Sprechstück*, that is, a "speech-piece." Its frequently sound contradictory sentences, unconnected clauses, catalogued, repetitive anaphoras, and seemingly irrational verbiage may stun and disorient those spectators who expect logically conceived situations and metaphorical approaches to stage happenings.

> You will hear what you have usually seen.
> You will hear what you have not usually seen here.
> You will not see a play . . .
> You will see a play without pictures.[9]

When and if spectators begin to shed their *a priori* attitudes and their structured and rational visions of life, they may be less perturbed, and begin to grasp the phenomemna of reality. In keeping with Wittgenstein's logical positivism, as delineated in his *Tractatus Logico-Philosophicus*, Handke does away with metaphysical innuendos, sanctioning only those things that can be proven via the physical senses. In his preface, Wittgenstein wrote:

> The aim of the book is to set a limit to thought, or rather—not to thought, but to the expression of thoughts. [It] will therefore only be in language that the limit can be set, and what lies on the other side of the limit will simply be nonsense.[10]

Language is limited, but as a force used with dictatorial powers, it can control thought and actions.

Theatrically speaking, Handke has also fostered a reappraisal or revisioning of the reality of stage happenings. Audiences no longer come to the theatre to be entertained, or to be invited to share the life of or "eavesdrop" on a family or an individual, or to become engaged in a movement or group. Identification has been banished, along with characterizations and representations. In *Offending the Audience*, Handke writes:

> You are sharing no experience. You are not sharing. You are not following suit. You are experiencing no intrigues here. You are experiencing nothing. You are not imagining anything. You don't have to imagine anything. You need no prerequisites. You don't need to know that this is a stage. You need no expectations. You need not lean back expectantly. You don't need to know that this is only playing. We make up no stories. You are not following an event. You are not playing along. You are being played with here. That is a wordplay.

> What is the theatre's is not rendered unto the theatre here. Here you don't receive your due. Your curiosity is not satisfied. No spark will leap across from us to you. You will not be electrified. These boards don't signify a world. They are part of the world. These boards exist for us to stand on. This world is no different from yours. You are no longer kibitzers. You are the subject matter. The focus is on you. You are in the crossfire of our words.[11]

Because language is crucial in conveying thought, the people, groups, or institutions that control language dominate the ideations of individuals and societies. Disconnected words, repeated in various sequences within a sentence or clause, using a variety of figures of speech (repetitions, anaphoras, enumerations, metaphors, and metonymies, etc.), and a complex of sonorities, rhythms, and amplitudes, arouse, excite, and confuse the protagonist. Intellectually unable to assess such linguistic power plays, the spectators experience their impact only through their senses, which increase their already potent feelings of disarray and malaise.

Handke seeks to provoke audiences, not in the Brechtian way, through the use of *Verfremdung* (distantiation as in *Man is Man*); nor in the Artaudian manner by means of shock, but rather by rejecting the Aristotelian concept of *mimesis* and by atomizing and exploding traditional and modern theatrical conventions. Once these are pared down to their essentials, a disparate, fractional, unrecognizable world emerges. Such a revisioning of approaches not only exposes spectators to new ways of *seeing* and *hearing*, divesting them of value judgments and conventional responses to people and objects, but encourages them to become cognizant of the *world of the theatre itself.* Theatre, for Handke, and for the spectator seeking to follow him along his innovative path, becomes a *linguistic adventure!*

As the curtains part on *Kaspar,* audiences view a second and similar curtain upstage. Soon it becomes obvious that someone is trying to find the opening in the back curtain—and does, after several futile attempts. "A hand is all one sees at first; the rest of the body follows." Handke's autistic character enters the stage space. He is terrified by the objects he sees about him (chair, table, closet, etc.) and by the disembodied voices (Einsager) speaking to him through public-address systems, megaphones, radios, telephones, televisions, and other mechanical devices. The words spoken by these Einsager (a Handkian concoction implying "insayers," and, by implication, "indoctrinators") will bring Kaspar, who utters only one sentence at the outset of the drama, "to speech by speech."

The drama revolves around Kaspar's linguistic evolution: his mental growth and therefore his dependence upon the mechanics of language forced upon him—rotelike—by the Einsager. The Prologue, consisting of "Kaspar's Sixteen Phases," enumerates the various steps he experiences during the developmental process: his use of one sentence at the outset, as opposed to other sentences, and the new dynamic such activity generates.

The Mechanics of Linguistic Conformity—Kaspar the Automaton

Handke's Kaspar is neither a protagonist nor an antagonist in the traditional sense. His personality is never defined, nor does he have normal mental apparatuses. Undeveloped intellectually and emotionally, Kaspar is unconscious of the world around him. All we know about him is that he came from the country and knows only one sentence. That Handke's character is given a proper name—Kaspar—individualizes him a little, at least for the spectator, thereby salvaging him from total anonymity.

Psychologically, we may say that Kaspar's ego (center of consciousness) cannot be distinguished as something apart from its surroundings. Ego and non-ego (or Self, the total psyche), then, are one and the same, as are inner and outer worlds. Existence is lived on the basis of a single totality. Like an infant or child, Kaspar exists in an original state of wholeness: an *ouroboric* condition. The word is borrowed from the Gnostics, and identified with the circular image of the tail-eating serpent; the *ouroboric* state implies self-containment or *primary identity* with the Self. Such a state exists prior to the birth of consciousness.

That Kaspar's psyche is primitive, and his perceptual process deviant, is obvious. He seems unable to discriminate between objects and since he only utters one sentence, his speech may be labeled idiosyncratic. Medically speaking, Kaspar's behavior has been identified as *autistic*. His symptoms are withdrawal from the objects onstage, then a kind of conflictual avoidance of them, followed by shifting responses: aggressive and angry approaches succeeded by unresponsive and apathetic attitudes.

That there is something of the clown, buffoon, and puppet in Kaspar's awkward fumblings, and sometimes rigid gestures and fixed glacial expressions, is also apparent. As Kaspar ambulates about the stage space, bumping into one object after another, he elicits laughter as well as pity from the audience. Handke's description of his protagonist supports the clown/Kaspar analogy. "His makeup is theatrical. For example, he has on a round, wide-brimmed hat with a band; a light-colored shirt with a closed collar; a colorful jacket with many (roughly seven) metal buttons; wide pants; clumsy shoes; on one shoe, for instance, the very long laces have become untied. He looks droll."

The clown, one of the most complex of creatures, is an archetypal figure: universal and eternal, and endowed with the extraordinary power of making people laugh. While indulging in bizarre antics or "pure play," the clown, drawing guffaws, is viewed as a joyful and ebullient creature. Beneath the mask, however, exists a diametrically opposed being: a sorrowful, pained, and victimized individual. Frequently a failure, the butt of ridicule, and the recipient of floggings, the clown wears his fear and hurt within while donning a smile without. Conveying neither dignity nor reverence nor authority, he may, as in *King Lear*, also utter truths under the guise of nonsense.

Like the clown's, Kaspar's entrance from behind the curtain upstage is awkward; his ungainly nature increases as he fumbles with his hat— antics reminiscent of Arlecchino in the *commedia del l'arte* or a comic performing a music-hall routine.

That Kaspar wears a mask, as do so many clowns, reinforces the dichotomy between outer and inner worlds, and the impenetrability of spheres. In that masks are archetypal, they represent unmodifiable and immutable nature. Since Kaspar wears such a suprapersonal and unchangeable disguise, audiences believe him to be unaffected by the world of contingencies, unadaptable and unmodifiable in his comportment. No identification exists between him and the exterior world. On the other hand, Kaspar's mask may also be looked upon as a protective device, the weakly structured inner being safely hidden behind an unchangeable expression, thereby pointing up a sense of mystery, ambiguity, and excitement.

When Handke further tells his audiences that Kaspar resembles Frankenstein's monster, a creature fabricated from human parts which runs amok, destroying itself and its creator; and King Kong, the giant gorilla brought from his natural habitat to the city, where he, too, kills people, we understand the horrors involved, both physical and emotional, accompanying the displacement of people or the creation of beings who do not conform to the norm. Yet how popular such creatures are and have been from time immemorial—whetting the imagination, titillating the senses, and generating ripples of laughter.

There is, then, something automated or machinelike in Kaspar—namely his speech and behavioral patterns. In that Handke had suggested that his play could be called "*Speech-Torture*," the introduction of a mechanical instrument at the very outset of the theatrical event is in keeping with the programmed, standardized, and computerlike approach to his character's *wordplay*. The apparatus in question—a type of "magic eye," designed to "formalize this torture"—is built above the ramp. Blinking during the performance, it measures "the degree of vehemence with which the PROTAGONIST is addressed."

Equally measured and consistent is the dialogue, divided between Kaspar and the Einsager. In book form, the former is printed on the left side of the page and the latter on the right. The Einsager's disembodied voices, speaking through loudspeakers, public address mechanisms, megaphones, telephones, televisions, and automatic answering devices, are trying to indoctrinate Kaspar and persuade him to follow their system and thereby "bring Kaspar to speech by speech." They are subverting outworn theatrical conventions by emphasizing language rather than mime; detachment instead of subjectivity; significations instead of reference to some relational reality.

Nor are the theatrical accessories and props onstage illusionist. There is the aforementioned backdrop (a curtain of the same fabric and dimensions as the front curtain) from which Kaspar emerges so unadroitly. There are also chairs, a broom, a cushion, a table, a sofa, a shovel, a wastepaper basket, and a closet, which, though unrelated to each other, are disposed in a normal position onstage.

Kaspar, the clown, the unadapted and autistic being who stumbles and falls, blusters about knocking over pieces of furniture, kicking the closet door open, spiraling back and forth, as he repeats his one sentence—"I want to be a person like somebody else was once"—lives in his own closeted world. His single sentence, like a litany, takes on different amplitudes, sonorities, modulations, and rhythms, conveying a variety of emotional reactions to each of the events experienced. A remarkable vehicle for an actor!

The ultramechanical voices of three or more Einsager break out from all sides of the stage; the loudspeakers emphasize their engineered, toneless, and impersonal words.

> Already you have a sentence with which you can make yourself noticeable. With this sentence you can make yourself noticeable in the dark, so no one will think you are an animal. You have a sentence with which you can tell yourself everything that you can't tell others. You can explain to yourself how it goes with you. You have a sentence with which you can already contradict the same sentence.

The world—outside of Kaspar's one sentence—is threatening. For someone who can neither direct nor adapt his thinking, he lives in an overwhelmingly subjective and distorted domain. He continues to walk about the stage, touching various objects here and there, discovering gaps between the cushions on the sofa. He throws these soft objects on the floor any which way. In that he is autistic, the repetition of his single sentence may be considered in part as an apotropaic mechanism: a means of insuring his safety.

Kaspar is in touch only with nature and the instinctual sphere—a kind of *prima materia*. If this primal stuff can eventually be assimilated—at least in part—by the conscious mind, it will summon a reactivation and reorganization of unconscious and conscious contents, leading possibly to psychological and intellectual evolution. If no integration of new contents pouring in from the unconscious takes place, Kaspar will continue living at the same stage of development.[12]

Once the Einsager begin their *Speech-Torture*, a dialectical process is generated between Kaspar and his single sentence (an expression of his emotional world) and the Einsager, whose goal it is to indoctrinate him. To teach Kaspar to speak conventionally, to think traditionally, and to behave morally, in keeping with societal codes, makes their efforts purposeful. The Einsager's instructional method is that of drill/propaganda: machinelike accuracy and measured precision.

Just as Kaspar sees the objects onstage as strange and incoherent, so, too, does he hear the Einsager's words as a hodgepodge of meaningless, irrational morphemes. Like a child in the presence of objects he neither knows how to use nor understands, Kaspar trips, staggers, and stumbles about the vocabulary which bombards him from all directions. As he begins to examine these entities, he is frightened, then surprised, and finally caught up by their sound, amplitude, meaning, and the power their presence invests in him. The Einsager say:

> You have a sentence you can speak from beginning to end and from
> end to beginning. You have a sentence to say yes and say nay with
> you. You have a sentence with which you can make yourself tired or
> awake. . . . You are the lucky owner of a sentence which will make
> every impossible order possible for you and make every possible
> and real disorder impossible for you: which will exorcise every
> disorder from you.

Subtle teachers, the Einsager take the initiative. They label each object,
thereby identifying it with the word, then inform Kaspar of its function. By
means of *word-forces* and *word-manipulation*, they teach him all the stereotypes and platitudes which make society society and culture culture.
Such is the method they use to manipulate and dominate their student.

The Einsager's key word is *order*. As indoctrinators of social views, they
use language as a disciplinary force, to inculcate order into Kaspar and
condition him to follow their rules, be they grammatical constructions or
otherwise. As their toneless mechanical voices drone on and on, like
plainchant, they "exorcise every disorder" from Kaspar. While the voices
from loudspeakers and microphones accentuate or diminish in pitch and
amplitude, also alternating their rhythmic beats, Kaspar's nerves and psyche are affected. Indeed, he reacts intensely and angrily to their continuous, rigid, and unflinching verbal assaults.

As the Einsager pursue their course, their lessons take on a more abstract
temper. Kaspar is taught to divide time into past, present, and future. To
understand linear time, they remark, will help him build up his memory
and thereby construct his life. That he had formerly lived his entire existence
enclosed in a blackened room with no exposure to the outside world, and
that his single possession consisted of one sentence, met all of his needs at
that time. Now, they inform him, his situation has changed: he has become
cognizant of the outside world and consequently of himself and of relationships. Such an expanded approach to life brings into being a complex of
opposites, including abstraction and concretion.

Words are no longer simple devices expressing pain or joy. They have
grown in dimension, density, shape, and form. Some may be used as
pacifiers, others like fetishes or hierophanies or instruments of torture,
putting Kaspar through one ordeal after another. Still others may be used
as suggestive devices, cajoling him to follow the Einsager's ways. If Kaspar
reacts fearfully to the advent of new words, the Einsager tell him how
morphemes can protect him: "You can still crawl off behind the sentence:
hide: contest it. The sentence can still mean anything."

The Einsager are always clear and concise; they say what they mean
during their *exorcistic* verbal assault. Language as they use it has activated

an all-important system—their system—a way of first disorienting and then controlling their student. Sometimes Kaspar regresses, reacting negatively to their indoctrination. He "would like to keep his sentence," he repeats childishly; until now it has answered all of his needs. The Einsager's reaction: renewed barrages of sentences. Confusion sets in, as does "hurt." Kaspar's limited and self-contained world, "unbeknown to him," has been corroded, dismantled, destroyed, displaced, and de-constructed. He is no longer the proud possessor of a sentence; nor can he speak it intact; and though he "defends himself with his sentence" against the constant and oppressive imperatives of the Einsager, his sentence slowly begins to break up into single words, incomplete emotions, disparate ideas.

> I want.
> I want to be like once.
> I want to be a person like once.
> Somebody else.
> Like a person else.
> Somebody.

A positive ushers in a negative: although Kaspar can utter a variety of words and sentences, his once unique possession, *his* sentence, he realizes, is no longer exlusively his. Nor is he, by implication, his own man. He belongs to something bigger, to which he must relate and *conform*. Emotionally affected by this agonizing realization, he starts to breathe rapidly. His self-confidence now gives way to fear. Terror takes over as Kaspar formulates a string of utterly meaningless letters/words: "Olce ime kwas askwike lein."

The Einsager are irate. What has happened to their machinelike order? They pursue their indoctrinating process. Kaspar again makes every effort to pronounce more and more words, and to correlate these with objects, thereby obliterating his fear of them. Kaspar, whose single sentence had served him apotropaically, now uses words to ward off evil. "The table stands. The table fell over? The chair fell over! The chair stands! The chair fell over and stands? The chair fell over but the table stands."

Because reality has been actualized by language, Kaspar feels a kind of serenity, as if he were linked, attuned, related to the world. But is not this a snare? To allow words to act as pacifiers and as security blankets is an overly simplistic notion. Words are signifiers, to be sure; they are coded depictions of objects in the *real* world. Nevertheless, in that they also possess their own material existence, each is subject to infinite interpretations or significations—actions and reactions on both a human and an inhuman level.[13]

Language, as viewed by the Einsager, yields only traditional constructs and prototypic relationships, which are themselves artificial concoctions of one sort or another used to discipline and to order. No sooner does Kaspar utter a normal sentence than the stage becomes dark. Fear envelops him.

The Photological Interlude and the Projection Syndrome

The lights go on again. Kaspar has been *awakened* to a differentiated and conflictual world outside of himself. That the educational process is a success is evident since his new sentences are *"normal;"* he can "compare" and "describe," and thereby "clarify" everything he perceives and senses. All seems to fall into its *rightful* and *ordered* place. He is told:

> Every object must be the picture of an object: every proper table is the picture of a table. . . . If the table is already a picture of a table, you cannot change it: if you can't change the table, you must change yourself: you must become a picture of yourself just as you must make the table into a picture of a table and every possible sentence into a picture of a possible sentence.

Not only are Kaspar's sentences rational and related, but for the first time, he is also able to coordinate his hands and feet with dexterity. As he bends down to tie his shoelace, thereby illustrating his newfound skill, a spotlight follows his hands and fingers, emphasizing the network or movements needed to intertwine and cross the laces.

A photological drama ensues. As he pursues his dexterous endeavors, tying his belt, buttoning his jacket, picking up a chair he had thrown down, arranging furniture the *right* way, a darkening and brightening spotlight guides his movements, showing him just how things must be accomplished and where objects must be placed. Soon two more spotlights join forces, not only adding to the photological histrionics onstage, but accentuating the conspirational factor: these are forces futhering the Einsager in their preaching/teaching lessons.

Lighting (*phos, photos* in Greek), like the loudspeakers and microphones used in the mechanization of words, increases the automatic, systematized, and engineered quality of the indoctrinating process. Power-driven machines, their tonalities veering from light to dark, work in consort with the Einsager's linguistic technique. Shadings either accentuate or obliterate the protagonist's movements and behavioral patterns, revealing his mood but also imposing the *right* approach to be used. In consort with the Einsager's *logos* ("reason," from the Greek) lighting procedures become mediating forces between Kaspar and the Einsager. Sound will be added to the spot-lights to disclose a panoply of moods and thoughts. The brighter the spot-lights, the more shrill and strident Kaspar's voice becomes; the darker the illumination, the more mellifluous.

The sameness in the lighting effects and the vocal tones emphasizes a paradoxical uniformity, predictability, and mechanical *order* in Kaspar's behavior. So certain are the Einsager of Kaspar's progress that they no longer accommodate their sentences to his movements. The reverse oc-curs: he coordinates his movements to their sentences. Such an alteration underscores the success of the *Word-Force* method and the immense power of language in molding a human being's emotions and thoughts as well as in creating stereotypes—creatures who conform, adapt, assimilate and transform themselves into collective images and act always in accor-dance with the dominant *signs* of their culture.

Kaspar glows again with self-confidence. At ease with the objects around him, understanding their values, he relates to their arrangement, shape, and codifications, and even looks upon them as beautiful. Now he is ready, the Einsager believe, to be given the model sentences that will help him through life. "You have model sentences with which you can get through life: by applying these models to your sentences, you can impose order on everything that appears chaotic: you can declare it ordered . . ." No longer estranged from the world of contingencies, Kas-par fits into the Einsager's order. He has grown accustomed to their world of images and signs. But, as suggested before, a growing aware-ness of the great void triggers feelings of anxiety which had, at least during his growing period, vanished. Along with the loss of *his* sentence, Kaspar now realizes that his individuality and his values have disap-peared. Whereas his sentence had formerly provided him with a secure and meaningful *whole* and *uniformity*, as had the Einsager's mechanized methodology which replaced it, Kaspar now finds himself *outside* of it all. No longer contained in either of the two enclosed systems, he feels himself opening up on a vast new world, without guidelines, without mechanical devices to point to the right path. No longer does he feel linked, related to the world at large.

Suddenly, a second Kaspar, identical in all ways to the protagonist, enters the stage space. As he begins sweeping the floor, his gestures and motions meticulously marked out by a spotlight, a third and fourth Kaspar, similar to the original, begin moving across the stage. Because the fourth Kaspar walks on crutches, the third one slows down to his pace. Two additional Kaspars then walk toward and away from each other, after which they step aside. The entire photological scene, like a choreo-graphed dance, is composed of sequences of rhythmical movements interspersed with an alternatingly blackened and brilliantly lit stage, emphasizing the drama inherent in forms themselves.

Who are these Kaspars? Like free-floating signs with no connecting principle, they keep colliding with each other, their movements accompanied by bumping and grinding noises.

Psychologically, the multiple Kaspars may be viewed as projections of a formerly whole and self-contained Kaspar. Just as his single sentence had been experienced as a unit, each word fitting into the composite grammatical construct or syntactical system, so had his psyche been apprehended as an entity—not alienated from either outer or inner worlds.

As projections of unconscious contents buried deep within Kaspar's subliminal sphere, the appearance of the Kaspars onstage indicates their actualization, or constellation. They are then perceived and reacted to by him as outer objects; as real and living factors—not merely as phantasms. That he sees these humanized forms outside of himself—sitting, walking, comporting themselves as human beings—serves to confuse him.

The *birth of consciousness* has inspired in Kaspar the desire to step out of the Einsager's single-purposed realm. He observes and questions their control over him, their simplistic answers. The world of differentiation emerges. Growing tension, anxiety, and conflict are manifested onstage by the grating, jarring, scraping sounds and brittle, mechanical gestures of the *other* Kaspars.

Kaspar senses that he must choose and mediate between words, objects, and the feelings they generate in him. Because he is no longer living unconsciously, systems and structures become suspect to him: they are fictions, artifices, manipulatory devices engineered to dominate individuals as well as societies. There is no single answer; there are no absolutes; nothing can be isolated or verified. Only a world of imponderables, of uncertainties, of indeterminacy, faces each individual, including Kaspar.

That the Einsager had ordered Kaspar to correlate word and object, that is, to name pain, thereby signifying the signified, adds to his disquietude because it no longer satisfies him. When existing in his undifferentiated or ouroboric but unique world with his single possession—his sentence—he felt imbued with a kind of paradisiac harmony. Malaise began corroding his being when he became cognizant that words have collective meanings: they belong to and are defined by the world at large, but they also change in value with the emotional impact individuals decant into them. Such reasoning is reminiscent of Eugene Ionesco's *The Lesson:* the teacher tells his pupil that the word *grandmother*, interpreted by different people, alters in meaning and feeling, since each person using it identifies the word with his or her own grandmother.

When Kaspar suddenly understands that words are not one person's possession, but must be shared with others, he feels displaced and dislodged. Insecurity and uneasiness take precedence. Aware that the Einsager have incarcerated him in *their* educational system, *their* closure, not unlike the one he knew in his autistic sphere, and that he has become a product of society, of the collective—a robotlike entity—he is overcome with a profound sense of isolation and alienation.

The Mechanics of Fractionality and the Schizophrenic Syndrome

An intermission is called for, but not the usual kind: an "INTERMISSION TEXT is piped through loudspeakers into the auditorium, into the lobbies, and even out onto the street if that is possible." Made up of a collage of fragmented and barely understandable clauses, the Intermission Text interpolates snatches of speeches made by party leaders, popes, and presidents, articulating on a variety of subjects such as dinner-table etiquette, the desire to overthrow the status quo, dithyrambs in favor of people beating others into obedience—all in one way or another replicating the Einsager's code of behavior.

During this medley of cacophonies, two Kaspars, joined by three others, are seated on the sofa, listening attentively to the mangled and distorted verbiage and medley of noises (a faucet gradually turned on full strength, people breathing, strident and deformed musical tones similar to those made by a record player playing at a very low speed) piped in through the loudspeakers. (The entire sequence is reminiscent of Dadaist and Surrealist filmstrips, where the rational and irrational vie for artistic supremacy.) The faces of the duplicate Kaspars, like glazed masks, wear "an expression of contentment," as does that of the original Kaspar: outwardly serene, complacent, and self-assured.

The latter, meanwhile, walks toward the microphone, stops in front of it, listens for a moment to the Einsager talk of the stipulations and restrictions imposed upon individuals by society, then begins his peroration. Using the microphone as the Einsager had the loudspeakers, amplifying his voice when intending to make a point, diminishing it for contrast, he controls audience and environment, bringing them to speech as he had been brought to speech.

Kaspar's elaboration of his etiology and epistemology is fascinating. He explains in elliptical phrases the grief and aching torment he experienced when opened up to the fearful and conflictual outer world. Reminiscent in some ways of Lucky's speech in Samuel Beckett's *Waiting for Godot*, audiences feel the pain he *knew* when coming into the world of being.

> I came into the world
> not by the clock
> but because
> the pain
> while falling
> helped me drive
> a wedge
> between me
> and the objects
> and finally extirpate
> my babbling:
> thus the hurt finally drove
> the confusion out of me.

Kaspar takes his audience from his autistic inner world of relative one-ness through his difficult birth into the domain of differentiation, the con-comitant shift in his response patternings, and his present rejection of order and closure as taught him by the Einsager. Language *is* a giant manipula-tor; morphemes condition behavior and consciousness; they dominate those who, while learning to apply words to objects and ideas, are in fact building constructs and systems—machinelike entities—thereby entrap-ping themselves in categories where predetermined meanings are as repres-sive as any political, religious, or other dogmatic power. Kaspar is now aware of the complexities involved in language—the baffling, capricious, even mysterious relationships existing between a word and the object it depicts, as signified and signifier perpetually alter and fluidify. Words be-tray, falsify, elude, and delude. Nor can they be humanized; they can only analogize and approximate feeling and sensations. As Artaud stated time and time again in *The Theatre and Its Double*, emotions cannot be transliter-ated verbally.

Whiler Kaspar continues articulating his ideas, the other Kaspars on the sofa begin making all kinds of dissonant, unexpected, and disruptive noises: sobbing, giggling, trilling, twittering, groaning, grumbling, rasp-ing, heckling, ululating, accompanied by falsetto and grating sounds, owl-like hooting, rustling leaves, roaring, laughter, humming, purring, war-bling, and a single sharp scream.

The din is so distracting that Kaspar keeps raising his voice higher and higher. When falsetto notes emanate from his mouth, the Einsager also chime into the symphony of cacophonies "in canon fashion." Apparently trying to outdo the screeching, yodeling, buzzing, trumpeting, grunting, burping, gurgling, barking, and nail-filing sounds from the other Kaspars, Handke's protagonist finds himself becoming more and more enmeshed

in a panoply of verbigerations. So striking is the irrationality of the interlude as a whole, and Kaspar's speech in particular, that he ceases to
indulge in his verbal contortions, only to question: "What was it/that/I
said/just now?"

Kaspar's mind has disintegrated. His memory, understanding, and
whatever potential rational principle existed in him during his autistic
period (and was developed in time by the Einsager) has vanished—along
with his concept of identity. Like the other Kaspars, and in concert with
them and the Einsager, Handke's protagonist begins to giggle, whine, and
snap his fingers against the microphone in rhythm with a medley of
incredible sounds punctuated by a panoply of disparate words. Rebelling
once and for all against the lessons taught him by his mentors, he says:
"Every sentence is for the birds."

Kaspar is undergoing a *schizophrenic* episode: his ego complex has exploded. Each of its disparate parts, manifested in the phenomenal world
as multiple Kaspars, expresses its own needs and wants. No central authority exists any longer in Kaspar's psyche: his discourse is free and undirected. Divested of authoritarian control, the splintered egos attempt to
impose their individual realities and their arbitrary values. In so doing, the
autonomous egos are depleting their energies and transforming the personality into insignificant and warring elements.

What caused this fractionalization of Kaspar's ego—this disintegration
of a central focus, or consciousness? When he first appeared onstage,
Kaspar was autistic, living within his own circumscribed world and unable to relate to *reality*. Despite his anxieties, however, his sentence with its
simile acted as a kind of pacifier, a palliative which helped him over the
hardships and terrors confronting a displaced and alienated person.
Kaspar's sentence, or group of words, or conventional unit of connected
speech or thought, acted as a boon for him, conveying as it did all of his
wants and needs.

What is the significance of the simile that such a figure of speech invited
Kaspar to feel wholeness, confidence, and a sense of accomplishment? The
simile is defined as a figure of speech "in which one thing is likened to
another, dissimilar thing by the use of *like* or *as*." Kaspar's undeveloped
mind adapted to the rudimentary comparison included in his sentence.
When, therefore, Kaspar pronounced his one sentence, "I want to be a
person like somebody else was once," the simile not only comforted him as
does a child's doll or rabbit (it was always there), he felt understandably
related to it. It stood as a mediating force between him and the world at
large. The Einsager took him out of his single-sentence domain—his
womblike realm—and taught him the more capricious aspects of language, including multiple figures of speech, then made insistent use of

repetitive devices, sound factors, and lighting procedures, which all worked in consort. After completing his rite of passage into the Einsager's world, he again began feeling secure, protected by their order. When, however, the Einsager lured him into the world of abstractions, their repetitive devices, sound factors, and lighting procedures had a dual effect: they forced complicated maneuvers to take root in his own intellect, whereupon Kaspar began to *think* on his own. Although they had oriented their pupil toward *logos*, their message spelled *order*. An instrument of order and a rational principle, words under their aegis became machinelike instruments capable of dominating, manipulating, disrupting, deforming, mishaping, twisting, and creating havoc within the psyche.

The Einsager taught Kaspar to perceive the outer world in a restricted, contrived, and shallow—though ingenious—way. Their notions were based on the belief that one thing resembles something else by association: that signifiers describe the signified and that one sign designates a panoply of others. The comparisons used in their educational process illuminate and instruct via the very polarities and differences enunciated.[14]

As representatives of society, systems, and concepts, the Einsager simply incarcerated Kaspar within another demarcated construct—no longer his autistic one-sentence realm but their own limited, authoritarian, linguistically centered world.

The Einsager's system fails at the end since Kaspar's mind explodes— thereby shedding the repressive measures they imposed upon him. *Logos* is subverted in favor of *anti-logos*; the irrational, the chance factor, now plays the decisive role. Instruction is no longer based on rote; no longer is word correlated to object or association based on resemblance; nor are there connecting principles which logify the universe. Deconstruction and divisiveness, rather than construction and unity, have become the operational factor.

When Kaspar rebels against the Einsager's "perfect" mechanical indoctrinating system through language, he falls into an irrational universe—an endless maw. No longer does he understand meaning or concepts. The single *word* alone remains. Endowed with great amounts of energy, this compact, condensed force works on his nerves and psyche, affecting him incisively, tearing and pulling at him.

Each of the other Kaspars onstage enunciates his power-words or power sounds; each adds to the original Kaspar's torment. Formerly he had reacted to the Einsager's linear commands and decrees in an orderly manner, adapting his thinking to theirs, bound and subjected to their picture of the world. After breaking out of their system, having not yet replaced it with another—unless it be that of the irrational sphere— Kaspar's ego-complex shattered and splintered. Schizophrenia took over.

The *ego-complex*, formerly the subject of Kaspar's experience, was transformed into only one of the experiencing subjects. When the ego-complex split into its disparate parts, or into many subjects, or into a "plurality of autonomous complexes," a central authority no longer reigned.[15]

In a well-adjusted and relatively normal person, the ego-complex is able to cope with most problems relating to the individual in question, and is considered "the highest psychic unity or authority." Moreover, the ego-complex gives direction to associations and ideas. In that it is the center of consciousness, it functions as *logos*. When a person is deeply disturbed, as in Kaspar's case, the psychic totality becomes fragmented, splitting into various complexes. When the split-off occurs, each complex, looked upon as a kind of "miniature self-contained psyche," develops "a peculiar fantasy-life of its own." When the egos in Kaspar's once cohesive complex became virtually autonomous, the resulting fantasies assumed abnormal proportions. Autonomous egos may be looked upon as vassals unwilling to give their suzerain "unqualified allegiance." They do not fit harmoniously into the conscious mind, and they may resist all attempts on the part of the will to cope with them.

Kaspar's autistic world, at the outset, was warped. Once the Einsagers gave it form (their form) through thought patternings, they succeeded in developing, to a certain extent, Kaspar's judgmental faculties. In so doing and much to their dismay, however, they inculcated in him a fundamental desire for freedom. The more hampered he felt, the greater grew his inner rage. His relatively feeble ego-complex split asunder under the strain, and with it his emotional order and the whole associative process.

Psychological mutilation and disjointed associations created secondary personalities, concretized in the Kaspars inhabiting the stage, each endowing the happening with separate consciousnesses or egos. The Kaspars onstage are materializations of a primordial drama being enacted within Handke's protagonist. Although conscious of their existence, Kaspar is unconscious of their relationship to him. He does not realize that they are constellations of his inner forces, or split-off egos. It is not surprising, therefore, that the noises and verbiage emanating from the Kaspars all over the stage are divested of meaning. That these grow louder and more strident—including fingernails scraping on slate or across a pane of glass, and files rubbing against tin, slate, stone— indicates Kaspar's inner agony.

Artaud, in the twenties and thirties, had suggested the use of disconnected verbigerations, fulgurating rhythms, and background noises to create a disturbing and inverted atmosphere. He succeeded—though few in the audience understood his prophetic technique—in his production of *The Cenci* (1935). Handke accomplishes a similar feat, but goes still further in fragmenting the whole by his provocative, subversive, linguistic and auditive methodology.

Kaspar talks on; but he is unable to bring the autonomous egos (the other Kaspars) under the control of one central consciousness. The disconnected powers are incapable of reintegrating into a psychic whole. As Kaspar falls further and further apart, an infinite play of significations comes into being: fractionality and dispersion take over, memory is obliterated, linear time schemes are undiscerned.

> What was it
> that
> I said
> just now?
> If I only knew
> what it is
> that I said
> just now!
> If I only knew
> what I said
> just now!

Kaspar's sequences become less and less comprehensible, more and more repetitive and manic, with slight and frequently unintelligible variations. With a sudden and last return to lucidity, we hear him say painfully: "I no longer understand anything literally. I cannot wait until I wake up, whereas earlier I could not wait to fall asleep. I have been made to speak. I have been converted to reality."

The stage is darkened, then brightened. Kaspar pursues his speech amid the din of the screeching autonomous Kaspars and dictatorial Einsager: "If only. If only . . ." Whereupon schizophrenia obliterates all sense/nonsense and we hear Kaspar utter "Goats and monkeys" five times, as the curtain jolts closed. The protagonist topples and then falls behind the curtain.

Handke's successful and brilliant dramatization of the mechanics used in the construction/deconstruction syndrome in both the linguistic and psychological spheres makes his play unique in theatre. His emphasis on the manipulation of thought and actions via the individual word, sequenced words, repetition and standardization of word and words, used alongside with loudspeakers, microphones, lights, sounds, television circuits and other technical devices, shed a terrifying picture of what can happen to an individual when a mechanized approach to language and education prevail in a society. Beware of the mechanics of indoctrination: beware of media.

11 Sam Shepard's *Operation Sidewinder*—The Mechanics of the Profane and the Sacred

Sam Shepard's *Operation Sidewinder* (1970) is a mystery play in the real sense of the word. Two religious ceremonies are enacted onstage: the Hopi Indian Snake-Antelope dance and the electrifying performance of a most up-to-date scientific invention: the sidewinder computer. Both are initiation rituals which lure audiences from the world of the profane to that of the sacred.

In dimension, *Operation Sidewinder* is apocalyptic (from the Greek, *apokalyptein*, "uncover" or "reveal"). It discloses the inner workings of the sacred mysteries hidden within the visible profane world that some label "reality." To this end, the staging, plot, images, songs, dances, dialogue, and protagonists work toward an Armageddon, the vast and decisive battle fought between the forces of good and evil. Such slaughter, which concludes the play, is foretold in many sacred books—among them, the Christian Revelation (16:14–16)—and in Hopi religious rituals. A destructive outcome suggests renewal for the Hopi Indian and for those who experience an affinity with the cosmic and with the instruments through which it is made manifest.

Because death and destruction are among the salient themes in *Operation Sidewinder*, the strongly patriotic Shepard speaks out openly in the play, urging viewers to become aware of the imminent dangers facing his country if new approaches to life are not forthcoming. Americans have reached a crossroads. In our increasingly powerful industrial society, a rampant mind-altering drug culture, meaningless killings, divestiture of moral values, and emphasis on immediate gratification spell decadence and downfall. If Americans are to survive as a creative people, they must take stock of their goals, actions, and ideals. *Operation Sidewinder* is apocalyptic in that it may lead some to greater understanding of themselves and the world around them, and it may help others to sort out confused or repressed values instead of being overwhelmed by them.

To "uncover" what is hidden in a culture, or in an individual psyche, is fraught with hazards. Such disclosures require exposure to an initiation ritual with its concomitant ordeals designed to test and scrutinize the spiritual, physical, and psychological health of a person or society in need. *Initiation* (from the Latin, "going within") allows acolytes to pass from one level of consciousness to another, thereby reaching the deepest of spheres within the psyche. Such a trajectory forces a descent into the Self—from *ego-consciousness* (awareness of the center of consciousness) to *Self-consciousness* (awareness of the existence of a total psyche)—and a reconnection with one's own past and concomitantly with humanity's primordial existence. Since the object of initiation is an illumination, the enrichment gained cannot be taught, nor can it be recounted to friends or acquaintances, nor handed down from one generation to another. It can only be *experienced*, as it is in *Operation Sidewinder*, through bizarre but spectacular events.

Shepard, if not overtly then covertly, was influenced by the writings of Antonin Artaud, most specifically his playlet *Jet of Blood* (1926). Like Artaud, Shepard attacks political, social, sexual, and religious attitudes, mocking them mercilessly but also suffusing them with a sense of dread and despair. His characters, like Artaud's, are for the most part collective, prototypal, divested of any personal trait, each cohabiting with ugliness in a dissolving world while yearning for beauty and purity. Sound and lighting effects are viewed as protagonists by both the French and American authors: thunder and flashing lights entering inexplicably into the stage happenings.

Unlike Artaud's playlet, Shepard's two-act drama is fullblooded. Its scenes are tightly knit, focusing as they do on specific problems which triturate the playwright and which he attempts to transform into nutritive forces. To this end he infuses with life the most advanced technical invention America has to offer—the sidewinder computer. This mechanical power is identified with the Hopis' traditional sacred snake. The vigorous respect with which a religious ritual focuses on both the machine and the snake fetish—one and the same—paves the way for the numinosum.

The Hopi Snake-Antelope ceremony as staged in *Operation Sidewinder* is also reminiscent of Artaud's *The Tarahumaras* (1936): an account of his incredible visit to the mountain home, near Mexico City, of Indians who claimed to have lived in these elevated regions since before the Flood. Like Artaud, Shepard enacts a religious ritual to reveal a world alive with magic, haunting rhythms, dazzling colors and images: an arcane dimension that invites the adventuresome to *reenter* a past existence.

Language for both Artaud and Shepard is of prime importance in a dramatic unfolding. As in days of old, words for them are not only instruments enclosing potential meanings, but harbingers of friendly and enemy forces, emanations of superior powers hovering about eternally. To recite poetry or prose, then, is a truly creative process in that it infuses morphemes and phonemes with the breath of life. Under the right circumstances, words and figures of speech become breeders of sorts, developing their own sexuality and spirituality which, in turn, trigger responses in both reciter and listener. Indeed, utterances iterated as an incantation or a chant, or even spoken in certain tones or rhythmic cadences, may call an entire universe into being, as electrical charges emitted during the process are transmitted from one body to the next. As libido is freed, emotions, sensations, and thought flow forth in an infinite array.

Shepard's language is American in the best and most authentic of its traditions: like Stephen Crane's straightforward and visceral cant, Walt Whitman's explosive poetic vision, Jack Kerouac's brutally expansive modernity. A world of mystery lies embedded in Shepard's incantatory language: the unknown in all of its terror and jubilation. As he noted: "I feel that language is a veil holding demons and angels which the characters are always out of touch with. Their quest in the play is the same as ours in life—to find those forces, to meet them face to face and end the mystery."[1]

Sam Shepard, born in Fort Sheridan, Illinois (1943), is somewhat of an *enfant prodige*, his first two plays, *Cowboys* and *Rockgarden*, having been produced when he was only twenty years old. Other theatrical works include *The Tooth of Crime, Geography of a Horse Dreamer, Icarus' Mother, Curse of the Starving Class*, and *Angel City*.

A kind of Renaissance man, Shepard is also the author of short stories, poems, monologues (*Hawk Moon*), and screenplays (*Zabriskie Point*). He has acted in *Days of Heaven* and *Resurrection* and been a drummer in the rock band Holy Modal Rounders. He is also the recipient of several Obie awards (for *La Turista* and *The Tooth of Crime*), and a Pulitzer Prize for Drama (for *Buried Child*).

Shepard's theatre, though derivative to a certain degree, as suggested above, is also innovative. Never flesh and blood, his protagonists, particularly in *Operation Sidewinder*, although stereotypic and abstract, are poetic and conventionally realistic. They are reminiscent of the two-dimensional hieratic Hopi drawings, which, though giving the impression of simplicity of form, convey a complex of feelings, not the least of which is infinite awe for nature in all of its manifestations. Although the emotions of Shepard's

characters run high, their seemingly exaggerated detachment and intellec-
tualization become butts for satire. Shepard's mélange of semi-fictional
and down-to-earth protagonists, each endowed with his or her own code
of honor, invites brittle and shocking confrontations on stage, violence and
brutality frequently taking over. Since such theatrical techniques as mimesis and empathy are rarely used by Shepard, the play's viscerality and
philosophical message rest to a great extent on the depth and impact of
the thoughts and images provoked in the spectator.

Two worlds are at odds in *Operation Sidewinder:* America's technological and materialistic aspect as opposed to its spiritual and cultural side.
Shepard's innovative vision in the play stems from his blending of science
and myth, the profane and the sacred. The intermingling of rough and
tough American cowboy, rock, drug, military, and hipster mores with
ancient Hopi religious customs and language makes his play unique in
theatre.[2]

Paradisiac Snake to Machine

As in Genesis, when "darkness was on the face of the deep" (1:2), *Operation Sidewinder* opens onto a black stage, creating a mood of mystery and
wonderment. The richest of non-colors or the sum of all colors, black
symbolizes undifferentiated primal material. From this great reservoir of
all things, this precreative substance, emerge vital and motivating forces.

Sound then comes forth from Shepard's stage: the protracted sharp and
strident noise of a rattlesnake grows disturbingly louder. Color next invades the proscenium in the form of flashing and glowing lights: "blue
light fills the ceiling of the stage . . . a bright flash of yellow light from the
center of the stage floor" encircles a large sidewinder rattlesnake coiled
and ready to strike.[3]

That Shepard has recourse first to the audible rather than to the visual
world not only activates the esoteric aspect of his drama, but also gives
primacy to the magic power of vibratory rhythms and tonalities. For
Shepard, following in the tradition laid out by Artaud in *The Theatre of
Cruelty*, concrete imitative sounds or nonrepresentative sounds produced
during the course of a play convey what words cannot. Flashing lights, for
Shepard, take on the power of a protagonist: they create an atmosphere
capable of moving the spectator to anxiety, terror, eroticism, or love.[4]

Because of its vibratory possibilities, its dazzling and dizzying effects,
lighting in *Operation Sidewinder* becomes a force that plays on spectators'
minds and psyches. Psychedelic luminosities, cast down in waves, sheets,
and fiery arrows, appear in conjunction with obscurity in the opening scene
of the play, emphasizing complementary values and suggesting cosmic

tension—even antagonism. The darker realms surrounding the lighted areas on the proscenium represent unredeemed primogenial spheres, where the light of understanding or knowledge has not yet dawned.

Strange, however, is the light which emanates from within the six-foot, thirty-pound sidewinder coiled inside the circle of yellow light ready to strike. In mystical and theurgic practices (and this is the case in Shepard's play as we will learn), the circle represents a protected and delimited area, isolating whatever is within its boundaries from foreign influences; in addition, everything within these womblike contours is encouraged to grow.

The containment of the rattlesnake within the circle separates it from all else onstage, creating a virtually sacred space, immune from danger and free from alien spirits. From within this *temenos* will occur the fundamental transformation: the actual religious unfolding.

Psychologically, we may say that the circle isolates the ego (center of consciousness) from the Self (the entire psyche), thereby protecting it from disparate psychic elements in the collective unconscious that might intrude and overwhelm it. What remains in the circle are those elements connected to the ego: the actual experience. In Shepard's play, if the ego's energetic factor (libido) were allowed to circulate freely, the power of this central force could easily be dispersed and the strength needed to persevere in the play's sacred ritual would diminish or simply vanish.

The sidewinder is an incredible apparition, reminiscent of those monstrous forces medieval people conjured up when confronted with fear and alienation. Its ruby red eyes, both animal and machine, blink on and off; its tongue spits, its rattle rattles, its body undulates to its own mechanical rhythms, its head sways from side to side, its bright yellow skin interspersed with black diamonds makes designs in space.

That the viper's eyes spit light—energy, electricity—transforms it into an *animator*. As such, it not only promotes life, but also sees to its duration. Iconographically, the serpent looks like a series of ligaments, linking together hours, events, and astral movements; its chainlike effect is comparable to an *imago mundi*.

What can we make of this formidable force? For the Westerner, Shepard's snake evokes Lucifer (*fiat lux*), Satan, and is synonymous with the dragon. As the viper rattles and stiffens on stage, ascending and descending in slow coiling movements, it arouses fear in the hearts of timorous audiences.

The Hopis, on the other hand, venerate snakes. As supernatural beings, they are cult objects, looked upon as agents of fertility, guardians of the springs of life and of immortality. The yearly shedding of their skin, which is replaced by a new one, identifies them with eternity. Because the sidewinder in particular is able to coil around a human or animal and is capable of strangulating them, it represents enormous power.

In the Hopi animist culture, the serpent is not only a cunning and venomous beast; because it slithers along in damp, cold, gluey subterranean regions and frequently vanishes from sight, it is identified with the underworld and the dead, even an ancestor. Because it inhabits two worlds, it attains cosmic stature. It is endowed with the ability to communicate with both visible and invisible domains; present and past.[5]

The sacred snake in *Operation Sidewinder* also has a technological aspect. Its ruby red eyes that blink on and off, as previously suggested, are symptomatic of high-powered energy. Hence its very existence is the product of an industrial society, and its mechanism, which triggers rhythmic undulations, indicates an engineered, and therefore unnatural quality.

The technological aspect is further corroborated at the outset of the play by a sonic boom which is heard as a jet passes overhead; by the noise of a car screeching to a halt, backing up, door slamming. The deafening cacophony, in addition to the nerve-wracking visual effects—the sidewinder's blinking ruby red eyes, the car's bright headlights, and the virtually blinding yellow luminosities flooding the stage—trigger tension and bewilderment. So harsh are these radiances that stage objects become difficult to see.

In the midst of this paradoxically automated but animistic vision, there appears a blatantly stereotypic individual. That he is called Man in Shepard's text, thus divesting him of a personal name and attributes, suggests his collective nature. He is just that: a typical tourist with the proverbial movie camera, cowboy hat, Bermuda shorts, Hush Puppies, open shirt, and hairy chest. Banal and unimaginative in his actions and dialogue, he is what he is.

As the Man's gaze focuses on the serpent, he calls to his wife. Equally stereotypical, she is categorized as a sex symbol, "with long blonde hair and tight pants, high heels." He asks her to bring him his tripod. Her pet name, Honey, ironically symbolizes a sweetness that does not exist in their relationship; his, Dukie, is equally sarcastic, indicating his nonexistent power over her and an elegance he does not possess. Indeed, the couple are married in name alone and are en route to divorce. Their relationship is as perfunctory and mechanical as the undulations of the snake, the sounds of the sonic boom and the car's motor, and the blinding lights blanketing the stage.

Contrary to the myth in Genesis, it is not the wife in *Operation Sidewinder* who drags the husband into evil; rather, she warns him to be careful of the sidewinder's venom. If poison is interpreted symbolically, it indicates an imbalance in a person's system that leads to infection or ill health. By extension, the same may be said of societies, as witnessed by the flies in Thebes, the plagues in Egypt, the aridity surrounding the Grail Castle. To approach the sidewinder in Shepard's play, as either a mythical or mechanical force, is to experience it as potentially death-dealing.

Honey peers at the sidewinder, making a wide circle around it, as physicians would draw a line with disinfectant around a wound or tainted area to guard against the spread of infection. Honey is mesmerized by the rhythmic swaying of this fearsome creature. Its hissing and rattling sonorities, its electrifying illuminations, dizzy and bewitch her. She begins to wonder why she has been brainwashed and taught to fear snakes. "I mean he's just out here trying to get a suntan or something. There's nothing awful about that. He looks kind of tense but I'll bet he'd loosen up in no time at all if he got the right kind of attention. . . . Little mice and stuff. I'll bet he'd make a nice pet."

Dukie, interested in getting a spectacular photograph of the snake that he can show off to his friends, asks Honey to "aggravate" it. As she stomps her foot, then hisses, the sidewinder's phallic attributes come to the fore. It suddenly leaps up, grabs her around the neck, and pulls her to the ground, while powerful energetic forces seem to shoot out from its red eyes. She screams. Dukie jumps away and runs down the road to get a Forest Ranger.

During the blackout that follows, sexual fantasies are conjured up in the spectators' imaginations, as the Holy Modal Rounders perform "Do it Girl," the first of several songs concluding each of the scenes in the play. These songs are not only reminiscent of the ancient Greek chorus that brought audiences up to date on theatrical events, but of rock culture as well as the techniques implicit in Hopi shamanism. Considered a "secret language" for the Hopis, their songs are sung softly, frequently improvised by shamans who use them to call forth titular deities, spirits of ancestors, and the like. When deeply immersed in song, a shaman may reach a state of ecstasy, thereby confirming the fact that the "power" alive within him is the direct inspiration for his vocal creation. If, during the period of protracted concentration required of this act, the shaman should reach a trance state, his voice may become unrecognizable: the strange and high-pitched tones emerging from him, it is believed, are those of some extraterrestial force that has taken over his body. Visions of all types may also come into his mind's eye. These may range from an inner light to whirlwinds, flowers, birds, or his own journey in the pursuit of a lost soul.[6]

Shaman magicians, healers, educators, adjudicators, and demiurges are all part of American Indian clans. Looked upon as "Master of Fire" and "Master of Spirits," the shaman is the virtual patriarch of the tribe, and the wisdom residing in him is believed to have been transmitted from extratemporal sources, his powers stemming in part from his ability to communicate with spirits and perform miracles. Unlike the priests of other religious groups who pray to God or gods, saints, or holy people, asking for their beneficence, shamans dominate these extraterrestrial forces. A shaman's effectiveness resides in his skill at relating to a world that lies beyond the visible domain: an invisible, animistic sphere tingling with life, where mysterious spirits make their feelings and intentions known in happy or sorrowful events.[7]

Just as shamans of old had attempted through song to exorcise sickness from their patients by invoking supernatural powers, so Shepard uses this same techinque to bring a couple's (and by extension, society's) pathogenetic ways into better focus, hoping to heal them more effectively. Not only are Dukie and Honey devoid of a common denominator, but their existence has no goal and feeling. To unmask the etiology of America's pathogenetic condition through ritual song, dialogue, and the mythical/mechanical experience would be to transform corrupt, decadent, and dehumanized America by restoring its nutritive and creative powers.

No sooner does the song fade out than the blinking red eyes of the sidewinder turn into yellow lights that slowly rise about ten feet off the ground. Is another supernatural/mechanical entity about to greet audiences? No. They are to be made privy to a garage. The yellow-tail lights blinking on and off are those of a small Volkswagen standing above ground on a hydraulic lift. Two stereotypic protagonists are deep in conversation: a mechanic wearing greasy coveralls and a Young Man with long blond hair, a bright purple T-shirt, tight leather pants, and bare feet.

The use of flashing lights—eyes that turn into headlights—not only lends continuity to the various scenes, but underscores both the miraculous and the mechanistic nature of worldly existence. Eyes symbolize perception and clairvoyance; be it with regard to the sidewinder and the shaman or when identified with the car. In these three cases eyes allow sight in darkness, as do glittering stars and infinite night; they likewise convey an inner spiritual glow which becomes visible in time to those who can peer deeply into matter—those whose sensibilities feel powerfully even through opacity. The protagonists in *Operation Sidewinder* need desperately to *see* into their subliminal spheres to better understand their desires and yearnings.

That the Young Man's car is in need of repair may be symptomatic of his own emotional ill health. A modern fetish, the car has become an obsession; the *sine qua non* of his life. That its lights cannot be turned off indicates a malfunction of both the machine and the Young Man's psyche. Strong lights have blinded him. He has no vision into himself and needs continuous highs to keep him from sinking into despair. When the Mechanic tells the Young Man that his voltage regulator or generator is out of order, he is alluding, symbolically, to the Young Man's denial of his own ill health. He does not recognize the fact that his use of drugs has debilitated him physically as well as psychologically. Like Honey and Dukie, the Young Man bears a collective nomenclature, because, like them and others of his generation, he is lost and identityless. Is it any wonder that human life has little meaning for him?

The sound of a car screeching to a halt is again heard. Now, however, we see not a joyous tourist but a virtually hysterical Man (Dukie) enter the garage. He asks the Mechanic to get help for his wife. Angry because of the interruption, the Young Man orders the Mechanic to continue fixing his car. When the Man rushes toward the Young Man, the latter takes out a revolver and shoots him to death.

Another stereotype now appears: Billy, an old prospector with long gray beard, floppy hat, boots, overalls, and pots and pans attached to him. A relic of America's past, this father figure is somewhat reminiscent of those driven men who long ago searched through thick and thin for precious mineral deposits, founded mining towns, and dreamed of possessing vast fortunes.

That Honey is "lying frozen" with the snake coiled around her body, its red eyes still blinking furiously, does not stop Billy from sitting down and spinning his own yarn. Using the jargon of the period in the early 1900s when the now-dead town was booming with excitement, he re-creates the American myth as it was once experienced and has since been realized in countless western films. Ensconced in his own world, Billy is oblivious to Honey's plight, nor is he aware of the orgasm she is having as the Young Man makes his unexpected appearance on the scene.

The Young Man is equally oblivious to the 'absurd' Honey, imprisoned in her sexuality and strangled by her overwhelming psychological and intellectual limitations. He focuses directly on Billy, whom he knows; hands him a gun to give to the half-breed Mickey Free. We learn later that the Young Man, with Billy's and Mickey Free's help, is intent upon carrying out an incredible scheme: he plans to seize Air Force planes on the desert by dropping dope into a military reservoir and poisoning the soldiers. The Young Man exits to the tune of the sidewinder's continuous hissing, spitting, rattling, and eye-blinking and the strains of "A Beautiful Bird in a Gilded Cage" and "Generalogy," anticipating the following scene, which takes place on an American military base.

In the military scene, the traditional Air Force Colonel, seated with one foot on his desk, is featured talking in his office to an equally conventional Captain. Both men, having imbibed a good deal of brandy, are so inebriated that during the course of their conversation they keep personifying animals, referring to them as "he," "she," or "brats," projecting whatever displaced emotion they feel, or whatever ideals they conjure up to remedy society's ills, upon "human" pigs and dogs. Nor do they, any more than the radical Young Man, feel guilty when they kill people. All rationalize their acts: they are perpetrated for the good of the cause—for whatever that is.

The dialogue next centers on a very special high-tech machine, a sidewinder computer invented by the mad Dr. Vector. This incredible engineering feat not only enables greater study of outer space—where UFOs have been spotted—but is endowed with human attributes. Its intelligence is such, however, that it has escaped the confines of the military base.

The sidewinder computer emphasizes *eyes* more than any other organ. The intent here is to see into the skies, into an impersonal world; it is a counterpart, psychologically, to the collective unconscious. To look for a round metallic object, which some have described as a "flying spider" coming from another planet and possessing a shell-like carapace that shines like metal, is its goal. That a snake computer should have the capacity to observe this brilliantly illuminated insect-like entity flying through space is possible for the speculative mind.

To get caught up in the coils of a snake, as is Honey's case, leads not to a broadening of vision, but to strangulation and, consequently, a divestiture of life. Indeed, such imprisonment, be it in an ethos, an attitude, or a religious or political creed, results in alienation, isolation, and an inability to reach out to the world at large. Such stricture may invite psychic catastrophe by allowing inertia or insanity to take over. On the other hand, humans have always wanted to visit the heights and the depths: to journey in a *katabasis* or an *anabasis*, intent upon finding a common denominator between polarities which would lead to increased self-knowledge.[8]

That the need to investigate UFOs, along with galaxies in general, places emphasis on nonearthly matters: a striving as in the collective visions in medieval times to lift oneself out of the dross of empirical reality into aerated or sublimated realms. The sidewinder computer, the most advanced high-tech instrument, focuses upward, and implies, along with space travel, humankind's need to pierce nature's mysteries. As a mechanical object, however, it must adhere to the laws of gravitation until the time comes when an "anti-gravity" entity is produced. Only one factor, as far as we know, is not subject to the law of gravity: the psyche, which is weightless. Visions of UFOs and the need to clarify their origins, then, are based for the most part on emotional foundations. They are projections, psychologically speaking, resulting in part from developments in science that make it possible to explore outer space but provoke fear in the explorers. After all, if humans are spying on others in space, it stands to reason that they might be spying on us. Didn't the ancient Hopis, along with Aztecs and Judeo-Christians, among other religious groups, believe that giants, superior to humankind in all ways, descended from the heavens and stalked the earth?[9]

The sidewinder computer, as a symbol, seeks an answer in the spheres above to fulfill a spiritual need. As a snake, it represents earthly and subliminal powers, the instinctual/natural realm. No matter what its origin, the sidewinder also depends upon unknown mysterious forces. Let us suggest in this regard that there is no development upwards without the aid of the unconscious. Consciousness can distinguish, probe, and plot the next steps in scientific discovery, but the subliminal sphere, in the last analysis, is the giant power that brings forth the creative act.

In its invention of the sidewinder computer, humankind uses the instrumentality of a snake whose habitat is the earth, rather than the airborne bird or dove. This suggests a need not only to regress to a long-forgotten or rejected stage of psychological evolution, but to discover a new philosophical and ideational turn of mind. The snake, a much maligned creature in Western religious tradition, takes on the attributes of a highly sophisticated mechanism in Shepard's play. As a metaphor for discovery and learning, it indicates the attempt in *Operation Sidewinder* to fuse the enormous split existing between spiritual and instinctual needs.

Deviation from the instinctual world is as dangerous as its counterpart, the cutting off of spiritual factors. In either case, a condition of *enantiodromia* may result: one pair of opposites in the continuous interplay between the energetic process (*libido*) in the psyche leads to its opposite. Good and evil, reason and instinct, love and hate, action and passivity, each in keeping with the personality's needs and motivations, will bring about a condition of dangerous one-sidedness. Such is the state of Shepard's stereotypic protagonists: each is ensconced in his or her own needs, blind to both outer and inner worlds, earth and heaven, suffering deeply from the schism tearing the psyche apart and unable to find a curative agent.

Suspense enters into the drama. What is the sidewinder computer doing out in the middle of nowhere? How this multimillion dollar marvel left the Air Force base and where it went are the questions implicit in the song "Catch Me," concluding the scene. Are machine and serpent one? Are reality and myth identical?

When the half-breed Mickey Free enters the stage area along with two Apache Indians, all dressed in typical renegade outfits of the late eighteen hundreds, they watch with unexpected intensity as the serpent sensually intertwines its coils around Honey, its red eyes flashing continuously. Mickey Free, blind in his right eye, squints constantly as he peers strangely at this undulating form. Is there an affinity between Mickey Free, who has sight only in one eye, and the Greek Tiresias, who was completely blind but could *see* within? Will the half-breed Indian be the *vates* of Shepard's drama? The one to resolve the situation via his own perception?

Roused from her agony-ecstasy, Honey calls to Mickey Free for help. Speaking in Apache language, he takes out his huge Bowie knife, kneels down behind Honey, strokes the sidewinder's head, soothing it with certain sounds emanating from his throat, then suddenly seizes and squeezes its neck, and, as the snake shows its huge fangs defensively, cuts off its head.

The Indians, making signs of approval, touch the viper's head, whereupon Mickey Free drops it into a beaded pouch which he has tied to his waist. Honey screams hysterically, then throws the snake's body downstage, after which she collapses.

The Young Man, who makes his appearance long enough to sit down with the Indians, takes two plasticene bags filled with white powder out of his crotch and gives them to Mickey Free, along with the promise of more guns to further his radical scheme.

Alone with Honey onstage, the Young Man takes up the sidewinder's body and uses it as a tourniquet, opens a vial, draws the liquid into a syringe and shoots himself with dope. Honey, who thinks he is a diabetic, complains of her diminishing energy. She, too, needs insulin. Whereupon he shoots her up, after which she screams "Euphoria"—to the tune of the next song.

The plot thickens when audiences are informed that the Young Man is a lackey for three black militants. Dressed in paramilitary uniforms, they drive onto the stage in a '57 Chevy convertible, stopping at a desert hot-dog stand. In pitifully puerile terms, they tell of their plans to overthrow the government. Their names, Blood, Blade, and Dude, are as stereotypic as those of the other Shepard protagonists. The bathos of their dialogue not only reveals a distressing emotional state, but an attitude toward their radical approach to empirical reality that is as self-indulgent as the Young Man's. Certainly this is not the stuff of which revolutionary leaders are made. Neither Lenin nor Marat nor Burke nor Condorcet nor Jefferson could have possibly been models for these undisciplined people. Unlike the leaders of the past, these modern characters seek immediate gratification, without the years of struggle and preparation needed to pave the way for the creation of a satisfactory form of government. Like the Weathermen or the Panthers, negativity is their byword, the ruckus and damage created by the noise to be used to draw attention to their views, giving them— under the guise of a new banner—a sense of identity while also endowing their lives with what they consider to be meaning.

Only at the conclusion of Act I do audiences realize the magnitude of the problems and questions arising because of the sidewinder's escape. According to Dr. Vector, the disappearance of this mechanical creation indicates, with no doubt whatsoever, the existence of another form of intelligence.

The machine is intended to transcend the barriers of human thought and penetrate an extraterrestial consciousness.

> This is when I began my studies of the Western rattlesnakes and experimenting with the possibilities of their rhythmic movements being directly connected with the movements of the planets and the flight patterns of the UFO'S. These studies resulted in the initial design for my sidewinder computer. . . . [I]f it succeeds . . . we will be in direct contact with these flying objects and eventually with those who operate and control them!

Sidewinder: Myth and Machine?

The enactment of the first Hopi ("People of Peace") religious ceremony in *Operation Sidewinder* takes place in a mountain cave, or *kiva*. It is not only gripping for its philosophical and spiritual impact, but for its spectacular theatricality.

The Hopis, who considered themselves the first inhabitants of America, lived in inhospitable and unyielding desert regions. Understandably, in view of the harshness of their environment, they emphasized fertility rituals which were regulated in keeping with the sun's trajectory, the rainfall, and other natural events. Their lives were lived in accordance with their belief in a universal plan which was manifested in the "Road of Life." The complex mythoreligious systems of the Hopis include sacred ceremonies, rituals, dances, songs, and prayers, the enactment of which permits them to adhere to their traditional ways.[10]

The kiva (world below) is an underground chamber in which sacred songs are learned, dances practiced, and religious rituals held. Cylindrical or rectangular in shape, kivas are sunk deep into the body of Mother Earth, thus nourishing worshippers who spend time in the *temenos* during their life and return there after death. A small hole in the floor of the kiva leads down into the underworld; while a ladder, opening through the roof, guides the hierophant to the world above.[11]

On stage, soft yellow candlelight illuminates the kiva in which Mickey Free sits cross-legged, holding the sidewinder's head in his cupped hand. The serpent's tongue still spits out its venom; its red eyes continue to blink on and off. Mickey Free has not made the drop as planned. Instead, he went to the kiva to speak with the Spider Lady, who now sits opposite him.

A motherly person as well as a wizened old Indian shaman with long white hair, the Spider Lady is a favorite among the Indians of the Southwest. It was she, according to the Hopi creation myth, who took some earth, mixed it with saliva, and molded it into two beings. Those in need seek her protection as well as her wise counsel. The candles surrounding her onstage are earthly counterparts of the heavenly life-giving sun, whose movements, under certain circumstances, she controls. Everything associated with the Spider Lady is not merely spiritual. She is very much involved in earthly matters, as attested to by the rifles and ammunition which are spread throughout the kiva, along with ribbons, red-fox tails, and religious artifacts. An eerie note is added to the scene as white smoke pours out of the bowls of incense placed in niches in the walls of the cave.[12]

The Spider Lady and Michey Free each sip a steaming sacred brew from a bowl they pass back and forth. He informs her of the great power he possesses—the head of the sidewinder—but says he has come for counsel because he lacks the wisdom to make good use of this force. Her obligation, he informs her, is to disclose the mysteries involved. Emanating from her very depths, her voice, a collective instrument for the Hopis, tells of the coming of a great war which will mark the end of the Fourth World and the preparation for the Emergence of the Fifth. The conflict will revolve around material and spiritual matters, the former being destroyed by the latter, thereby paving the way for the creation of "one world and one nation under one power, that of the Creator." The serpent's head is a *sign* for that which will come to pass. As for Mickey Free, he is destined to play a part in this Emergence: "Those who are at peace in their own hearts already are in the great shelter of life."

The magic brew imbibed has expanded the Spider Lady's consciousness, inspiring her to trace the cosmogony of the Hopi people. She counsels that the sidewinder's head must be allowed to speak to Mickey Free's heart. Only then will he experience the truth of Hopi reality.

The Spider Lady may be looked upon as a totemic form, like the Fate Spinner of Greek mythology (Moera or Athena), or the Hindu Maya, sitting at her Wheel of Fate, weaving the web within which the future can be foretold. As the spinner of old ways, however, she is not considered a creative force, and this is as it should be since she is old. As the eternal voice of wisdom, the Spider Lady cautions clan members to be on guard and never allow the Life Pattern given to the Hopis by the Great Spirit to vanish. Because detachment marks her ways, her advice is considered objective and prophetic rather than admonitory. As the keeper of the fire, the sustaining force of her culture, she carries its torch, and in so doing preserves its fragile but authentic relationship with nature. It is she who appears to believers in times of trouble, be they relatives, friends, or strangers.[13]

The thundering sound of pounding feet penetrates a blackened proscenium as low moaning chantings in Hopi language cascade forth. The atmosphere of the group-Self, past, present, and future, living out its destiny on arid, wind-beaten mesas, is most evident. As the hierophants sing and thump their feet, they seem to be endowed with the sustenance needed to heal their frequently aching souls—the mood absorbing the individual into the group, interweaving the many into the one.

The Hopi chants, with their repetitive vocal responses, their intricate rhythms, stark imagery, and continuous footwork, open the worshippers up to outerworldly spheres. Thus are participants invited to return to a mythical past: to an *illud tempus*, where a new beginning is experienced and thought and feeling come together. So, too, do other conflictual spheres, such as abstraction and earthiness, good and evil, fuse into a cohesive whole. To regress to a primordial past, through song and dance, allows a Hopi to know the "Spirit of the Breath" or "Breath Body," the "Mighty Something," viewed as a composite concept of divinity. The emotionality of the experience anchors him to both his inner world and the cosmos. The interaction between the two, viewed as the pull and tug between the individual and the collective, and, psychologically, as the struggle between the ego (household and clan) and the Self, helps him carry the burden of empirical reality.[14]

A change of scene: at its center is Mickey Free's *wikiup*, described as "a small oval-shaped structure made out of bent twigs, old sheets of metal, mud, strips of cloth and a dark blanket covering the door." Eight chanting Snake Priests are seated in a semicircle around an old pit. The Chief, in the center, holds a ceremonial standard. Three large pottery jars, the tops of which are covered with antelope skin, have been placed in front of the priests.

> Behind them is the snake altar: a large screen of antelope skin stretched on four long sticks. Three large Hopi Kachina dolls are painted on the skin with other symbols, semicircles and figures. Large snake bodies and heads protrude from the skin in bright colors; these operate like hand puppets from behind the screen, so at a certain point in the ceremony they will come alive and wriggle to the dance.
>
> In front of the screen are several stalks of corn and tall poles with feather and ribbon streamers dangling from their tops. Encircling the entire group and the altar is a line of sacred yellow cornmeal.

Kachinas (*Ka*, meaning "respect"; *china*, defined as "spirit") are invisible forces of life which are invoked to help humans pursue their eternal journey. These spiritual beings have existed since humankind's earthly beginnings. After the Emergence from the Underworld, the Kachinas, through their songs and dances, sustained the Hopis through their many wanderings and the ordeals these entailed.[15]

The Hopis in Mickey Free's wikiup, having donned their Kachina masks, are so imbued with the power infused in them by these supernatural visitors that they lose their personal identities, moving about on stage alone, aloof, and awe-inspiring, weaving a variety of spatial patterns about the proscenium.

Masks are not only believed to be invested with outerworldly power, but are deeply involved in the very life of the clan: they are, so to speak, its heart.[16] So sacred are some Kachina masks that they are fed daily, prayers and songs are recited by their guardians, and the right to wear them is hereditary.[17]

The sacred corn and cornmeal, also part of Shepard's staged cere-mony, represent the Corn Mother. Indeed, so crucial is this vegetable to the Hopis (it was created by divinity during the First World), that no ceremonial is conducted without it. The Hopis believe that corn unites two principles of creation: male and female. The stalks, growing up-wards in spirals along with the first tassels, symbolize the male element; the ear, which is female, is ready to be fertilized by the male element. In that the Corn Mother serves as nourishment, it stands for earth; because it was divinely created, it also serves as spirit. Sprinkled frequently around kivas to warn of a ceremony in progress, and equated in impor-tance with mother's milk, cornmeal is also used to circumscribe the entire performing group, as in Shepard's play—keeping the participants within a sacred mandala.

The white streaks and circles decorating the faces of the Indians per-forming in the ritual represent a symbolic ascension to heavenly spheres; the black tones stand for the fertile moist earth in its capacity for transfor-mation. Like the mask, the black-and-white designs (ovals, circles, and wavy lines) represent protective imagery. The dancer wearing the ritual object (mask, costume) or painting his body becomes so identified with the supernatural power he calls on for aid (sun, moon, water, animal, ancestor) that he feels the actual transformation taking place during the performance. A supernatural relationship between the dancer and the tutelary being comes to pass, and this intimacy with primary forces en-dows both the individual and the clan with greater power and authority.

The spectacular nature of the Snake-Antelope ritual as enacted in *Opera-tion Sidewinder* is unforgettable. The variety of rhythmic patternings in the Hopis' songs and their lilting, crooning, high- and low-pitched monotones, are reminiscent of wind passing through crags, corn, or bean blossoms, mesmerizing believers and non-believers alike.[18]

The colorful accoutrements worn by the priests—turquoise and shell necklaces, blue loincloths with black snake designs, fringed belts around the waist, a fox-skin tail fastened to the belt in back, a turquoise shell rattle tied to the right knee, moccasins and other ornaments—are symbols of a deeper reality, a primordial mystery, as unfathomable to them as to contemporary observers.

Now the Chief, followed by the other priests, "removes the skin from the top of the jar and tips the jar toward the pit. The chanting mounts in volume and intensity. Suddenly, on cue from the Chief, they all dip the jars down into the pit. Dozens of snakes of all sizes and colors slither from the jars into the pit. The chanting keeps up until all the snakes have disappeared into the pit."

The jars, containers of life and immortality, representing a kind of physical and intellectual womb and paving the way for a return to the clan's origins, enclose the sacred snakes. As phallic symbols, the snakes have penetrated the pit, or burrowed deeply into the Great Mother. Fetishes for tutelary spirits, Gods, or ancestors, and agents of fertility who can communicate between upper and lower worlds, the serpents gathered for the Snake-Antelope ritual, one of the Hopis' most holy ceremonies, are protected from harm in the votive jars.

Shockingly antithetical to the profoundly religious liturgy enacted onstage is Honey's and the Young Man's abrupt arrival. Their conversation, mundane as usual, centers on such material questions as apple pie and coffee, movies, Elvis Presley, money, taxes, cars, and refrigerators.

Suddenly, two Indians armed with knives jump Honey and the Young Man and pin them down. Mickey Free, dressed in ceremonious attire, his face painted with white zigzags, emerges from the wikiup and has them released. He informs them, however, of his change of heart: no longer is he interested in guns or drugs, nor does he plan to impose his views on the world. When he notices that the Young Man is carrying the sidewinder's body, he screams shrilly, "You are the Pahana! Lost White Brother, the Salvation," grabs the Young Man, and begins dancing with him.

The Hopis believe that after the Fourth World emerged a guardian spirit (Masaw) told them how and where to migrate, settle, and enact the laws that were to regulate their lives. These had been written down in symbols—some featuring snakes—on four sacred tablets, one given to each of the clans. Only with the appearance of the Pahana would suffering cease and universal brotherhood be possible.

It is fated that the Young Man should bring the snake's body to Mickey Free for reattachment. Hadn't the Spider Lady predicted the advent of the Pahana, a power instrumental in the unification of the snake?

Mickey Free reaches such a state of ecstasy that he grabs the sidewinder's body, holds it over his head, and continues his frenetic dancing, joined moments later by the other two Indians. The unification ceremony can now begin, he states. "My brothers and I have followed many separate ways, sometimes killing each other. Tonight we shall all see the kingdom. Tonight the spirit snake shall become one again and with it shall join all its people."

Although the Young Man tells him that the sidewinder is a computer and not a God, Mickey Free invites the nonbelievers to join in the ceremony. "You have brought us to our emergence. It will take us to a place we will never come back from. You are welcome to enter and follow us there or stay here on this earth and follow your will. The stars will watch you as you go."

The ever-louder chanting fills the temenos with a mood of sacrality that has a mesmerizing effect upon Honey. No longer is this flesh-pot woman interested only in hamburgers and Elvises. A spiritual power now inhabits her being, and after remarking that the monotonous chanting she hears around her is "like hearing wind," she enters into a trance state, rises, and walks toward the wikiup. As she reaches this sacred inner space, a blue flash of light fills the heavens, followed by the sound of a jet. The Young Man, alienated from society and from himself and unable to cope with the harrowing alternative of loneliness, also walks toward the wikiup as he recites the Lord's Prayer.

The entire stage area crackles with the intensity of the new reality brought into being. Time is no longer linear; it has stretched, deepened, kineticized, enveloping in its paradoxically etherealized grasp both the sensate and nonmaterial world. The eternal present which now prevails invites acolytes and hierophants to experience upper and lower spheres as but a single totality—as if winter were blending into summer, day into night, life into death—the All perpetually decanting into the reservoir of Universal Being.

As blue lights flash about, casting ominous shadows on the floor, walls, and ceiling, sacred songs are droned with increasing amplitude until the voices reach a peak of frenzy. Eight Antelope Priests leave the wikiup in single file. They are dressed like the Snake Priests described previously, but painted with ash-gray and white zigzag lines, the former tone an annunciation of death, or of an eternal return, since it is magically linked to the world of germination. The gourdlike rattle carried by each of the priests symbolizes gestation, the womb. One priest beats on a large antelope drum, its primordial tones and rhythms replicating universal sonorities and pulsations, as well as echoing the sacred thunder which precedes the much-wanted rain. Used by shamans to invoke protective forces, drums, like song and dance, pave the way for ecstasy: the fusion of duality which permits fluid access from upper to lower worlds, visible to invisible spheres—inviting divination to become a reality.

Chanting in pronounced rhythmic sequences continues as the Snake and Antelope Priests proceed single file toward the snake pit, then stop on either side and face each other. The sacred space begins to reverberate as the hierophants stomp with their right feet, sway in unison while shaking their rattles, then gather in a round, fan out single file, and circle the stage four times, singing their incantations in slow cadenced patterns.

Identified with the earth, the foot and the leg ensure equilibrium: they support the body and keep it upright. They are also endowed with phallic significance, for as they hit the earth they seem to be inseminating it with raw vital energy, feeding it with their own specific elements—universal substances—in the same way as the farmer pounds the ground to encourage germination when planting his seeds.

The Priests move toward the snake pit, which they encircle while linking arms. As they bend over this most sacred area, mouthing sounds which range from low pitches to high shrieks, they experience the most holy part of the ritual: a psychic happening which ushers in a cosmic discharge.

> The CHIEF PRIEST of the snake group kneels down and puts his head into the pit. He comes up with a snake in his mouth. The others fan back and the CHIEF SNAKE PRIEST dances with the writhing snake in his mouth. The ANTELOPE PRIESTS fan off and dance to the right side of the stage. . . . One of the SNAKE PRIESTS dances out from the line toward the CHIEF and waves two long eagle feathers over the snake's head as the CHIEF dances with it. The snake goes limp and the CHIEF lets it drop to the floor. A third SNAKE PRIEST dances out with a stick and waves it over the snake then bends down, picks it up with both hands, holds it aloft and dances over to the ANTELOPE PRIESTS.

The moment of deepest concentration (*pavasio*) occurs as the Snake and Antelope Priests, each in turn, put their heads into the pit—the place of Emergence from the lower to upper worlds—as if summoning the very essence of life. So powerful is the grip of faith on the psychic system that as the hierophant withdraws his head, a snake clutched tightly between his teeth, the depth of meaning of the event takes precedence over all else and the reptile is rendered harmless. The canalization of libido which occurs at this juncture engulfs the act in a holiness, greatness, and livingness which is all-pervasive.[19]

At the height of the ceremony, Mickey Free, wearing a blue kachina mask and holding the sidewinder's head in his left hand and its body in his right, enters the stage space. He is accompanied by Honey and the Young Man. Honey, whose face is painted like that of the Snake Priests, indicating her link with fertility, wears a long black dress and a white and red cape; her hair is loose, with eagle feathers attached to the back. The Young Man is identified with the Antelope Priests, suggesting his association with more spiritual matters; he has an eagle feather tied to the front of his hair. Both hold earthen jars containing sacred oil in preparation for initiation into mystery, which will endow them with group protection and feelings of continuity, counteracting the rootlessness and aridity of their world.

The enactment of an ancient ceremony, that of the mystic marriage between the Snake Maiden and the Antelope Youth, will endow their lives with purpose and direction. A union of another kind is also assured during this ceremony, that of the Snake and Antelope clans: the lowest vibratory centers or generative organs of being are linked to the highest or most ethereal spheres. The head or crown is the "open door" by means of which a mortal communicates with deity: that area where gross and spiritual life eternally become one.

Honey kneels facing the Antelope Chief, receiving his hands in blessing on her head; the Young Man kneeling before the Snake Chief experiences the sacrament in like manner and simultaneously. Hands are used to transfer energy, activity, or power from one being to another, and for the Hopi they also indicate the manifestation of a new sacred force entering into initiates. Compared frequently to the eyes, hands are likewise believed to be a means of perception: an added way of seeing into difficult opacities.

Once the acolytes are blessed, the priests push their heads into the jars of oil. This sacramental ritual is repeated twice during the course of the ceremony, after which Honey's hair is twisted together with the Young Man's as if joined for eternity. Sacred oil, a symbol for light and purity, is used by the Hopis, along with many other peoples, as nourishment for the acolyte who seeks admittance into the fraternity. Not only is hair part of a person, but, when identified with the head, stands for that individual's spiritual as well as virile qualities. Certain groups, among them Indians and Christians, venerate the hair of saints for the powers they believe they contain. Like a fetish, hair enables its possessor to participate in the qualities identified with the person to whom it originally belonged.

Wracked with fear and anguish prior to their participation in the religious ritual, Honey's and the Young Man's features are now marked with serenity and beatitude.

Enacted simultaneously with the mystic marriage is Mickey Free's rejoinder: the reattachment of the sidewinder's body to its head. The electric charge accompanying this cataclysmic event generates a thunderbolt of blue light from the serpent's body, followed by a mighty thunderclap and then a brilliant illumination in the heavens above.

Myth and machine are one—the fusion of the religious and the technical inviting outerworldly events to act in consort with motion, sound, and gesture, thereby releasing feelings associated with joy, fear, grief, and love.

The abrupt entrance of the Desert Tactical Troops, with their machine guns, pistols, and helmets, stuns audiences and readers, but not the initiated. The Hopis, whose bodies have become the instrument of experience, and who have through dancing and mimed metamorphoses established an intricate relationship with the cosmos, are oblivious to such agitation. Even when the paratroopers attempt to grab the sidewinder, a blue light suddenly emanates from the reptile, another from the sky, the two working together, no longer divergently. What is above is below, said the ancient Egyptian mystic Hermes Trismegistus; the same belief is inherent in Hopi religious practices.

Still holding the sidewinder above his head, Mickey Free—along with the Indians and the just-initiated Honey and Young Man—begins moving slowly toward the Desert Tactical troops; then, chanting their litanies, the ceremonial group encircles them. Fearful of strangulation, not by the sidewinder this time but by the group, the paratroopers attempt to break away, then order the group to hand over the reptile. As the Hopis continue swaying and chanting, closing in all the while on the paratroopers, they are so identified with their ancestral spirits that they are oblivious to the fact that the soldiers have opened fire on them. Suddenly a paratrooper reaches up and grabs the sidewinder, separating its body and head once again. Then,

> Bright bolt of blue light from the sky. The D.T.T.'s scream as though being blinded. The lights go to black after the blue light, then back to bright blue. Each interval of light and dark lasts about five seconds. . . . Huge gusts of wind blow from upstage directly out into the audience, changing from hot to cold. . . . Streams of smoke come from all around. . . . The chanting increases. A high frequency whine. The chanting becomes amplified. The bright blue light flashes on, the INDIANS are in ecstasy as they chant. The D.T.T.'s are cringing on their knees center stage. The lights go to black. The blue light again and this time all the INDIANS plus the YOUNG MAN and HONEY are gone. Just the DESERT TACTICAL TROOPS holding their ears and shielding their eyes. The lights stay up and become brighter. The whine and the chanting get louder, then everything goes black.

The horrific sparks aroused by the friction between the Indians, who experience transcendence, and the paratroopers, who are killed, fulfill the Hopis' prophecy. Because they believe in the continuation of life after death, the distinction between the living and the dead is minimal. Not only do they visit each other in the form of a cloud or Kachina, in their respective worlds, but they recall these experiences and recount them. Indeed, life in the Underworld is virtually the same as on earth.[20]

Even when gunned down at the play's conclusion, the Hopis do not die, but rather move off the stage as they set out on their eternal journey, in unison and in dignity, retaining as they walk the circular pattern destined for them since birth.

The apocalyptic image which concludes *Operation Sidewinder* underscores the exaltation experienced by those who respond to the notion of sacrality. A modern mystery play, it calls for the incorporation of the old and the new, the wedding of science and the most primitive identification with nature. Honey and the Young Man, symbolizing those who have lost their way in today's drug culture, in baseless idealism, or in fantasies designed to bring them instant gratification in all domains, have experienced redemption. Not so for the paratroopers, who remain incarcerated—strangulated—choked by their own limitations.

A disturbing and frightening work, *Operation Sidewinder* may be viewed as a rite of passage which compels contemporary acolytes to awaken and deal with life-threatening perils—not necessarily "out there," but within their own being.

The archetypal transformations which occur through the complex religious ceremony in Shepard's play encourage a new adaptation to an inner reality. The snake, be it a theriomorphic deity or a computer, participates in the fabulous events onstage, accentuating both the mythical and mechanical powers called into question.

The apotheosis in the last sequences of *Operation Sidewinder* makes for a mind-altering theatrical experience. As a combination of spirit and matter, the sidewinder becomes an object of awe: a manifestation of the divine as conveyed through His creation.

Like the shaman, whose wisdom came from extratemporal sources and was transmitted to the Hopis via the venomous rattlesnake in tribal ceremonies,[21] the playwright has created the sidewinder computer, a modern machine—as *contemporary fetish*, working in consort with the individual's spirit and intellect to produce a theatrical epiphany.

Conclusion

The impact of concrete, abstract, or human machines has been the focus of our attention in each of the works explored in *Machine, Metaphor, and the Writer*. Because our goal was to adopt a universal point of view so as to assess more broadly the reactions of creative people to the machine, we chose dramatists, novelists, and short-story writers from both the east and the west. They all posed questions. They all brought problems into the open. These revolved around the interaction between human beings and the mechanical, technological, and programmed world of which they were and are a part. Few answers were forthcoming. They preferred, as I did, to arouse thought, to awaken perceptions, to trigger curiosity and perhaps action.

In Jarry's *The Supermale*, the sex machine, the food machine, and the bicycle play such a powerful role in the life of the protagonist that he allows these relentless powers to overwhelm him and is eventually destroyed by the very objects which were not only designed to further his well-being, but also bring technological advances to society.

In Joyce's "A Painful Case" the man-machine whose robotlike personality dictated his ways awakened to the profound meaning of a *real* relationship with a woman, but only after a concrete machine, in this case a train, had caused her demise.

The Crazy Locomotive by Witkiewicz, a surrealistic work with apocalyptic implications, dramatized the fate of certain elements in society if the rule of the machine is allowed to continue. Here, too, annihilation is the outcome.

Pirandello's *Tonight We Improvise*, less drastic in its conclusion, presents a conflicting picture of a director who views the theatre as a mechanical force—"the yawning mouth of a gigantic machine that is—hungry"—and the actors who consider the dramatic event as a creative force plowing through uncharted terrain.

In a more positive and perhaps mystical vein is Saint-Exupéry's vision of a pilot who, when airborne, ascends to astral spheres where imagination roams unimpeded. From these vertiginous heights he gains access to another mode of existence. Feelings of transcendence open him up to a new poetics of space.

Arreola's "The Switchman" uses the train as an allegorical device to underscore eternality as opposed to linearity. In its machinelike capacity, the train also serves to heighten feelings of alienation and powerlessness of finite beings living in the infinite vastness of an impersonal universe.

In Yizhar's *Midnight Convoy*, the action revolves around the safe conduct of a convoy of trucks, half-trucks, and jeeps carrying crucial supplies to the army. The drama, symbolically viewed, involves more than the machine and the patriarchal sphere with which it is usually associated. It invites nature in its human and nonhuman form, along with the feminine principle, to participate in the events, thereby expanding and deepening religious values.

Osaragi's *The Journey* uses the machine—train, boat, car, bus—as a means of depicting contemporary society. Each in its own way underscores a complex network of displacements and equivocations. These mechanical vehicles not only encourage Osaragi's protagonists to shift perpetually from one area to another, but the velocities of the machines used also reflect psychic conditions ranging from frenzy and anguish, to serenity and even beatitude.

Narayan's *The Man-Eater of Malgudi* focuses on the printing press not as a producer of unending masses of volumes, newspapers, cards or the like, but rather as a mystical device. The letters, syllables, words, and sentences set down in type are viewed as meditative devices, factors activating and actualizing a secret initiatory language.

Handke's *Kaspar* treats language as machine. The dangers involved in the mechanics of language, particularly when power-hungry individuals or groups stamp the human brain with programmed instructions, are dramatized. Such a manipulative approach to language and education— the thought processees—by dictatorial individuals or groups cannot but grow increasingly fearsome in contemporary society given the autonomy of media today.

Shepard's *Operation Sidewinder* takes readers into two worlds: that of a mechanistic computerized society with its drug and rock groups, and that of the sacred and mythical domain of the Hopi Indians and the respect they feel for all living things. The common denominator of these antagonistic views is projected onto the sidewinder: considered the latest and most effective computer by contemporary society, for the Hopi Indians, it is looked upon as a fetish of sacred power which must be approached with awe.

Writers and creative artists in general, are, as Erich Neumann has suggested, the prophets of the future. The messages of the authors included in *Machine, Metaphor, and the Writer*, be they utopian, mythical, or mystical, or warning society of possible demoralization and degradation, must be evaluated, taken seriously, and dealt with accordingly.

Jarry, Joyce, Witkiewicz, Pirandello, Saint-Exupéry, Arreola, Yizhar, Osaragi, Narayan, Handke, and Shepard were deeply affected by the changes occurring in their lives and times and because they were artists were able to transform raw, unchanneled energy from their collective unconscious into novels, plays, and short stories. Their ability to channel feelings and sensations into the word, image, character, and plot, creating monstrous and robotlike individuals or humans able to soar into celestial spheres or walk the earth amid endless sands, has taken their work out of an individual frame of reference and placed it into a suprapersonal and nonindividual sphere.

The machine was the catalyst in all of the works explored in *Machine, Metaphor, and the Writer*. The machine was that factor which triggered the creative impulse in the above-mentioned authors, thus activating the archetype of transformation in the writings analyzed. When the uncreated idea or insight manifests itself in the concrete object, in our case, the machine, the psyche grows and alters in definition and course. The machine, therefore, is viewed variously by our authors. Each depicts the world as he sees it: monstrous or beautiful, robotlike or helpful, with healing or destroying powers.

The creative process allowed the writers whose works figure in *Machine, Metaphor, and the Writer* to point out the problems involved in megalithic societies with their machine-oriented focus. In so doing, the reader may perhaps better understand the complexities, dichotomies, and virtually infinite modes of organizational and power systems facing the environmental and human elements in contemporary society. Then, it is hoped that each in his or her own way may help avoid the collective collapse of civilization as we know it.

The psychological and ideational analyses in the writings of the eleven authors whose works have been explored in *Machine, Metaphor, and the Writer* may be viewed as one way of responding to the traumas plaguing our megatechnical society. For Lewis Mumford, such a course may bring forth a new consciousness and concomitantly, a new and creative dynamics—

"something like a universal awakening sufficient to produce an internal readiness for a profounder transformation" to take place.[1]

There is no one answer to the perplexities inherent in today's world. Although increasing, they are also perpetually transforming, as does everything in the life process. So individuals and nations must be ever-vigilant in determining the *right path* or the *right course* to take in order to be in a position to rectify what has gone awry in society's approach to the machine, be it concrete, abstract, or human.

Human initiative, whatever its form, may hopefully respond vitally, dynamically, critically, and creatively to situations as they arise. To do so is to awaken society to the possibility of catastrophe. The fear of extinction, viewed as a catalyst, may be used to generate fresh avenues of discovery and new fields of endeavor, thus transforming the alienated individual into the fraternal one, the detached view into a deeply committed approach to the well-being of humanity in general.

To listen to the creative artist and respond to his or her call for awareness when the need is acute, as it is today, is no longer a hope or wish, but *a necessity*. As Jung said:

> The Romans were familiar with all the mechanical principles and physical facts which would have enabled them to construct a steam engine, but all that came of it was the toy made by Hero of Alexandria. The reason for this is that there was no compelling necessity to go further.[2]

Will we allow humanity to be swept along mindlessly by the momentum of technology? Or will we attempt to find a balanced course. The problem is ours. Do we face it or walk away?

Notes

Introduction

1. Lewis Mumford, *Technics and Civilization*, p. 4.
2. Ibid.
3. C. G. Jung, *Collected Works*, 8, p. 42.
4. Ibid.
5. Ibid.
6. Ibid.
7. Erich Neumann, *Depth Psychology and a New Ethic*, pp. 30, 107.
8. Horst de la Croix and Richard G. Tansey, *Helen Gardner's Art Through the Ages*, 6th edition, pp. 717–20.
9. Phil Patton, "How Art Geared up to Face Industry in Modern America, " *Smithsonian*, 1987, p. 156.
10. Alan Trachtenberg, "The Art and Design of the Machine Age," *New York Times*, September 21, 1986.
11. Patton, p. 157.
12. Edward Edinger, "An Outline of Analytical Psychology" (unpublished), pp. 1–29.
13. Ibid.
14. Ibid.
15. Ibid.
16. C. G. Jung, *Collected Works*, 10, pars. 148–96.

Chapter 1

1. Alfred Jarry, *Le Supermale*, p. 147. All quotes come from this edition.
2. C. G. Jung, *Collected Works*, 10, p. 268.
3. Charles Baudelaire, *Oeuvres Complètes*, p. 981.
4. James Feiblemen, *In Praise of Comedy*, p. 88.
5. See Jacques Henry Levesque, *Alfred Jarry*, pp. 12–64.
6. *Helen Gardner's Art Through the Ages*, 6th edition, Horst de la Croix and Richard G. Tansey, eds., p. 733.
7. Henri Bergson, *Le Rire*, pp. 4, 5, 20.
8. Esther Harding, *Psychic Energy*, pp. 208–18.
9. Ibid., p. 107.

10. Sigmund Freud, *The Basic Writings*, p. 77.
11. Mircea Eliade, *Yoga*, p. 260.

Chapter 2

1. James Joyce, *Stephen Hero*, pp. 211–13. "A Painful Case" was written in 1904 but revised because of early weaknesses in 1906. See Richard Ellman, *James Joyce*, p. 205.
2. Bruce Bidwell and Linda Heffer, *The Joycean Way*, p. 126.
3. John Ryan, "Anna Livia Plurabelle," *Ireland of the Welcomes. James Joyce Centenary Issue*, p. 21.
4. Richard Ellman, *James Joyce*, p. 205.
5. James Joyce translated *Michael Kramer* in 1901. He hoped that it would be produced by the Irish Literary Theatre. It was not.
6. Yolande Jacobi, *Paracelsus*, p. 105.
7. C. G. Jung, *Psychological Types*, p. 583.
8. *Joyce Letters*, I, ed. Stuart Gilbert, p. 226. Joyce wrote: "Every Power in nature must evolve an opposite in order to realize itself and opposition brings reunion."
9. C. G. Jung, *Collected Works*, 8, par. 931. When synchronistic situations occur, an exterior situation may be said to coincide with an inner condition. Such a happening suggests that the archetype needed to constellate a certain luminosity manifests itself: "It is certainly not a knowledge that could be connected with the ego, and hence not a conscious knowledge as we know it, but rather a self-subsistent 'unconscious' knowledge which I would prefer to call 'absolute knowledge.' . . . It is not cognition but, as Leibniz so excellently calls it, a 'perceiving' which consists—or to be more cautious, seems to consist—of images, of subjectless 'simulacra.' These postulated images are presumably the same as my archetypes, which can be shown to be formal factors in spontaneous fantasy products. Expressed in modern language, the microcosm which contains 'the images of all creation' would be the collective unconscious."
10. Ibid., 12, p. 250.
11. Joyce, *Stephen Hero*, pp. 212–13.
12. Friedrich Nietzsche, *Le Gai Savoir*, p. 260.
13. Edward F. Edinger, "An Outline of Analytical Psychology," p. 2.
14. C. G. Jung, *Collected Works*, 7, p. 26.

Chapter 3

1. C. G. Jung, *Collected Works*, 14, p. 415.
2. Joshua C. Taylor, *Futurism*, pp. 11, 124, 126.
3. Stanislas Ignacy Witkiewicz, *Instability*, trans. with an introduction by Louis Iribarne, xxi.
4. Bernard F. Dukore and Daniel C. Gerould, eds., *Avant-Garde Drama*, p. 484.
5. Ibid., pp. 484, 491.
6. Marie-Louise von Franz, *On Dreams and Deaths*, pp. 144–45.
7. Fritjof Capra, *The Tao of Physics*, pp. 62–63.
8. *The Madman and the Nun and Other Plays by Stanislas Ignacy Witkiewicz*, trans. and ed. Daniel C. Gerould and C. S. Durer.
9. Victor Zuckerhandl, *The Sense of Music*, p. 15.
10. C. G. Jung, *Collected Works*, 7, p. 214.
11. Marie-Louise von Franz, *Alchemy*, pp. 99–100.
12. Rivkah Scarf Kluger, *Satan in the Old Testament*, p. 25.
13. Esther Harding, *Psychic Energy*, pp. 282–86.
14. Raffaele Carrieri, *Futurism* (Milan: Edizioni del Milione, 1963), p. 11. See also "Preface to the Initial Manifesto of Futurism," from Daniel C. Gerould's introduction to *The Crazy Locomotive* in *The Madman and the Nun*, p. 81.
15. C. G. Jung, *Collected Works*, 7, p. 144.

16. Harding, p. 419.
17. *The Madman and the Nun*, pp. xiii ff.
18. *The Tao of Physics*, pp. 201–3.
19. Taylor, p. 124. *The Madman and the Nun*, p. 82.
20. Harding, p. 243.
21. H. G. Baynes, *Mythology of the Soul*, p. 3.
22. *The Madman and the Nun*, p. li.

Chapter 4

1. Luigi Pirandello, *Tonight We Improvise*, p. 9.
2. A. Richard Sogiazzo, *Luigi Pirandello, Director: The Playwright in the Theatre*, p. 76.
3. Marie Louise von Franz, *Creation Myths*, p. 171.
4. Massimo Carra, *Metaphysical Art, p. 12.*
5. See Marinetti's poem, "A mon Pegase," and "L'Aviatore Futurista parla con suo Padre, il Vulcano," 1914.
6. C. G. Jung, *Collected Works*, 5, pp. 158–59.
7. Barbara G. Walker, *The Woman's Encyclopedia of Myths and Secrets*, p. 304.
8. C. G. Jung, *Collected Works*, 5, p. 6.
9. *The Woman's Encyclopedia of Myths and Secrets*, pp. 602–13. See also Geoffrey Ashe, *The Virgin* (London: Routledge and Kegan Paul, 1976), p. 151.
10. Ibid. See Amaury de Riencourt, *Sex and the Power in History* (New York: Dell Publishing, 1974), p. 150.
11. *The Woman's Encyclopedia of Myths and Secrets*, pp. 599–602. See Vern L. Bullough, *The Subordinate Sex* (Chicago: University of Illinois Press, 1973), p. 112.
12. Marie Louise von Franz, *Shadow and Evil in Fairy Tales*, p. 35.
13. Lyn Cowan, *Masochism. A Jungian View*, p. 2. See also St. Teresa of Avila, *Spiritual Relations*, in *The Complete Works of St. Teresa of Jesus*, I (New York: Sheed and Ward, 1946), p. 307.
14. Ibid., p. 21.
15. C. G. Jung, *Collected Works*, 10, p. 314.
16. Bettina L. Knapp, *Dream and Image*, pp. 52–53.
17. Liliane Frey-Rohn, "Evil from the Psycholocigal Point of View," *Evil*, p. 156.

Chapter 5

1. Marie Louise von Franz, *Puer Aeternus*, III, p. 3.
2. Lewis Mumford, *The Myth of the Machine*, p. 46.
3. Ibid.
4. Curtis Cate, *Antoine de Saint-Exupéry*, p. 48.
5. Antoine de Saint-Exupéry, *Lettres à sa Mère*, p. 18.
6. Cate, p. 103.
7. Antoine de Saint-Exupéry, *Wind, Sand and Stars*, trans. Lewis Galantière, p. 12. *Terre des Hommes*, p. 12.
8. Cate, p. 190.
9. Erich Neumann, *The Origins and History of Consciousness, pp. 432–33.*
10. Such notions are erroneous since we know today that no water exists on the moon.
11. Marie Louise von Franz, *On Divination and Synchronicity*, p. 53.

Chapter 6

1. Jose Gomez Sicre, *Three Artists of the Americas*, p. 73. Juan José Arreola, *Confabulario*, "The Switchman," trans. George D. Schade.
2. Seymour Menton, *Hispania*, 42 (Sept. 1959): 295–300.
3. Marie Louise von Franz, *On Divination and Synchronicity: Psychology of Meaningful Chance*, p. 54.

4. Jacques Soustelle, *Daily Life of the Aztecs*, pp. 108–12.
5. Ibid., p. 115.
6. Marie Louise von Franz, *Time*, p. 6.
7. Ibid., p. 10.
8. *New Larousse Mythology*, p. 436.
9. Soustelle, p. xv.
10. Yolande Jacobi, *Complex Archetype Symbol in the Psychology of C. G. Jung*, p. 48.
11. Laurette Séjourné, *Burning Water*, p. 89.
12. Ibid., p. 48.
13. C. G. Jung, *Psychogenesis of Mental Disease*, p. 40. See *Rufino Tamayo* (New York: Rizzoli, 1982).

Chapter 7

1. S. Yizhar, *Midnight Convoy and Other Stories*. S. Yizhar, a man who knows the meaning of death and destruction, has steadfastly and paradoxically fought against war his whole life. Born in Rohovot (1916), where he also taught, he participated as a soldier when the need arose in Israel's tumultuous history.

Let us glance for a moment at the traumatic events accompanying the birth of Israel in 1948, after the General Assembly of the United Nations established the United Nations Special Committee on Palestine (UNSCOP). A plan designed by UNSCOP to divide Palestine into a Jewish state, an Arab state, and a small internationally administered zone including Jerusalem was adopted on Nov. 29, 1947, by the necessary two-thirds majority of the General Assembly led by the United States and the USSR. Great Britain abstained and the Arabs left the meeting, informing those concerned that they would resist. The British began their withdrawal in 1948 as the Arabs and Jews were preparing for war. No sooner had the British high commissioner for Palestine departed than the state of Israel was proclaimed at Tel Aviv, given *de facto* recognition by the United States, and awarded *de jure* recognition by the USSR. As the combined armies of Lebanon, Syria, Jordan, Egypt, and Iraq invaded Israel, the Jews surrendered the Old City of Jerusalem to the Arab Legion of Jordan, but held on in the New City. Despite the armistice signed in late 1949, guerilla attacks, incursions, and wars—in 1956, 1967 (Six-Day War), and 1973 (Yom Kippur War)—have plagued Israel ever since.

2. Edward F. Edinger, *The Bible and the Psyche*, p. 68.
3. Aryeh Kaplan, *Meditation and the Bible*, pp. 39–42. Robert H. Pfeiffer, *Introduction to the Old Testament*, pp. 539–59. Gershom G. Scholem, *Major Trends in Jewish Mysticism*, pp. 41–79.
4. Kaplan, p. 39.
5. C. G. Jung, *Collected Works*, 11, p. 420.
6. Ibid., 5, p. 77 f. Yolande Jacobi, *Complex Archetype Symbol in the Psychology of C. G. Jung*, p. 84.
7. Bettina L. Knapp. *A Jungian Approach to Literature*, p. 329.
8. C. G. Jung, *Collected Works*, 5, p. 66.
9. Ibid., p. 85.
10. C. G. Jung, *Psychological Types*, p. 545.
11. Marie Louise von Franz, *Alchemy*, p. 8. Jacobi, pp. 62–63.

Chapter 8

1. Jiro Osaragi, *The Journey*, p. 23.
2. Ibid.
3. Ibid., p. 351.
4. William Bruce, *Religions in Japan*, p. 45.
5. Daisetz T. Suzuki, *Zen and Japanese Culture*, p. 228.
6. Introduction by Harold Strauss to Jiro Osaragi, *Homecoming*, V–VIII.

7. Ibid.

8. Yolande Jacobi, *Complex Archetype Symbol in the Psychology of C. G. Jung*, pp. 5–12.

9. Jiro Osaragi, *The Journey*, p. 3.

10. *Nagel's Encyclopedia Guide*, p. 399.

11. Suzuki, p. 298.

12. Ibid., pp. 113, 181.

13. Ibid., p. 220.

14. Noritake Tsuda, *Handbook of Japanese Art*, pp. 367–68.

15. Bettina L. Knapp, *Theatre and Alchemy*, p. 193.

16. Suzuki, p. 111.

17. Knapp, p. 195.

18. *Nagel's*, p. 541.

19. Donald Keene, ed. *20 Plays of the No Theatre*, p. 251.

20. Suzuki, p. 242.

21. *New Larousse Encyclopedia of Mythology*, p. 404.

22. Introduction to *Homecoming*, p. vi. See also Charles S. Terry, *Masterworks of Japanese Art* (Tokyo: Charles E. Tattle), p. 42, and Peter C. Swann, *A Concise History of Japanese Art* (Tokyo: Kodansha International, 1959).

23. Suzuki, p. 67.

24. Ibid., pp. 220, 222, 226.

Chapter 9

1. C. G. Jung, *Collected Works*, 6, pp. 535–36, 540, 616; 9^1, pp. 283–86. All references to Narayan's *Man-Eater of Malgudi* from Penguin Books edition, 1983.

2. Mircea Eliade, *Le Profane et le sacré*, pp. 15–19.

3. Printing was an art practiced in China from 868 B.C.; in Babylonia, where seals and stamps were used for making impression in clay; and in Korea, where movable type was made from molds at least fifty years before they were used in fifteenth-century Europe.

4. Yolande Jacobi, *Complex Archetype Symbol in the Psychology of C. G. Jung*, p. 48.

5. Mircea Eliade, *Yoga*, p. 215.

6. Aryeh Kaplan, *Jewish Meditation*, pp. 10–15.

7. Ibid., pp. 10–12.

8. *Rig-Veda*, 10.9.

9. The etymology of the word *type* is significant: in Latin, *typus* means image. This derives from the Greek *typos*, indicating a blow, impression, or model.

10. Jacobi, p. 49.

11. Heinrich Zimmer, *The King and the Corpse*, p. 239.

12. C. G. Jung, *Collected Works*, 9^1, p. 283.

13. *Sources of Indian Tradition*, I, pp. 44–60.

14. Ibid., p. 53. From Sutrakrtanga, *The Book of Sermons*, I, i–5.

15. Thomas H. Hopkins, *The Hindu Religious Tradition*, 92. From the *Bhagavad-Gita*, 4, 8.

16. So, too, may the collective unconscious be tapped if great need is experienced; while sinking into the mythical sphere, subliminal contents are reshuffled, and new signs frequently point toward the way to follow.

17. *Sources of Indian Tradition*, p. 67.

18. Wendy Doniger O'Flaherty, *Women, Androgynes, and Other Mythical Beasts*, p. 136.

19. Ralph Metzner, *Maps of Consciousness*, pp. 43–44.

20. Eliade, *Yoga*, pp. 123–24.

21. *Sources of Indian Tradition*, pp. 3–6.

22. Ibid., p. 63.

23. Marie Louise von Franz, *On Divination and Synchronicity*, p. 56.

24. Heinrich Zimmer, *Philosophies of India*, p. 384.

25. C. G. Jung, *Collected Works*, 5, pp. 50 ff. See also W. H. Wilkins, *Hindu Mythology* (Calcutta: Ruppa, 1981), and *Hindu Myths* (New York: Penguin Books, 1978).

Chapter 10

1. *Kaspar and Other Plays by Peter Handke*, p. 59.
2. Jerome Klinkowitz and James Knowlton, *Peter Handke and the Postmodern Transformation*, p. 2.
3. Ibid., p. 4.
4. Ibid., p. 19.
5. Ibid., p. 9.
6. Nicholas Hern, *Peter Handke*, p. 12.
7. Samuel Beckett, "Dante . . . Bruno. Vico . . . Joyce," *Transition*, (June 1929): 14.
8. June Schlueter, *Plays and Novels of Peter Handke*, pp. 172–73.
9. Ronald Hayman, *Theatre and Anti-Theatre*, p. 96.
10. Hern, p. 71.
11. *Kaspar*, p. 9.
12. C. G. Jung, *Collected Works*, 5, pp. 442, 408.
13. Klinkowitz and Knowlton, p. 109.
14. Ibid., p. 115.
15. C. G. Jung, *Collected Works*, 3, p. 227.

Chapter 11

1. Bonnie Marranca and Gautam Dasgupta, *American Playwrights. A Critical Survey*, p. 82. John Lahr, "Spectacle of Disintegration *Operation Sidewinder*," *American Dreams*, pp. 49–56.
2. The Hopi tribe of the Pueblo Indians, formerly called the Moki or Moqui, occupy several mesa villages in northeast Arizona. Their geographical isolation enabled them to survive invasions by Spaniards and remain relatively independent of American influence. See *Sun Chief: the Autobiography of a Hopi Indian*, by Leon W. Simmons.
3. Sam Shepard, *Four Two-Act Plays*, p. 152.
4. Bettina L. Knapp, *Antonin Artaud: Man of Vision*.
5. Edward Edinger, "An Outline of Analytical Psychology," p. 18. John Lahr, "Spectacle of Disintegration *Operation Sidewinder*."
6. Mircea Eliade, *Shamanism*, pp. 290–303.
7. Ibid.
8. C. G. Jung, *Collected Works*, 10, p. 352 ff.
9. Ibid., p. 329.
10. Frank Waters, *Book of the Hopi*, p. X, and Natalie Curtis, *The Indians' Book*, p. 473.
11. Waters, p. 126.
12. Ibid., p. 4.
13. Hamilton A. Tyler, *Pueblo Gods and Myths*, p. 97.
14. *The Dream and Human Societies*, eds. G. E. Von Grunebaum and Roger Caillois, p. 242.
15. Natalie Curtis, *The Indians' Book*, p. 473.
16. Edwin Earle and E. A. Kennard, *The Hopi Kachinas*, pp. 1–5.
17. Elsie Clews Parons, *Hopi and Zuni Ceremonialism*, pp. 36–43.
18. Curtis, pp. 473–77.
19. Tyler, pp. 224–26.
20. Waters, p. 220.
21. *Papers*, XXII, Peabody Museum of American Archaeology and Ethnology, Harvard University, pp. 152–54. H. R. Voth, *The Oraibi Summer Snake Ceremony*, Anthropological Series, Vol. III (no. 4): 344–53. J. W. Powell, *1886–87*, Bureau of Ethnology to the Secretary of the Smithsonian Institution, pp. 16–21. Ruth Benedict, *Patterns of Culture*, pp. 95–127.

Conclusion

1. Lewis Mumford, *The Myth of the Machine*, p. 411.
2. C. G. Jung, *Collected Works*, 10, pars. 148–96.

Bibliography

Arreola, Juan José. "The Switchman." *Confabulario*. trans. George D. Schade. Austin: University of Texas Press, 1974.

Ashe, Geoffrey. *The Virgin*. London: Routledge and Kegan Paul, 1976.

Avila, St. Teresa. *Spiritual Relations*. In *The Complete Works of Saint Teresa of Jesus*. I. New York: Sheed and Ward, 1946.

Barry, Theodore de, ed. *Sources of Indian Tradition*. I. New York: Columbia University Press, 1958.

Baynes, H. G. *Mythology of the Soul*. London: Rider and Rider, 1969.

Beckett, Samuel. "Dante . . . Bruno. Vico . . . Joyce." *Transition*. June 1929.

Bergson, Henri. *Le Rire*. Paris: Presses Universitaire de France, 1969.

Bidwell, Bruce, and Linda Heffer. *The Joycean Way*. Baltimore: Johns Hopkins University Press, 1982.

Bruce, William. *Religions in Japan*. Tokyo: Charles E. Tuttle, 1970.

Bullough, Vern L. *The Subordinate Sex*. Chicago: University of Illinois Press, 1973.

Capra, Fritjof. *The Tao of Physics*. Berkeley: Shambhala, 1975.

Carra, Massimo. *Metaphysical Art*. New York: Praeger Publishers, 1971.

Carrieri, Raffaele. *Futurism*. Milan: Edizioni del Milione, 1963.

Cate, Curtis. *Antoine de Saint-Exupéry*. New York: Putnam's Sons, 1970.

Cowan, Lyn. *Masochism. A Jungian View*. Thalwil, Switzerland: Spring Publications, 1982.

Croix, Horst de la, and Richard G. Tansey. *Helen Gardner's Art Through the Ages*. 6th Edition. New York: Harcourt Brace Jovanovich, 1975.

Curtis, Nathalie. *The Indians' Book*. New York: Harper and Brothers Publishers, 1907.

Dukore, Bernard F., and Daniel C. Gerould, eds. *Avant-Garde Drama*. New York: Thomas Y. Crowell, 1976.

Earle, Edwin, and E. A. Kennard. *The Hopi Kachinas.* New York: J. J. Augustin, 1938.

Edinger, Edward. "An Outline of Analytical Psychology." Unpublished.

———. *The Bible and the Psyche.* Toronto: Inner City Books, 1986.

Eliade, Mircea. *Le Profane et le Sacré.* Paris: Gallimard, 1965.

———. *Shamanism.* Princeton: Princeton University Press, 1972.

———. *Yoga.* Princeton: Princeton University Press, 1973.

Ellman, Richard. *James Joyce.* New York: Oxford University Press, 1982.

Franz, Marie Louise von. *Puer Aeternus.* New York: Spring Publications, 1970.

———. *Creation Myths.* Zurich: Spring Publications, 1972.

———. *Shadow and Evil in Fairy Tales.* Zurich: Spring Publications, 1972.

———. *Time.* London: Thames and Hudson, 1978.

———. *On Divination and Synchronicity.* Toronto: Inner City Books, 1980.

———. *Alchemy.* Toronto: Inner City Books, 1980.

———. *On Dreams and Death.* Boston: Shambhala, 1986.

Frey-Rohn, Lilian. "Evil from the Psychological Point of View." In *Evil*, edited by the Jung Institute Curatorium. Evanston: Northwestern University Press, 1967.

Giudice, Gaspare. *Pirandello. A Biography.* trans. Alastair Hamilton. London: Oxford University Press, 1975.

Grünebaum, G. E. von, and Roger Caillois, eds. *The Dream and Human Societies.* Berkeley: University of California Press, 1966.

Handke, Peter. *Kaspar and Other Plays by Peter Handke.* trans. Michael Roloff. New York: Farrar, Straus and Giroux, 1969.

Harding, Esther. *Psychic Energy.* Princeton: Princeton University Press, 1967.

Hayman, Ronald. *Theatre and Anti-Theatre.* New York: Oxford University Press, 1979.

Hern, Nicholas. *Peter Handke.* New York: Ungar, 1972.

Hopkins, Thomas, H. *The Hindu Religious Tradition.* Encine, California: Dickenson, 1971.

Jacobi, Jolande. *Complex Archetype Symbol in the Psychology of C. G. Jung.* trans. Ralph Manheim. Princeton: Princeton University Press, 1959.

———. *Paracelsus.* Princeton: Princeton University Press, 1973.

Joyce, James. *Stephen Hero.* New York: A New Directions Book, 1955.

———. *Dubliners.* ed. Robert Scholes. New York: Penguin, 1983.

Joyce Letters. I. ed. Stuart Gilbert. New York: Viking, 1966.

Jung, C. G. *Collected Works.* trans. R. F. C. Hull. Vol. 5, 9 (Parts 1 and 2), Vols. 3, 5, 7, 10, 11, 14. New York: Pantheon Books, 1960, 1956, 1953, 1956, 1977, 1959, 1963. Vol. 6. London: Pantheon Books, 1964. Vol. 8, 13. Princeton: Princeton University Press, 1969, 1967. Vol. 12. London: Routledge and Kegan Paul, 1953. Princeton University Press now publishes Jung's *Collected Works.*

Kaplan, Aryeh. *Meditation and the Bible.* New York: Samuel Weiser, Inc., 1978.

———. *Jewish Meditation.* New York: Samuel Weiser, 1981.

Keene, Donald, ed. *20 Plays of the No Theatre.* New York: Columbia University Press, 1970.

Klinkowitz, Jerome, and James Knowlton. *Peter Handke and the Postmodern Trans-formation*. Columbia: University of Missouri Press, 1983.

Kluger, Rivkah Scärf. *Satan and the Old Testament*. trans. Hildegard Nagel. Evan-ston: Northwestern University Press, 1967.

Knapp, Bettina L. *Dream and Image*. Troy, New York: Whitston Press, 1977.

———. *Antonin Artaud: Man of Vision*. Athens, Ohio: Ohio University Press, 1980.

———. *Theatre and Alchemy*. Detroit: Wayne State University Press, 1980.

———. *A Jungian Approach to Literature*. Carbondale: Southern Illinois University Press, 1984.

Lahr, John. "Spectacle of Disintegration *Operation Sidewinder*." In *American Dreams*, ed. Bonnie Marranca. New York: Performing Arts Journal Publica-tions, 1981.

Marranca, Bonnie, and Gautam Dasgupta. *American Playwrights. A Critical Survey*. New York: Drama Book Specialists, 1981.

Menton, Seymour. *Hispania '42*. Sept. 1959.

Metzner, Ralph. *Maps of Consciousness*. New York: Collier Books, 1971.

Mumford, Lewis. *Technics and Civilization*. New York: Harcourt, Brace and Com-pany, 1934.

———. *The Myth of the Machine*. New York: Harcourt Brace Jovanovich, 1970.

Nagel's Encyclopedia Guide. Geneva: Nagel Publishers, 1979.

Narayan, R. K. *Man-Eater of Malgudi*. Middlesex, England: Penguin Books, 1983.

Neumann, Erich. *The Origins and History of Consciousness*. New York: Pantheon Books, 1954.

———. *Depth Psychology and a New Ethic*. New York: G. P. Putnam's, 1969.

New Larousse Mythology. Hong Kong: The Hamlyn Pub. Group, 1973.

Nietzsche, Friedrich. *Le Gai Savoir*. Paris: Gallimard, 1950.

O'Flaherty, Wendy Doniger. *Women, Androgynes, and Other Mythical Beasts*. Chi-cago: University of Chicago Press, 1982.

Osaragi, Jiro. *The Journey*. trans. Ivan Morris. Tokyo: Charles E. Tuttle, 1980.

———. *Homecoming*. trans. Brewster Horwitz, introduction by Harold Strauss. Tokyo: Charles E. Tuttle, 1980.

Papers, XXII. Peabody Museum of American Archaeology and Ethnology. Harvard University. Cambridge: Published by the Museum, 1944. Kraus Reprint, Millwood, New York, 1974.

Parons, Elsie Clews. *Hopi and Zuni Ceremonialism*. Printed in the United States of America (monograph), 1931.

Patton, Phil. "How Art Geared Up to Face Industry in Modern America." Smithso-nian. November, 1986.

Pfeiffer, Robert, H. *Introduction to the Old Testament*. New York: Harper and Row, 1948.

Pirandello, Luigi. *Tonight We Improvise*. Revised and Rewritten by Marta Abba. New York: Samuel French, 1932.

Powell, J. W. *1886–1887*. Bureau of Ethnology to the Secretary of the Smithsonian Institution. Washington: Government Printing Office, 1891.

Riencourt, Amaury de. *Sex and the Power in History*. New York: Dell Publishing, 1974.

Rig-Veda. trans. and annotated by Wendy Doniger O'Flaherty. Middlesex, England: Penguin Books, 1981.

Rufino Tamayo. New York: Rizzoli, 1982.

Ryan, John. "Anna Livia Plurabelle." *Ireland of the Welcomes. James Joyce Centenary Issue.* Vol. 31 (no. 3). May-June, 1982.

Saint-Exupéry, Antoine de. *Wind, Sand, and Stars.* trans. Lewis Galantière. New York: Reynal and Hitchcock, 1939. *Terre des hommes.* Paris: Gallimard, 1939.

————. *Lettres à sa mère.* Paris: Gallimard, 1955.

Schlueter, June. *Plays and Novels of Peter Handke.* Pittsburgh: University of Pittsburgh Press, 1981.

Scholem, Gershom G. *Major Trends in Jewish Mysticism.* New York: Schocken Books, 1965.

Séjourné, Laurette. *Burning Water.* Berkeley: Shambhala, 1976.

Shepard, Sam. *Four Two-Act Plays.* New York: Applause, 1980.

Sicre, Jose Gomez. *Three Artists of the Americas.* trans. George C. Compton. Washington, D.C.: Pan American Union, 1957.

Simmons, Leon W., ed. *Sun Chief: the Autobiography of a Hopi Indian.* New Haven: Yale University Press, 1967.

Sogiazzo, Richard A. *Luigi Pirandello, Director: The Playwright in the Theatre.* Methuen, New Jersey: Scarecrow Press, 1982.

Soustelle, Jacques. *Daily Life of the Aztecs.* trans. Patrick O'Brien. Stanford: Stanford University Press, 1981.

Suzuki, Daisetz T. *Zen and Japanese Culture.* Princeton: Princeton University Press, 1973.

Swann, C. *A Concise History of Japanese Art.* Tokyo: Kodansha International, 1959.

Taylor, Joshua C. *Futurism.* New York: Museum of Modern Art, 1961.

Terry, Charles S. *Masterworks of Japanese Art.* Tokyo: Charles E. Tuttle, 1959.

Trachtenberg, Alan. "The Art and Design of the Machine Age." *New York Times.* September 21, 1986.

Tsuda, Noritake. *Handbook of Japanese Art.* Tokyo: Charles E. Tuttle, 1970.

Tyler, Hamilton A. *Pueblo Gods and Myths.* Norman: University of Oklahoma Press, 1964.

Voth, H. R. *The Oraibi Summer Snake Ceremony.* Anthropological Series. Vol. III (no. 4). Chicago, U.S.A., 1903.

Walker, Barbara G. *The Woman's Encyclopedia of Myths and Secrets.* New York: Harper and Row, 1983.

Waters, Frank. *Book of the Hopi.* New York: Viking, 1963.

Wilkins, W. H. *Hindu Mythology.* Calcutta: Ruppa, 1981.

Witkiewicz, Stanislas Ignacy. *Instability.* trans. with an introduction by Louis Iribarne. Urbana: University of Illinois Press, 1977.

————. *The Madman and the Nun and Other Plays by Stanislas Ignacy Witkiewicz.* trans. and ed. Daniel C. Gerould and C. S. Durer. Seattle: University of Washington Press, 1968.

Yizhar, S. *Midnight Convoy and Other Stories.* Jerusalem: Israel University Press, 1969.

Zimmer, Heinrich. *The King and the Corpse.* Princeton: Princeton University Press, 1973.

———. *Philosophies of India.* ed. Joseph Campbell. Princeton: Princeton University Press, 1974.

Zuckerhandl, Victor. *The Sense of Music.* Princeton: Princeton University Press, 1971.

Index